GW01606288

Jim Downes
Berthold Daum

The Indian-Pacific

From Coast to Coast

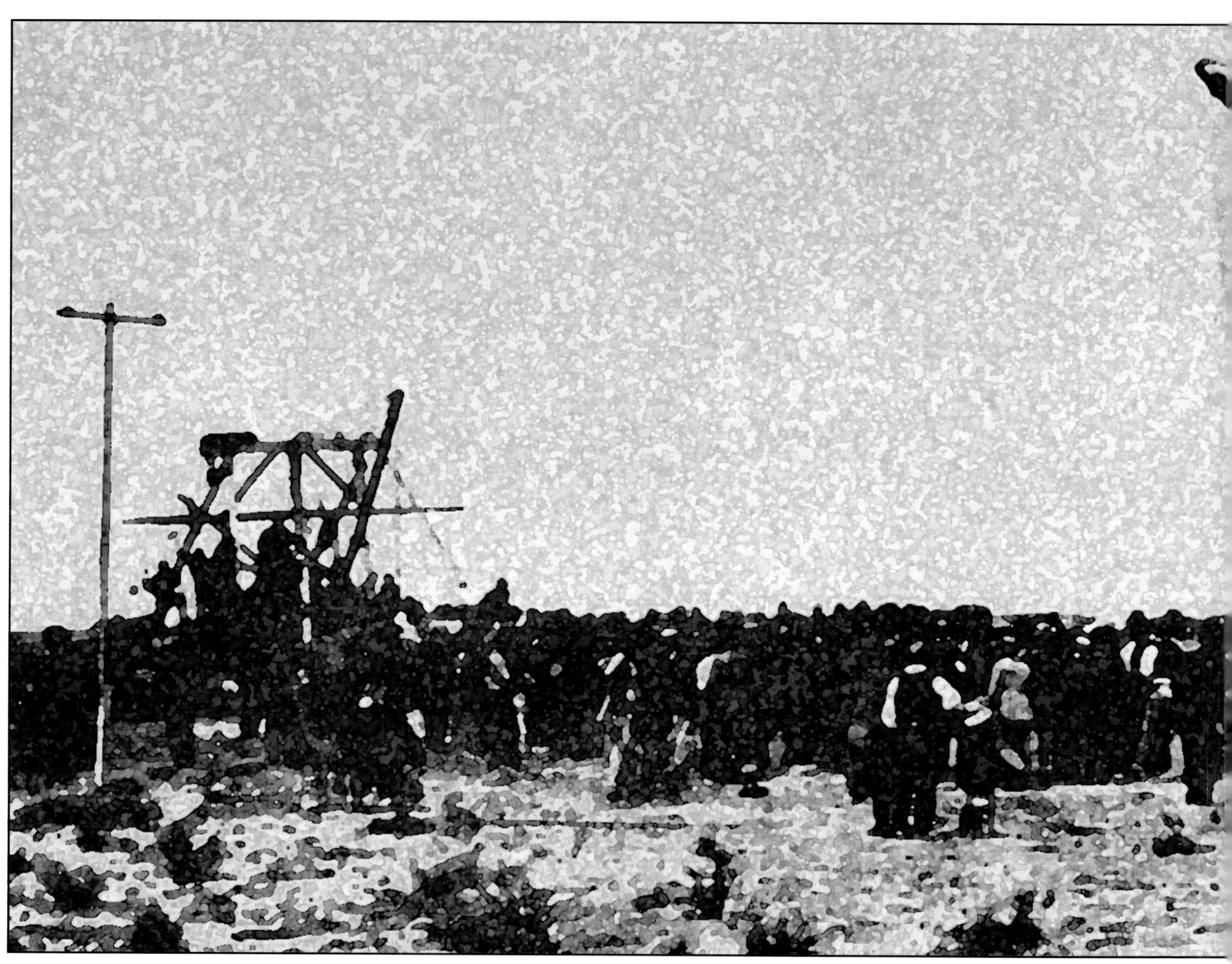

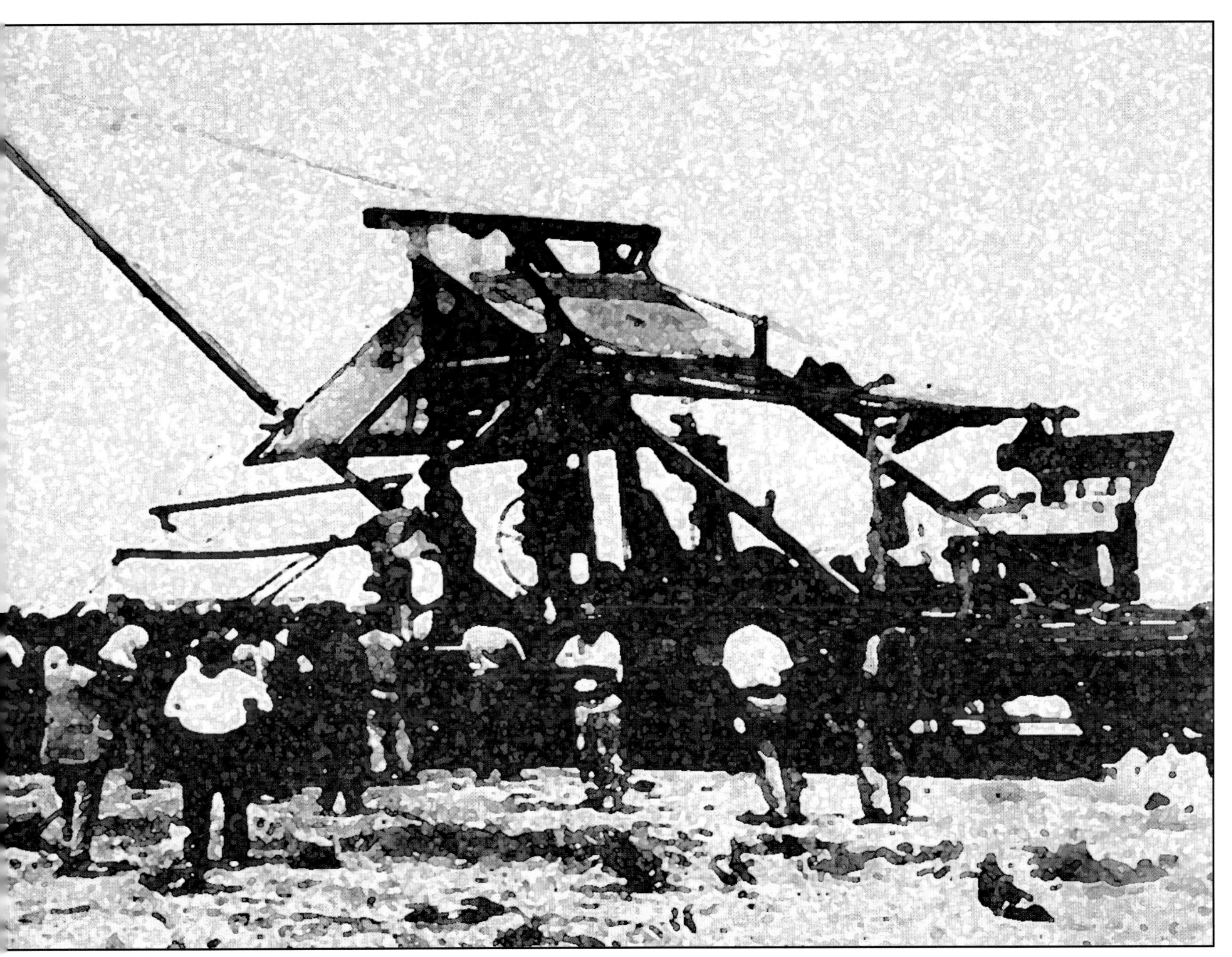

Work gangs from the East and the West meet near Ooldea, SA, on October 17th, 1917

First published in 1997 by
lichtbild pty ltd
LPO Box 6011
Cromer, Vic 3193
Australia

phone: (03) 9584 9638
email: lichtbild@compuserve.com
http://ourworld.compuserve.com/homepages/lichtbild

Typeset in Berthold Baskerville
Printed in Australia by Southbank Book

Cover image: The eastbound Indian-Pacific at Forrest, WA.
Back image: Graffiti on a freight car.

National Library of Australia
Cataloguing-in-Publication data:

Downes, J. (Jim), 1934 –
Daum, B. (Berthold), 1949 –

ISBN 0 646 31263 4

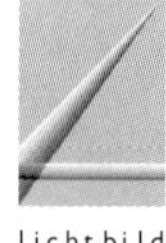

Contents

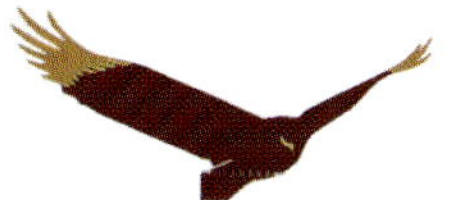

For more than a quarter of the 20th Century, one of the world's great passenger trains has made, twice a week, one of the world's great train journeys: 4,348 kilometres (2,700 miles) from coast to coast of the Australian continent.

The oceans gave the train its name: The Indian-Pacific. Its countless thousands of passengers have seen a cross section of Australia visible to no-one else. The view from the wide double glazed windows of the Indian-Pacific takes in the cramped back yards of three inner-cities and the wide emptiness of Australia's vast outback.

Either journey, eastbound or west, brings some understanding of the nature of Australia. The round trip is better because the view is subtly different each way, and there's double the travelling time in daylight hours.

The rolling hours across Australia – the one-way trip takes two and a half days – are a chance to do some sums about this big island, to clear up some misconceptions and debunk some myths.

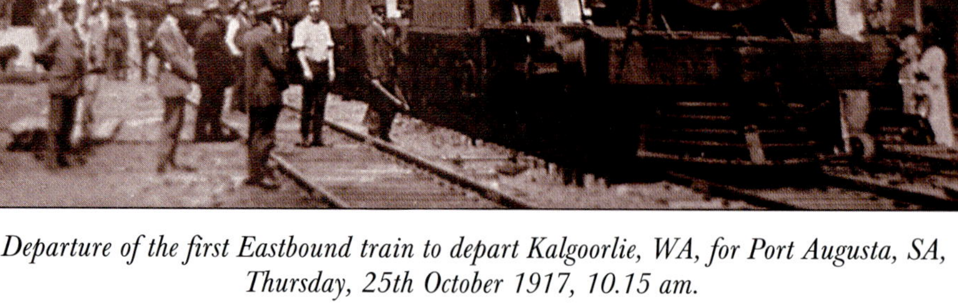

Departure of the first Eastbound train to depart Kalgoorlie, WA, for Port Augusta, SA, Thursday, 25th October 1917, 10.15 am.

Big it certainly is. Australian kids learn early on that they live on the biggest island on earth: The Indian-Pacific's route maps show the vast spread east to west. And from north to south Australia extends from ten degrees south of the equator down to the roaring forties, well on the way to Antarctica.

The land mass is 7.7-million square kilometres, and it's shared by only eighteen million people – fewer than three people for every square kilometre, so the figures say.

What the figures don't show, but the journey of the Indian-Pacific does, is how little of this island can be used for human occupation, animal and food production. Allowing for climate, soils and terrain, only one tenth of Australia is suitable for agriculture and suddenly the image of our island shrinks. Agricultural Australia, farmable Australia, is about the size of the island of Borneo, smaller than Papua New Guinea.

There are no great mountains, no

massive melt of snow, therefore few worthwhile rivers. The one powerful impression of Australia through the windows of the Indian-Pacific is how dry the country is, how few the streams, how rare the fresh water, and how harsh the environment beyond the air conditioning and double glazing of the train. It is water that limits the growth of production and therefore of population. And even the water we do have is at risk. Rivers are polluted, excess irrigation restricts their flow. As this story explores the track of the Indian-Pacific, the theme of water will occur again and again. It is the most vital element, the most significant factor, in the equation of Australia's future.

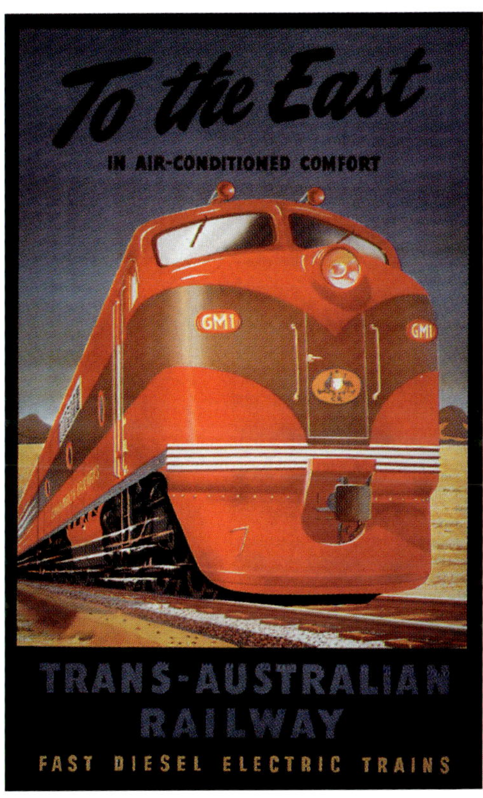

The book rides the Indian-Pacific westbound. The choice of direction was largely historical: The first Indian-Pacific started from Sydney, and the serious history of railways in Australia started hereabouts. In fact, the history of Australia itself started half an hour's walk from where the Indian-Pacific begins its westbound journey.

For a place that began as a prison, Sydney's done very well.

It's site, on its famous harbour, was originally second choice, because Arthur Phillip, the English sailor who commanded the First Fleet of warships, supply ships and convict transports, had been ordered by his masters at the Admiralty in London to establish a settlement down the coast a bit at Botany Bay, where James Cook the great and revered navigator had landed and declared the place the property of the British Crown eighteen years before.

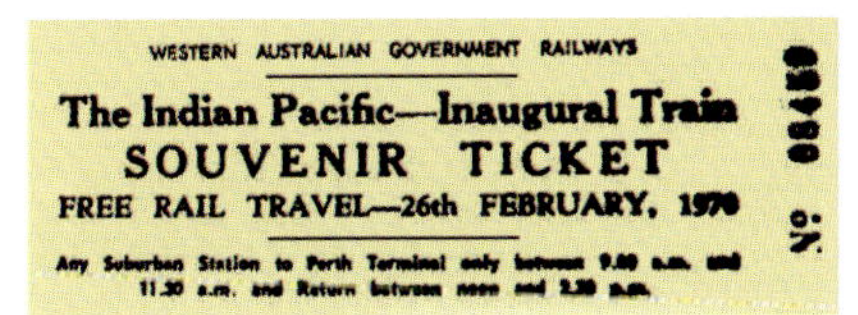

Phillip found Botany Bay an unpleasant, barren place. Now the site of oil refining, a container port and the country's biggest airport, it has, if anything, gone downhill.

Phillip's search for something better led him to explore an inlet between high cliffs to the north of Botany Bay. Cook had sailed by, noting just the inlet. But as Phillip's scouts rounded the southern headland, one of the finest sights of the world, then as now, came into view: they called it Port Jackson, and in a deeply sheltered bay with a creek feeding in fresh water they made a camp site.

The fleet followed. Again the flag went up, and His Britannic Majesty was declared the King of this Terra Nullius, no-one's land. Two centuries later, and in belated recognition of prior ownership, serious questioning of this procedure began occupying Government time and furthering legal careers.

Phillip named the place Sydney Cove. Sydney was an English politician, Home Secretary at the time, and the middleman in all dealings between His Majesty the King and the convicts who would be encouraged, at the end of the whip wielded in the King's name, to set about building here the visible proof of British ownership before someone else laid equally spurious claim to it.

The French were the fear, though since Willem Janszoon in 1606, the Dutch had been visiting the island marked Terra Australis (Southern Land) on the maps which guided their trading ships round the tip of Africa and northeast to the Spice Islands, later called the Netherlands East Indies and later again the Republic of Indonesia. Occasionally, the Dutchmen got lost, or turned too late out of the Roaring Forties and found themselves coasting Terra Australis. Or curiosity overcame trading and they ventured deliberately far to the east, to see what was there.

So Abel Tasman found the southernmost island of Australia and called it Van Dieman's Land. But being less acquisitive that the sailors of England, he staked no lasting claim.

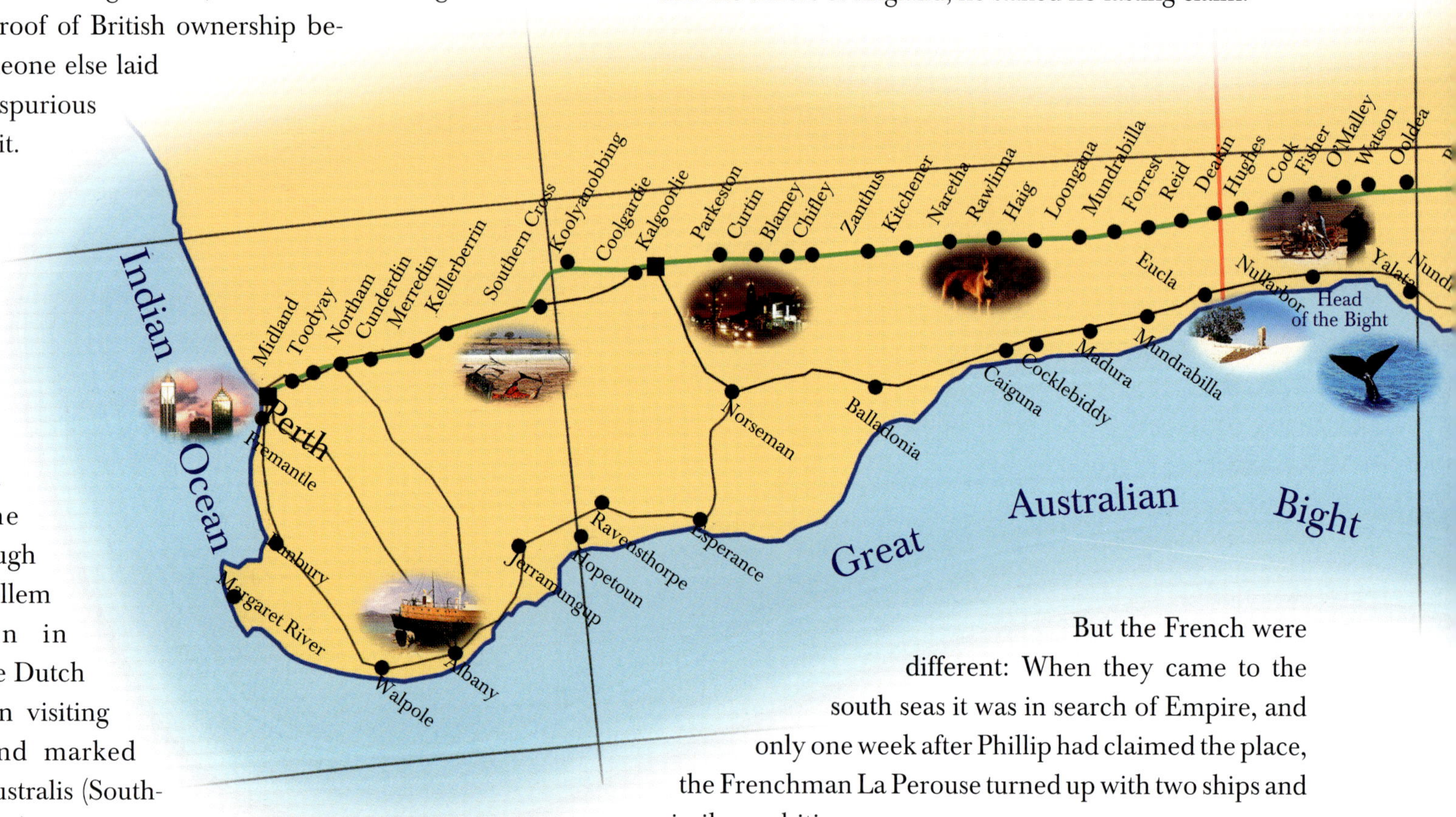

But the French were different: When they came to the south seas it was in search of Empire, and only one week after Phillip had claimed the place, the Frenchman La Perouse turned up with two ships and similar ambitions.

That week decided the future of Australia: British convicts, not French settlers; stodge rather than food for 150 years; the noose not the guillotine for serious bucking of the system; British Law not the Code Napoleon; Government from Whitehall not the Quai d'Orsay; Norfolk Island and Port Arthur, not Guyana. And looking at the subsequent history of French ex-colonies, perhaps it was a lucky week for the future Australia that delayed the arrival of the Count of La Perouse.

In time, the British colony that was still called New South Wales was subdivided into other colonies. Phillip had set the naming pattern at Sydney Cove: British notables, especially British Royalty, might be made well disposed by the naming of far-off places in their honour: An orgy of name-giving began, all of them totally inappropriate and most of them lasting to the present day: Victoria, in honour of a long term occupant of the British throne; Queensland, similar motivation; and a hundred, many hundred, similar examples as colonial administrators filled in the blanks on the maps of the fiefdoms.

From England came the idea of railways. A company was set up in Sydney to build a railway to the interior of the Colony, to encourage settlement and to carry to the seaport the wealth that was bound to come. It set the pattern for many subsequent Australian companies: It got into financial trouble, and it called for Government help.

Government took over the railway enterprise.... and that was the real origin of the track which carries the Indian-Pacific across this island, Australia. In the beginning.....

In The Beginning...

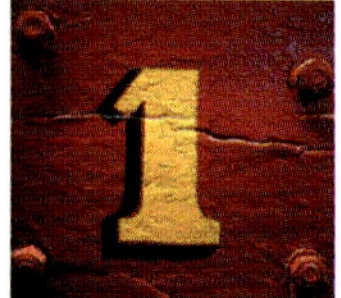

......there was great confusion. Australia's railways were born of colonial rivalries (the place was – some say it still is – more a collection of warring principalities than a united nation) and while each of the British colonies that were the nascent Australia agreed that railways were a necessary part of a modern society, they couldn't agree on the shape and size their proposed railways should be.

The proponents of railways, the colonial administrators and would-be politicians circling in the background, hired what they considered 'expert' help to design the transport network that would replace horse and bullock teams and camel trains.

The experts, engineers mostly, were hired from the true source of railways, England, Ireland and Scotland. Imported with the experts, unfortunately as things turned out, were old ideas, old prejudices, old solutions to old problems and not a lot of ideas for the unimagined problems presented by this large and very distant island begging to join the railway world.

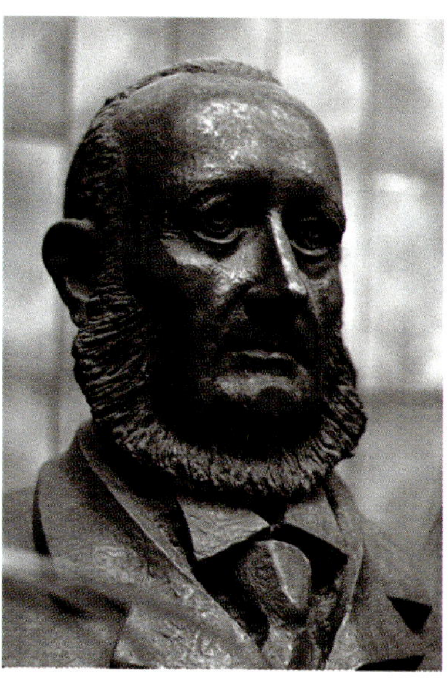

John Whitton, Father of NSW railways.

There is one truly vital measurement in railways: The distance between the steel extrusions called rails. Legend has it that the one International standard, four feet eight and a half inches or one thousand four hundred and thirtyfive millimetres, was derived from the distance between the first wheels ever to roll in primitive England: the wheels of the horse-hauled vehicles of the occupying Romans. How that standard was reached, no-one knows: Enough to conject that when the pioneers of railways sought stout foundations for the machines of the age of steam, the Romans had paved the way.

But because of some rebellious genes that seem part of human nature not all the early railwaymen (and history records no early railwaywomen) agreed the Roman standard should apply. Other standards were declared. In Ireland, five feet and three inches seemed a good enough spacing between the wheels. The legendary British engineer Isombard Kingdom Brunel decreed his own broad, broad gauge for his Great Western Railway.

It was found that sometimes a narrower gauge was cheaper to build. So three feet six inches between the rails appeared as an economic alternative. Parts of Europe, led of course by the French, wanted nothing to do with anything measured in inches. Another gauge developed, metre gauge, a thousand millimetres between the rails, easy to remember but further confusing the developing chaos.

Enter the United States of America, another British colony which had the sense in 1776 to declare itself out of the British Empire via the War of Independence.

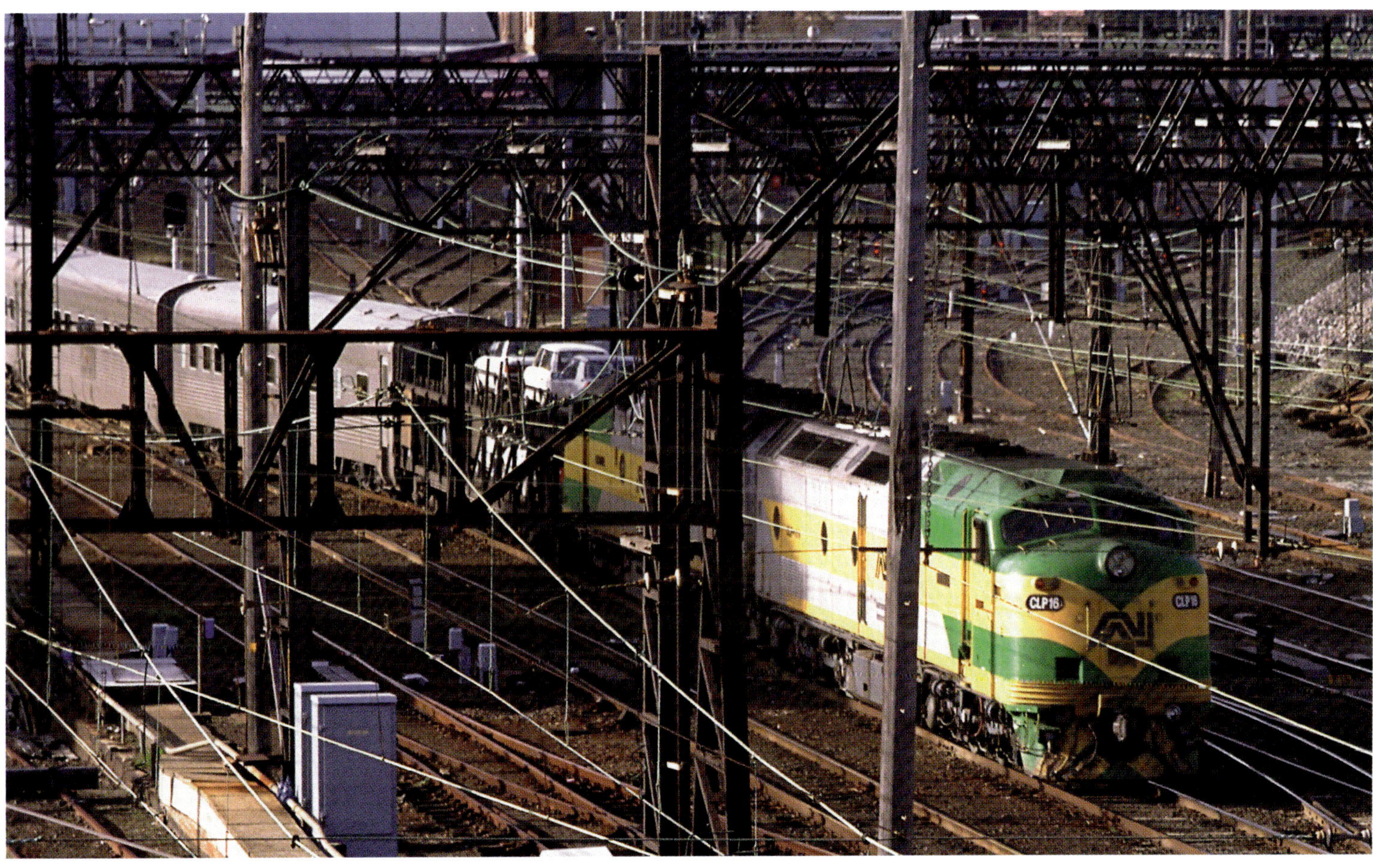

The Indian-Pacific, headed by a CLP class locomotive, leaves Sydney Central Station.

If ever a place were ready for railways, it was North America. It had money, it had entrepreneurs, it had compliant politicians with hands out for rewards in exchange for laws that smiled upon the new railways. Yet from this apparent morass of self interest there emerged a standard gauge railway system which came to span the continent. Sure, there were substandard gauges everywhere, small lines that either fed the developing big ones or served their own isolated areas, but the essential national network was there: A freight car could load at New York and unload at Seattle or San Francisco, hauled across the tracks of a dozen different railway companies by the engines of a dozen others.

The administrations of colonial Australia seemed determined that no such co-operative efficiency could ever happen here.

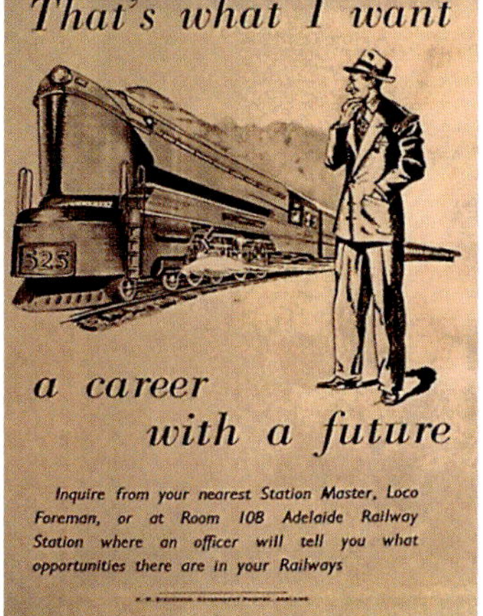

Times change.

The hired engineers from Britain built railways of standard gauge from the coastal cities to the inland of the oddly named colony of New South Wales. An engineer from Ireland came with the broad gauge five three between his ears to plan railways for Victoria and South Australia. And in Queensland and Western Australia the short term view of cheap and quick construction brought the curse of the narrow gauge: Lightweight rail on lightweight roadbed condemned the systems to a future of lightweight trains. One state, South Australia, bought the worst of both worlds to its one state system: Broad gauge and narrow gauge and a problem of interchange between the two that would last a hundred years.

But in the Colony of New South Wales, some forgotten soul had the good sense to hire as Engineer of Railways the Yorkshireman John Whitton. It was a choice some in Government had cause to regret, while later generations of railway builders and railway users had cause to bless.

Few engineers achieve honour in Australia: If honour is measured by statuary and the naming of public places, Australian honour is bestowed most commonly upon home grown and eminently forgettable politicians, and imported civil servants and minor royalty even less worthy of marble or bronze.

In the case of John Whitton, someone in the unreal realm of Government devoted to honours, statuary and the like, seriously erred and caused a bronze bust of the bluff Yorkshire engineer to be cast and exhibited at Sydney's Central railway. And there, described with total accuracy as the Father of NSW Railways, the stern, bewhiskered bust of a true Man of Ingenuity (the origin of the word Engineer) gazes across to Sydney Central Platform One, where the return transcontinental journey of the train called the Indian Pacific begins and ends.

In Railways terminology, the end of the line in Sydney is called Sydney Terminal. That's logical enough, but for generations it's been called Central Station, and the platforms the long distance trains use are often called the Steam Platforms, though no steam train, apart from historical and tourist specials, has graced Central Station for a

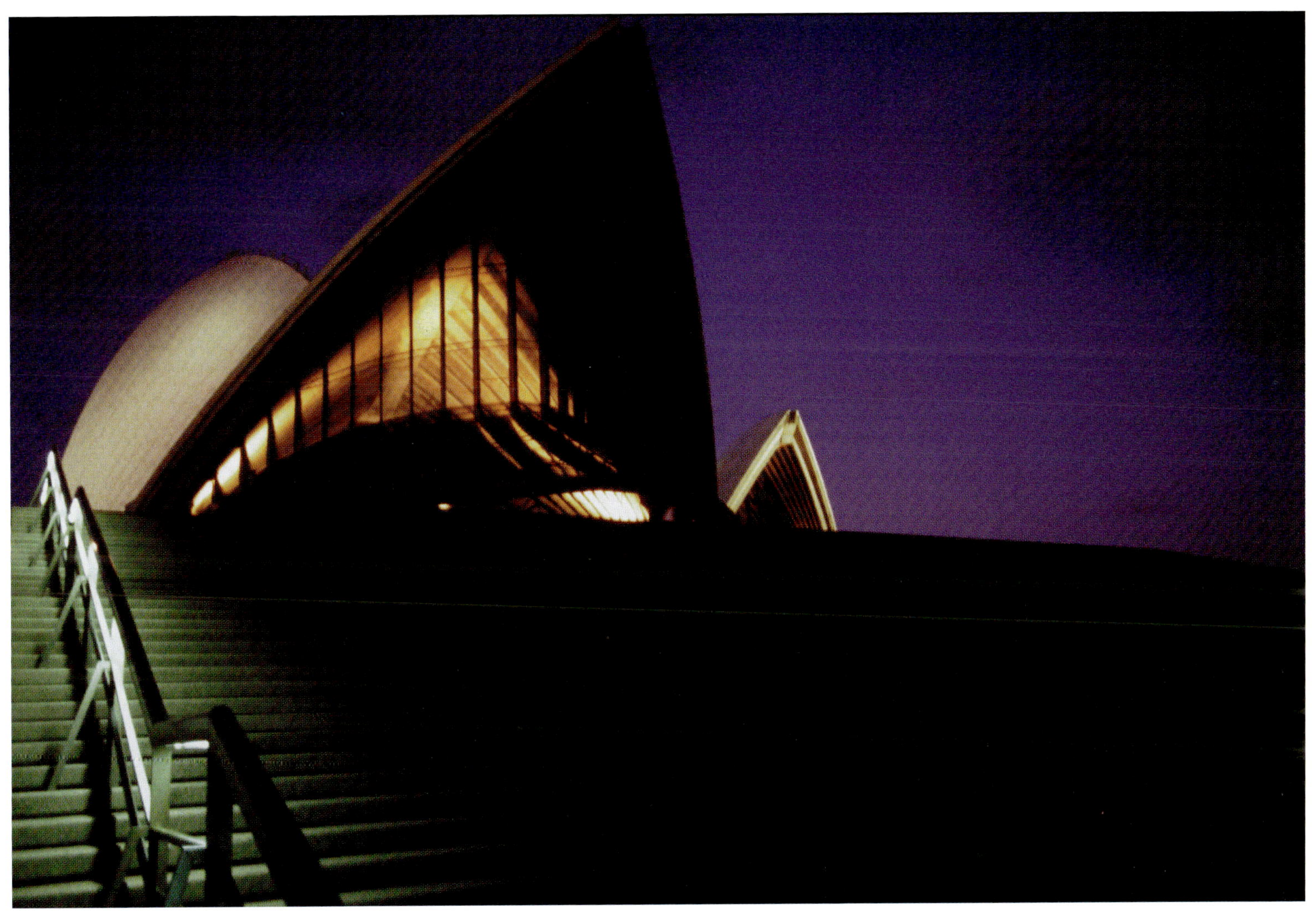

The Sydney Opera House.
Designed by Danish architect Joern Utzon and opened in 1973, it joined the famous Harbour to form the twin icons of Sydney.
The dramas of its building, the budget blowouts, the political and professional intrigues are part of the city's folklore.

generation. Indeed, the Indian Pacific is the last locomotive-hauled train to use the grand old sandstone building that recalls the long gone peak of railway effort and prestige.

Platform One at central has seen some of the great trains of Australia come and go, and eventually depart for ever: The overnight Melbourne Expresses, hauled through the night by the mighty 38 class as far as Albury where in the cold early morning passengers in the elegant teak and cedar lined sleepers would be rudely disturbed and made to carry their belongings across the platform to the broad gauge train for the run on to Melbourne.

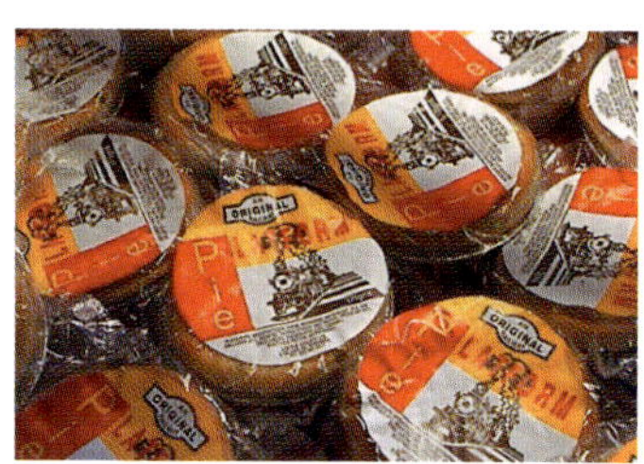

Food to Go:
The famous Railway Pie has sustained generations of travellers through Sydney Central.

The Brisbane Limited, which once ran overnight from Sydney on a standard gauge line that intruded into Queensland's narrow-gauge system as far as South Brisbane Station. To go further north, or to proceed anywhere on Queensland railways, passengers had to make their own way across town to the Roma Street Station where the state's 3'6" system began.

In time, a new standard gauge track from Albury to Melbourne ended the travellers' trials on the cold and cheerless Albury platform, and to celebrate, new trains of stainless steel sleepers, lounge cars and dining cars appeared at Central's Platform One. These were the Southern Auroras, glamour trains of a system from which glamour was quickly fading. Passenger trains were an endangered species, expensive to operate and losing money year after year. One by one services were withdrawn. The night mails ceased. Regional passenger trains were cancelled or replaced by light railcars, and on longer runs the self-powered XPT sets. The Southern Auroras overnight sleepers to Melbourne and back were withdrawn. Central Station's Platform One had only one train left to serve: *The Indian Pacific.*

It would not be true to say that without the Engineer John Whitton, the journey of the Indian Pacific could not be achieved. Later engineers would no doubt have reached the same conclusions that made possible the railway crossing of the Blue Mountains. But Whitton was first to send surveyors in search of a rail way over the mountains, and to devise from their measurements a practical path for steel wheel on steel rail.

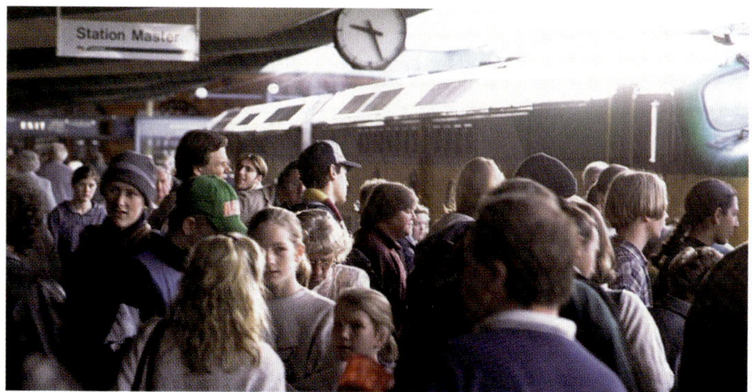

Sydney Central, Platform One:
The Indian-Pacific has just arrived from Perth. In about five hours it will start again for the trip across the continent.

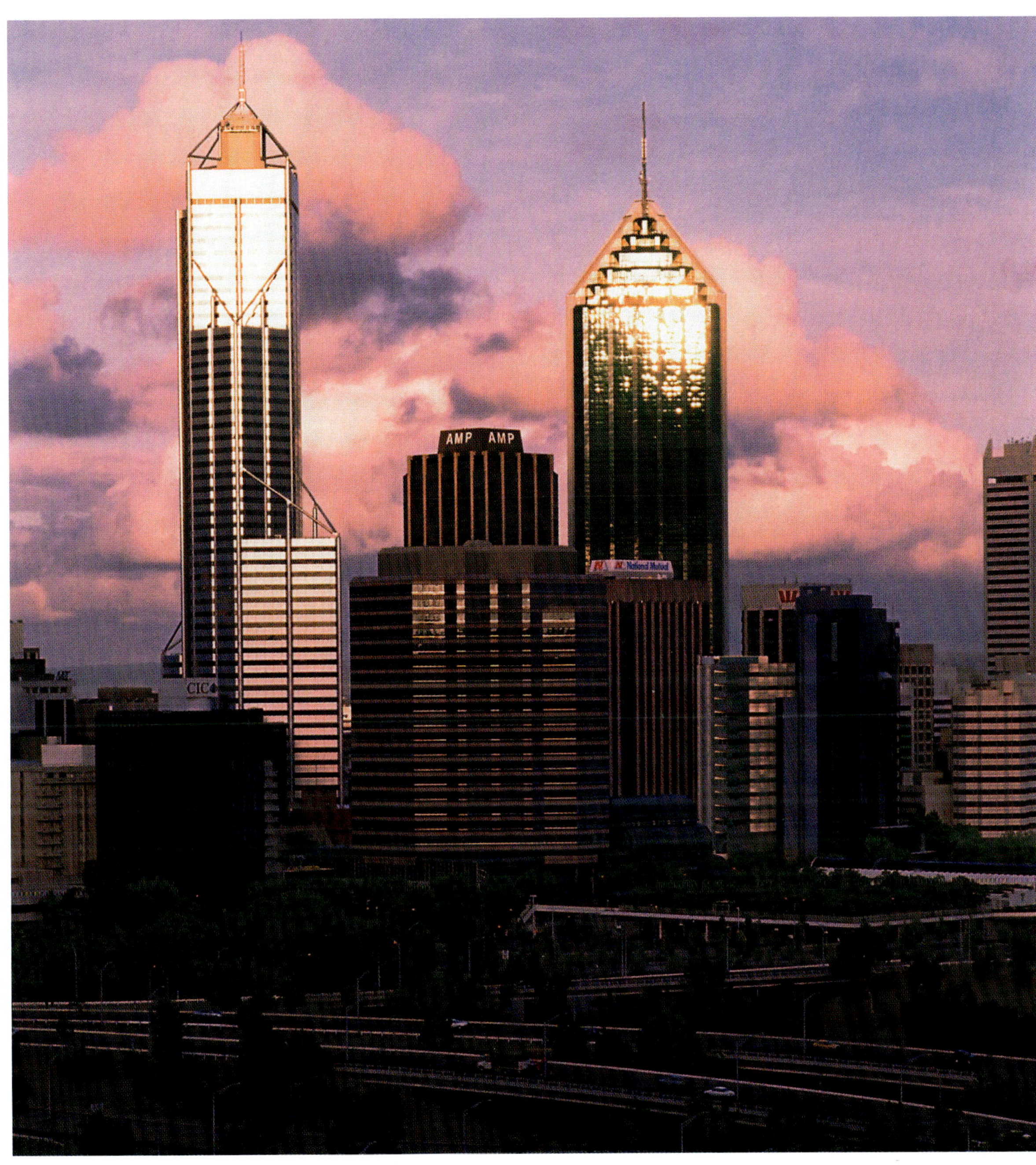

The skyline of Perth, Australia's most isolated capital. Perth from space, one astronaut said, looks like a shimmering pearl on black velvet.

The Train

The Indian Pacific is by any measure the most comfortable train ever to use Central Number One. Not that it's luxurious: despite the advertising, utilitarian is a better word to describe its appointments. Things are pretty basic even in the highest priced first class twin cabins, and in the sitting cars up the front signs of luxury are few indeed.

It's an elderly train now, and most of the cars are a quarter of a century old. The designs go back even further, to the passenger trains of fluted stainless steel developed in the United States by the Budd Corporation of Philadelphia for some of the great name trains of North America. The car sets which make up the Indian Pacific were built under licence from Budd by Commonwealth Engineering in Sydney at the end of the 1960s in time for the inaugural journey to depart Central Number One on the night of 23 February, 1970. The train was the symbol of a long overdue rail link, a celebration of the completion in 1969 of a standard gauge railway from Australia's Pacific Coast to the Indian Ocean. It was said at the time that the Indian Pacific was a symbol of nationhood, but the four Governments which had a say in its running squabbled for years over principles and details of its operation.

Hannan's Lounge: Patrick Hannan discovered the gold of Kalgoorlie.

Finally, Australian National, which had developed from the Commonwealth Railways and was showing signs of entrepreneurial skills notably lacking in the several state systems, took the Indian Pacific cars into its carriage workshops at Port Augusta, South Australia, and spent $13 million on overhaul and refurbishment. Australian National then negotiated total management of the Indian Pacific over the tracks of Western Australia, South Australia and New South Wales, potentially ending the inter-system differences which had long been in the way of an efficient, tourist orientated, Great Train Journey.

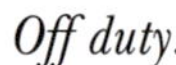

Off duty.

No sooner had this been achieved than an inexplicable Federal Government manoeuvre took away the revenue base of Australian National, its profitable long haul freight traffic. AN had shown innovation and business skills. It was offering real competition to road transport. It bought from the U.S. rights to build and operate on its network the revolutionary Road-Railer vehicles which changed in minutes from rail vehicle to road trailer and effectively extended the railways to wherever there were roads. The Government demolition of Australian National's profit making capacity left the railway with huge debts accumulated from years of rebuilding long neglected tracks, modernising locomotives and rolling stock, and totally overhauling facilities from communications to workshops.

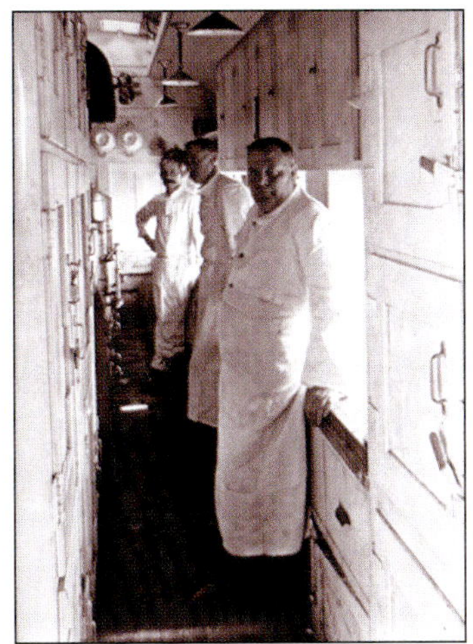

Kitchen and chefs – 1918.

Three mainland passenger trains remained under Australian National control: The Overland on the Melbourne-Adelaide route, The Ghan, a popular tourist train between Adelaide and Alice Springs, and the Indian Pacific on its epic coast to coast run.

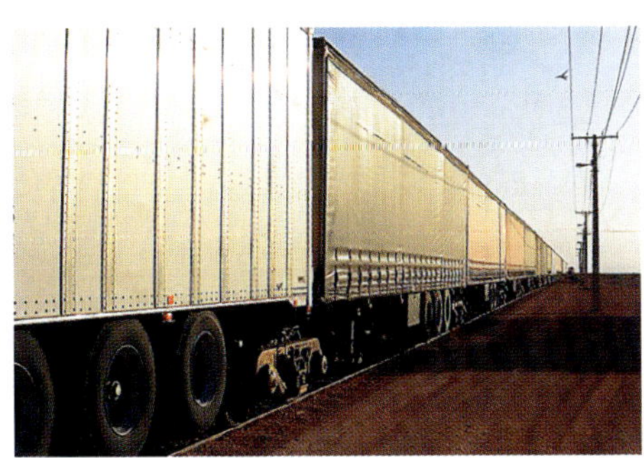

Road-Railer across the Nullarbor: Longer than a road train.

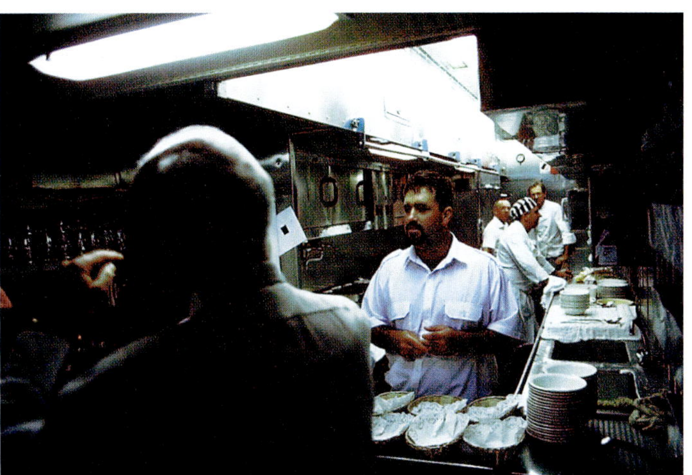

Kitchen and chefs – 1996.

Like passenger trains everywhere, the Indian Pacific is under a cloud of uncertainty. For how much longer it will offer travellers its special perspective of Australia is unclear.

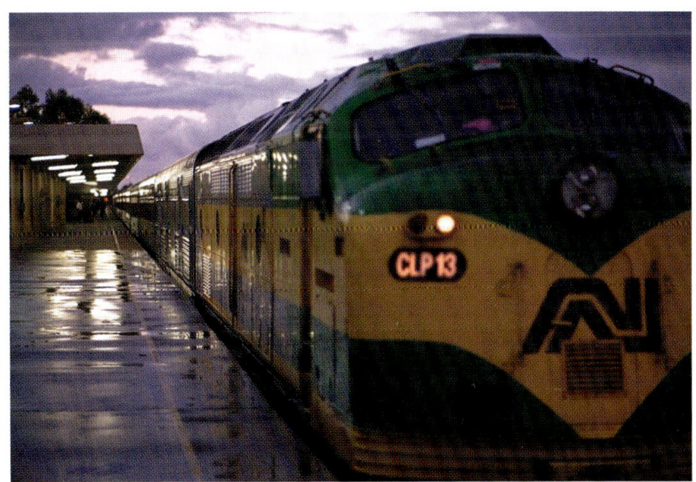

The Overland connects Melbourne with Adelaide.

Locomotives

In the years of joint management of the Indian Pacific, its power came from whatever locomotives the four separate railway systems had available.

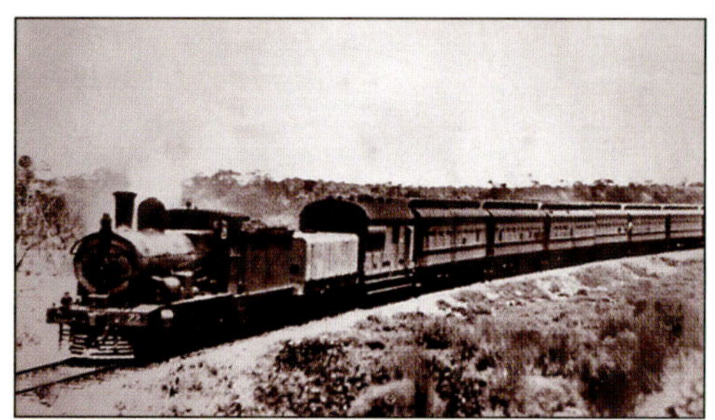

"G" 22 on an early train near Kalgoorlie (ANR c1920).

The inaugural Indian-Pacific left Sydney behind a pair of box-like 46 Class electric locomotives which hauled it over the Blue Mountains to Lithgow, where the overhead electric wiring system ended. Two diesel-electric locomotives of the 44 Class took over at Lithgow, and ran the train to Broken Hill. South Australia contributed its 600 Class from Broken Hill to Port Pirie, where a Commonwealth Railways' CL diesel took over for the run across the Nullarbor. At Parkeston, the C.R. terminus near Kalgoorlie, L260, the 3,000 horsepower pride of the W.A. Railways, was coupled on, and this was the locomotive whose nose broke through the streamers at East Perth Terminal as the inaugural Indian-Pacific completed its crossing of the continent.

Locomotive power followed a similar pattern through the 1970s and 1980s, with new classes of electric and diesel-electric power appearing in turn at the head of the Indian Pacific. But the spit and polish of early days did not last long, and shifts at the front of Australia's premier passenger train became just another chore for whatever locomotives were available.

Shabby diesels, just off a long haul freight, made a poor showing ahead of 12 or 16 shining cars of stainless steel. But there was little attempt, or little time, to run the locomotives through the car-wash the carriages enjoyed at each end of the journey.

Australian National, when planning to assume full route management of the train, wanted its own locomotives all the way from Perth to Sydney. It had a batch of elderly, but active, diesel-electrics, the Clyde Engineering (Sydney) built CL Class, a 3,000 hp (2,240 kW) workhorse dating from 1970. One of the class had hauled the inaugu-

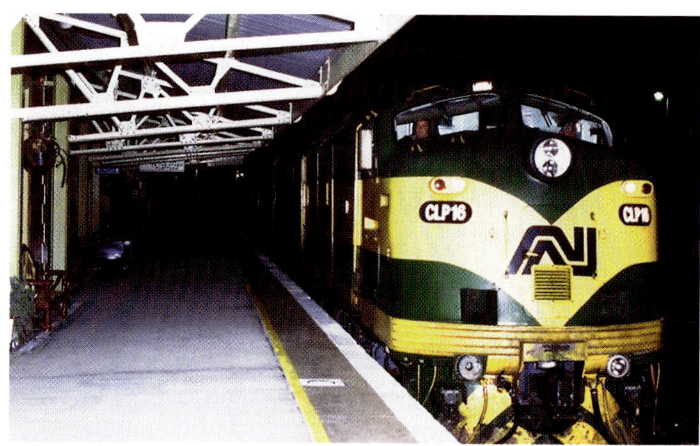

CLP16 at Katoomba, Blue Mountains, NSW.

ral Indian Pacific across the Nullarbor. A very effective locomotive, the 17 members of the class bore a hybrid body design: The traditional cab profile of General Motors (Electro-Motive Division) diesels from the 1930s, '40s and '50s, leading a more modern Mansard roofed body.

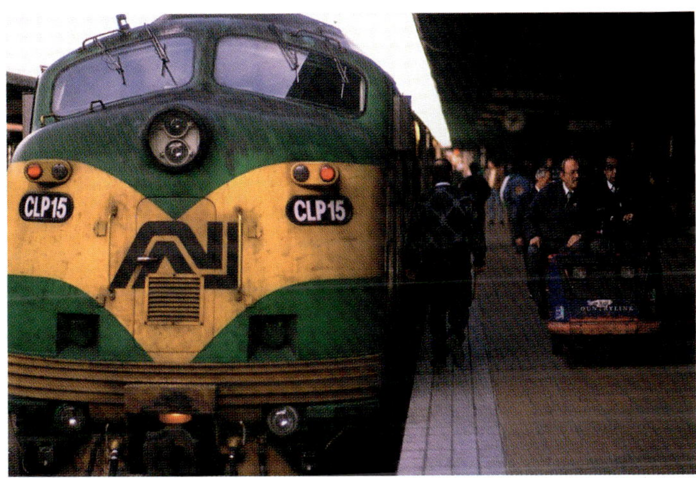

In need of a wash: CLP15 arriving at Sydney Terminal.

CLs had hauled all manner of trains for Commonwealth railways for 20 years. Their original maroon and silver paint scheme had gone through the evolutions first of CR then its successor Australian National. In 1992, AN negotiated a deal, the first of its kind in Australia, with the Morrison Knudsen Corporation, an American firm which had set up a locomotive rebuilding plant at Whyalla, South Australia, just down the track from AN's headquarters at Port Augusta. Morrison-Knudsen contracted to buy the 17 CL locos, rebuild and modernise them and lease them back to the railway, charged by the hours used.

'Power By The Hour', the deal was called. Seven locomotives were to be rebuilt for freight service, and the other ten, greatly modified, would power AN's three passenger routes. Eight freight locomotives of the CL class were also involved.

The locomotives that emerged from the Whyalla plant from June 1993 are handsome machines: To some eyes the best looking diesel locomotives ever built, anywhere. Classed as CLP (the P for passenger) the ten locomotives on the Indian Pacific, the Ghan and the Overland roster retain the body styling of their CL class forebears, but painted now in a classy design of silver grey, green and yellow, and bear brass nameplates honouring Aboriginal tribal areas along the routes of Australian National: Wiljakali, Mirning, Kaurna, Ngadjuri, Nukunu, Barngarla, Kokatha, Murunitja and Arabana. One loco is named City of Port Augusta, the South Australian railway town that's a part of AN's history.

WILJAKALI

Under the stylish outside skin of the CLPs are some of the most advanced mechanics and electronics available. The driver sits at a console, and all functions are controlled from his desktop. Computer microprocessors monitor and control major locomotive functions. Horsepower is up, to 3,300, and as well as the traction power engine and generator, each CLP carries aboard two 140kW generating sets to drive train air conditioning and services, from the hot water in the showers to the ice for drinks in the bars.

The Backyards of Sydney

Every Monday and Thursday afternoon two of Australian National's handsome CLP class Diesel-electric locomotives, rumble and whine their way out of Sydney's Platform One and haul up to sixteen newly cleaned, provisioned and peopled cars along an orderly steel path through the apparent confusion of tracks, points and crossings that mark the entrance to the biggest railway station south of the Equator.

There's history on both sides of the track: To the right, the elegant old Mortuary station, sandstone-arched, and once the departure point for funeral trains making the ultimate train journey.

On the left, a new Technology Park occupies the site, and some of the buildings, of the once-great Eveleigh Locomotive Depot. The tracks follow the approximate alignment of the first railway planned for New South Wales, the Sydney Railway Company's proposed line to Parramatta, built eventually by the Colonial Government when the railway company failed.

Like growth rings on a tree, the stages of Sydney's growth and development are clear to see as the Indian-Pacific cuts a cross-section from the sea to the mountains. There are occasional signs, too, of the change in the population mix brought about by immigration in the last half century. One of the most obvious is at Auburn, about 20 minutes after departure, where the minarets of a Muslim Mosque, one of the biggest outside the Arab world, point to the future of a changing society.

There's social history in the suburbs on both sides of this main railway line. In the early years of railways, it was both fashionable and sensible to live close to train services and some very grand houses were built along the line. Fashions changed, so did transport. Roads and streets came to prominence, the motor car to dominance, and the suburbs strung out along the western and southern lines declined in social

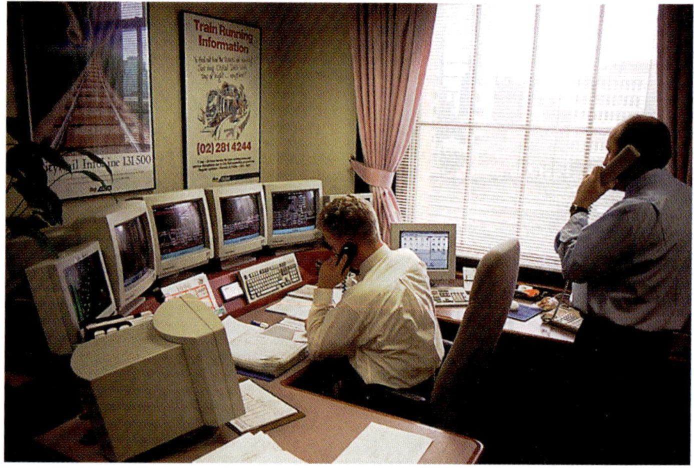

Train control Sydney: On seven screens controllers play a complex video game which allows no mistakes.

favour. Grand houses fell into neglect, or were partitioned in the middle years of the 20th century into inadequate and overpriced 'flats,' and given slapdash paint jobs in whatever colour was cheapest at the time.

Sydney, at the end of the second world war in 1945, came under population pressures it was ill-prepared to meet. Farmland was hurriedly cleared and government housing thrown up as quickly and cheaply as building contractors could devise. There were whole streets of near-identical houses, timber framed, tin roofed, paling fenced and clad in a material called fibro-cement. Cheap and nasty they may have been, but they were safe from grasping landlords and a generation grew up in them. The houses exist still, and line the railway as the Indian-Pacific builds speed and heads towards the western limits of Sydney.

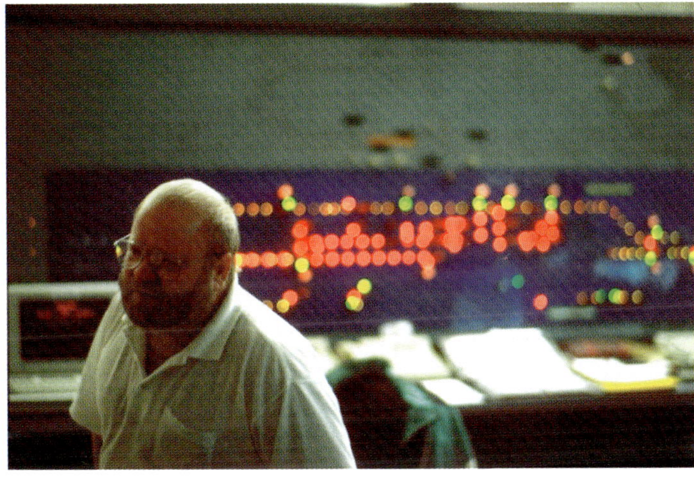

Sydney signal box.

But now, many of them are owned by the people who live in them. They've been extended, modernised, often made unrecognisable from their basic origins. They have gardens, mature trees, character, identity.

And back in closer to the city, it's again smart to live near the railway – steam's long gone, the railways now are electric and relatively clean – and some of the old houses that fell from elegance by neglect or exploitation again have loving owners intent on bringing them back to their old grace. Restoration is a Sydney industry. The search for styles, materials and techniques of past times is a hobby, often a dedication, of people who have made themselves the occupants, the owners for a while, of a piece of the past. While, sadly, the custodians of the future, the planners, the politicians, the architects and the money- makers who pay them, create an environment that generations to come are likely to find more worthy of demolition than of restoration.

A few minutes after the Mosque of Auburn, the Indian Pacific passes in seconds a place that has influenced Australia for two centuries: Parramatta. By now the train is moving so fast that the station's Aboriginal nameplate, so long and so complicated, may be unreadable.

Australian farming began at Parramatta, when one of the first land grants was made to a farmer, James Ruse, and here he grew the first Australian wheat. A couple of years after his first crop, Ruse and his family were self-sufficient for grain, and therefore, for flour and bread. The Australian wheat industry exists as his principal memorial. Another, named much later in his honour, is the James Ruse Agricultural High School, one of the best schools in Australia.

Now, Parramatta is the business centre of western Sydney, and so rapid has been the development of these western areas that hereabouts, at a place called Blacktown, is the geographic centre of Sydney.

This is a big town, this Sydney: Its parts may be called other things on the map: The City of This or the Municipality of That, according to local government boundaries, but from the sea to the Blue Mountains, from the Hawkesbury River down the coast half way to Wollongong, it's all Sydney. As the Indian-Pacific heads west, some of the pleasures and the problems of this sprawling city are clear to see: Building allotments are generously sized, luxurious by the standards of much of the world. Houses are bigger than they need to be, and they sit on land that is more often decorative lawn than productive garden. Such a life style costs a lot to service: Water, sewerage, electricity, telephones, roads are expensive to provide for relatively few users. Transport is a problem: most people have cars, but the road system can't cope in busy times. Public transport is inadequate, people complain; but when it's provided, few use it. They want hospitals close by, and schools, but such facilities are economically possible only if there's the population density to support them.

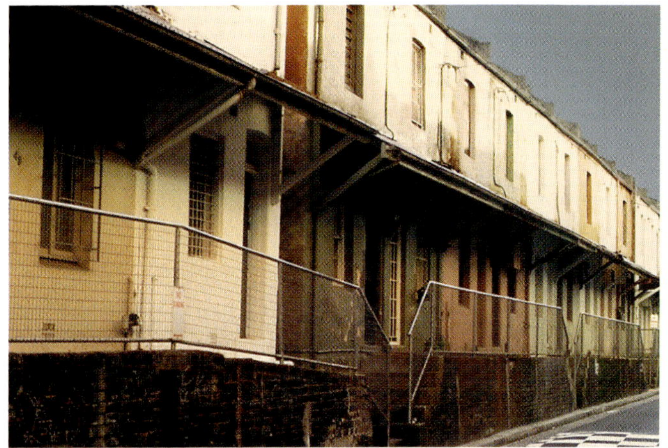

Older houses in Ultimo, Sydney.
Street signs are bilingual: English and Vietnamese.

It's not exclusively a Sydney problem: Indian-Pacific passengers will see it again, on a smaller scale, in Adelaide and Perth.

But because Sydney is the biggest, its problem is the most acute, and the contrast between overcrowded city and under-populated bush is seen from the windows of the train than covers the continent.

The Australian image – whether we claim it ourselves or others cultivate it for us – is of a nation of wide open spaces. In fact, we are dedicated city livers. Take, as an example of Australia, as far removed as can be from the mythical outback, the strip of coast between Newcastle, north of Sydney, and Geelong, west of Melbourne, and fifty to sixty kilometres inland: In this relatively small part of our big island, coincidentally shaped like a boomerang, live two-thirds of all our people. Nearly half of us live in two cities, Sydney and Melbourne and their environs. We are a nation of city dwellers.

In the case of Sydney, the sheer number of people who want – or through economic circumstance need – to live close to it has pushed the price of housing so high that Sydney is now one of the world's most expensive cities for housing, and that has pushed people to the very edges of town, across the natural barrier of the Nepean River and into the foothills of the Blue Mountains.

The westward expansion of houses and people makes it hard to define where Sydney begins and ends, but the lovely Nepean River, which the railway crosses at Penrith, is a good geographical boundary.

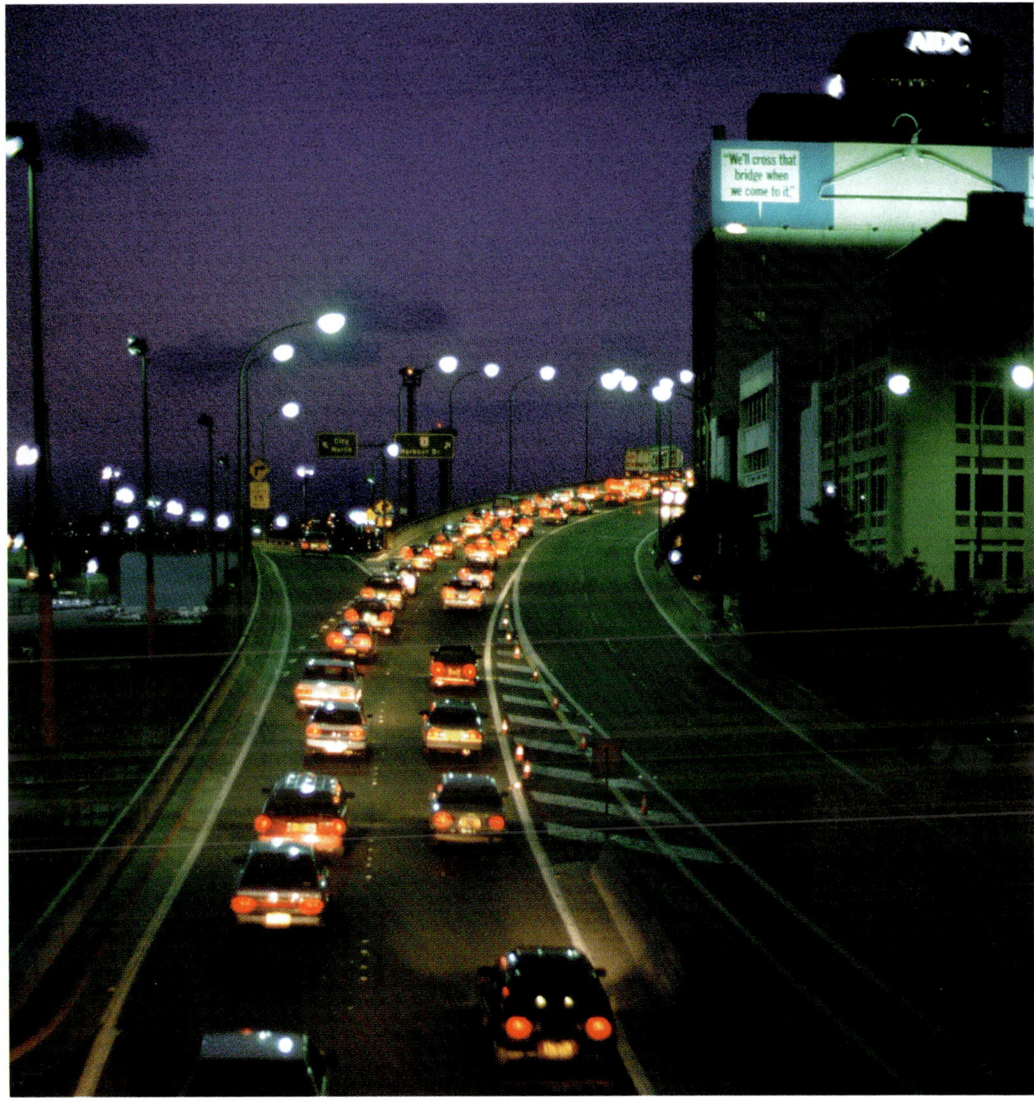

Sydney freeways at Ultimo - the more roads we build the more traffic is attracted, the more our cities become congested.

Downstream a little way from the railway bridge, the Nepean changes name and becomes the Hawkesbury, and under that name flows spectacularly through deep sandstone gorges and rich river plains to the sea at Broken Bay. The Hawkesbury and Nepean are part of the recreational waterways of the Sydney region, popular for power boat racing and water skiing. But they're also the drain and sewer for river front communities upstream, and their waters, long unfit to drink, are now unsafe for swimming or washing the dog. Pious sounds are frequently made on their behalf, but little of lasting value has been done to protect them. The Nepean is the first, but not the last, of the sick rivers of Australia the Indian-Pacific will cross.

Across the Nepean, the Blue Mountains abruptly begin. The diesels heading the Indian-Pacific notch up their power to defeat the hills which for years were the barrier to inland expansion of the colony on the coast.

Up Whitton's Way

Sometimes, the railway across the Blue Mountains is called 'Whitton's Way,' an unofficial tribute to the Engineer, John Whitton, who is credited with its construction.

It was Whitton who sent railway surveyors along the cattle track, later a road, that had been blazed across the barrier hills in 1813 by an expedition led by three gentlemen of the colony, Blaxland, Wentworth and Lawson. History credits the three with the discovery of a way over the mountains, and railway stations are named in their honour. But some of today's historians are inclined to think the honour belongs elsewhere, perhaps even to a convict named Wilson who was in no position to dispute the social pressures of the time that decided where honours should be bestowed.

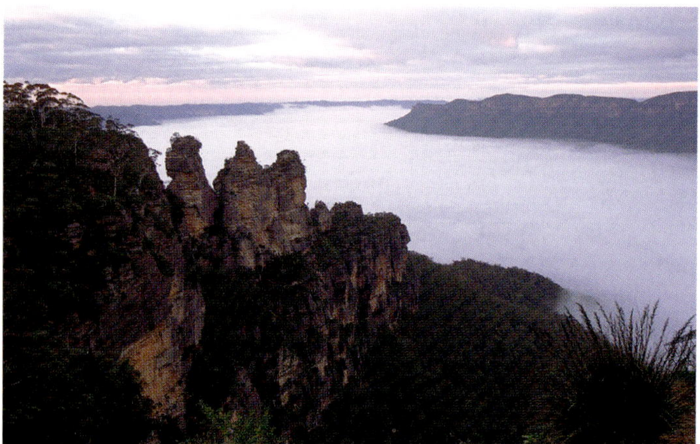

The Three Sisters – an early winter morning fills the valley with fog.

That first track succeeded because the explorers, or explorer, sought a track along the top of the complex of ridges that comprise the Dividing Range west of Sydney.

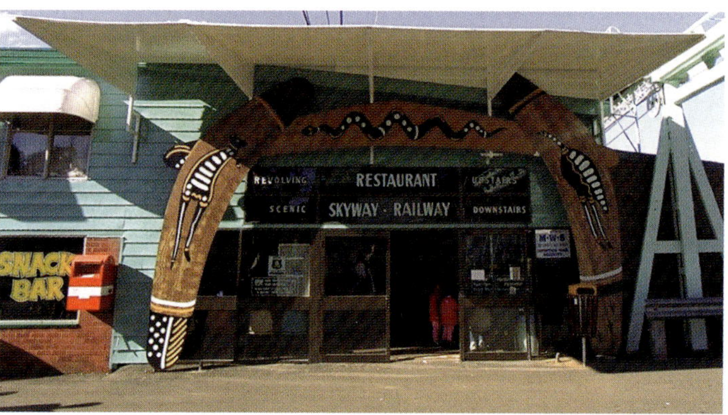

The 'Three Sisters' tourist station – a Kitsch design classic.

Others failed because they had followed valleys which brought them to dead ends. The track over the mountains, once established, became the trade route to the inland, and convict labour made of it a road fit for the coaches of Cobb & Co., the Australian transport legend only the railways would destroy.

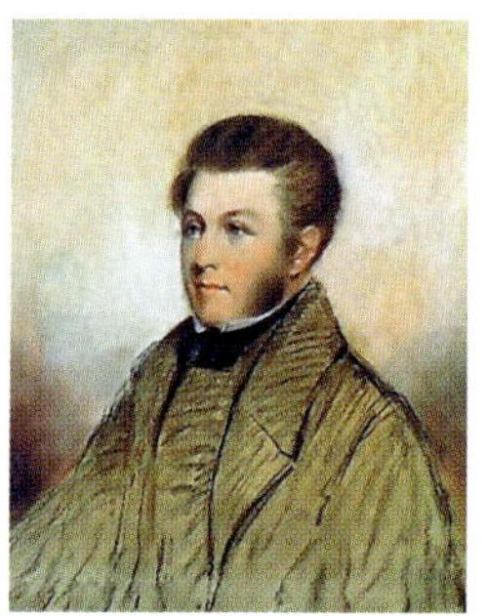

Gregory Blaxland

The railwaymen followed the ridges, too, but their task was infinitely more difficult for they had to find a route whose grades and curves were within the capacities of small steam locomotives and the adhesion of their wheels on rails.

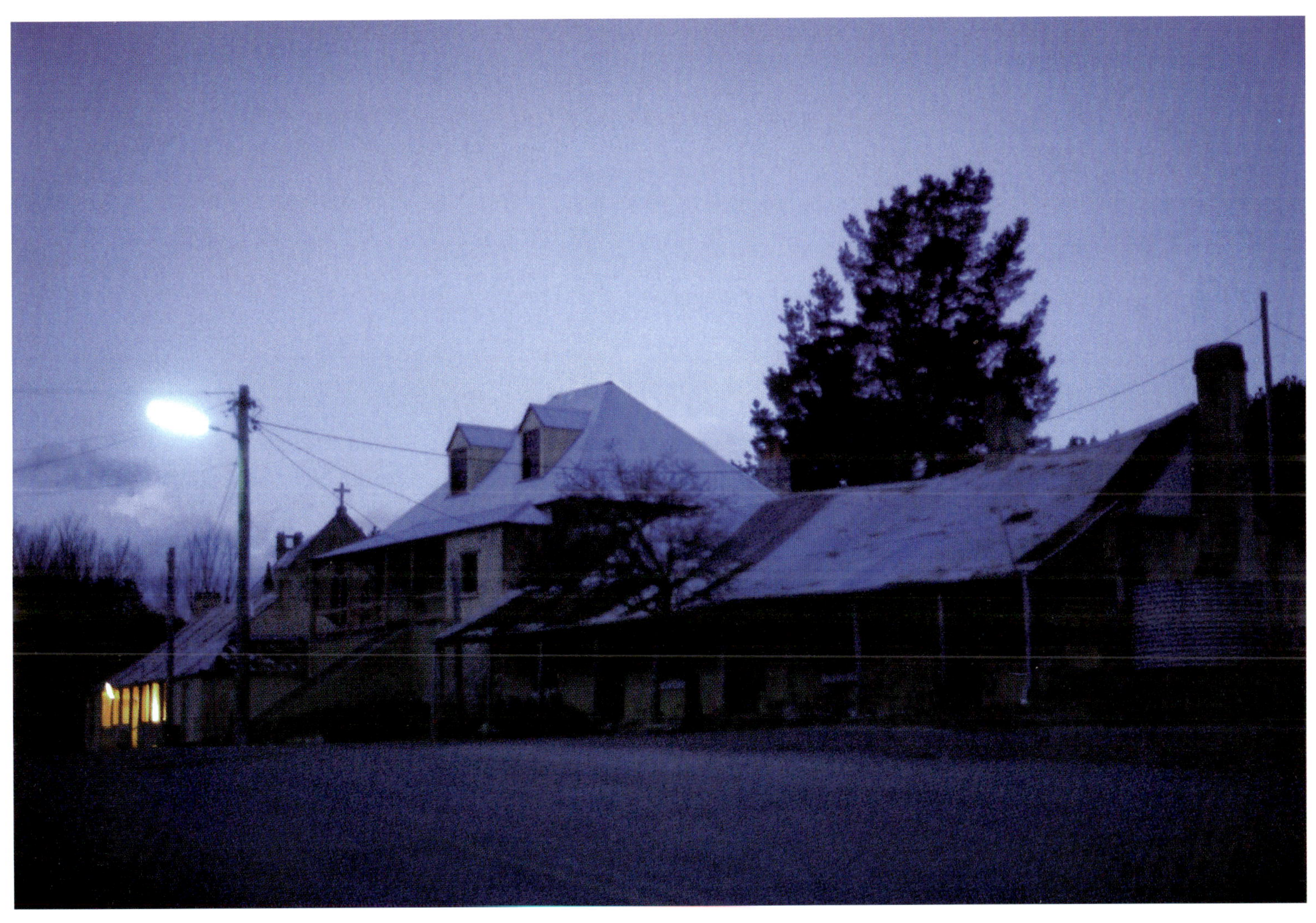

Australia as it was: The historic village of Hartley, NSW.

'It can't be done' was a catch cry of the times. A Parson, J D Lang, proposed that trains should stop when the going became too steep, and passengers could walk up stairways, and goods be lifted by rope, to another train higher up. Lang's Stairway to Heaven barely got past his pulpit, but an equally ratbag idea caused engineer Whitton some serious problems, because this was the pet plan of His Excellency the Colonial Governor.

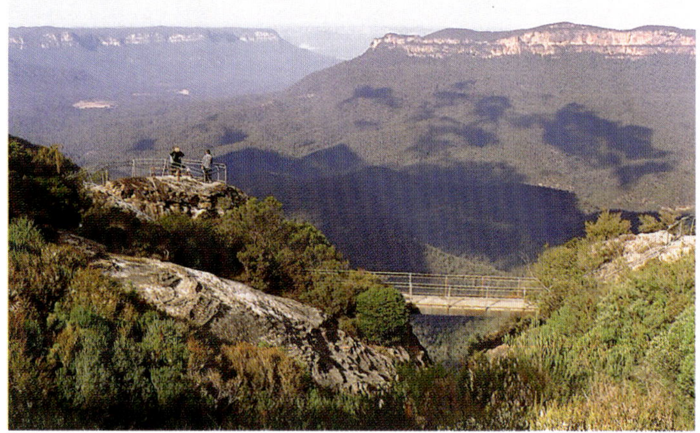

Leura, Blue Mountains, NSW.

The Governor, Denison, was a military man – Colonial Governorship was a way of rewarding military careers while at the same time keeping old soldiers out of British politics – and he was fond of horses. He wanted a horse-drawn tram across the Blue Mountains.

The Engineer, Whitton, usually described as a 'Bluff Yorkshireman,' was a man of uncompromising standards. Almost as old as railways themselves, he'd begun his apprenticeship only five years after the great locomotive trials at Rainhill, where, in 1825, Stephenson's steam engine, The Rocket, showed the way of future transport.

Whitton saw his job in New South Wales as the building of a standard gauge railway system, steam powered, and equal to the best of British practice. He would accept no less. Certainly, he would have no part of horses and trams. Showing foresight not always apparent in later railway developments, the Powers That Were agreed that Whitton's Way was best. Not that it would be made easy for him: The money allocated for railways was trimmed and pared and halved and eventually quartered. Whitton steepened his grades, tightened his curves, milled his own timber, cut his own stone and pushed his railway, a real railway, over the mountains.

A horse drawn tram ....
This one operates in Victor Harbour, SA, but is what the good Governor had in mind.

His international reputation in engineering was made by his solution to a sheer ascent on the coastal side of the range and an even more savage descent on the inland side. Whitton designed two switchbacks (zigzags, to the excited local press) and had incorporated in them a series of elegant sandstone viaducts which stand to this day as a monument more telling than the bronze bust at Sydney Central Station.

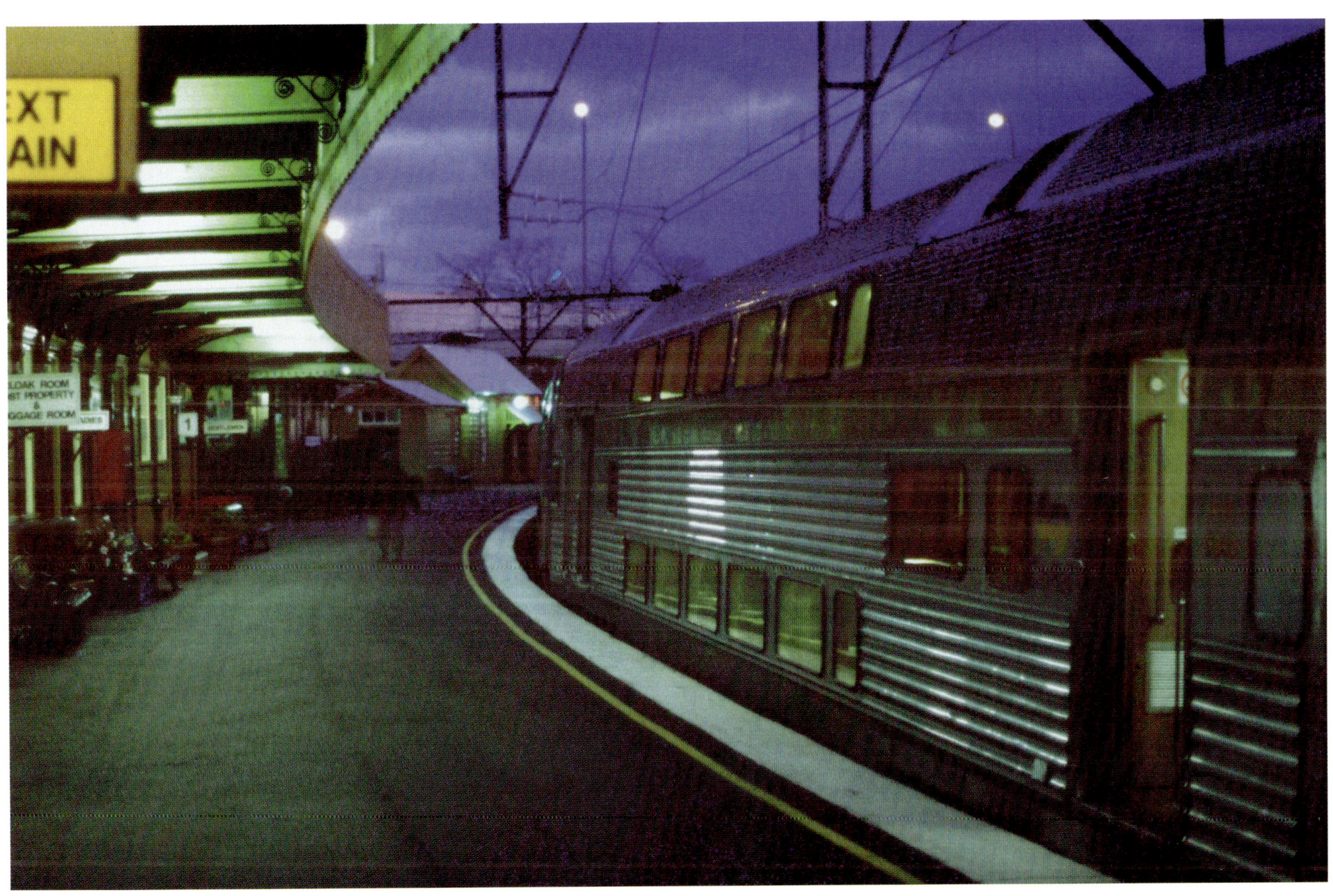

An early morning commuter train passes Katoomba. On the Blue Mountains real estate is still affordable, so people take the daily ride down the mountains to Sydney.

And as the ultimate monument to a railwayman, some of his great stone viaducts still regularly carry trains. The main lines have long since bypassed the switchbacks by a series of ten tunnels (called the Rat Holes by steam engine men who found them a preparation for hell) but a tourist line called the Zig Zag Railway ensures that the sights and sounds of steam live still along Whitton's Way. Ironically, the Zig Zag is a narrow gauge (3'6") line, for good practical and economic reasons.

Settlement of the Blue Mountains inevitably followed the railway. An Australian tradition measures the size of a town by its number of 'pubs' (hotels), and one-pub villages grew along the coach routes of Cobb and Co.

Cobb worked on a forty-mile day: After forty miles in a coach, passengers were more than ready for a night in an unmoving bed. So came the coaching inns, and around them the villages which were there and waiting when the railways came. In between the overnight stages, perhaps ten miles apart, were meal stops and stables where horses and drivers changed and passengers ate and drank.

And again, villages grew and some of them were lucky enough to be along the railway, and they prospered.

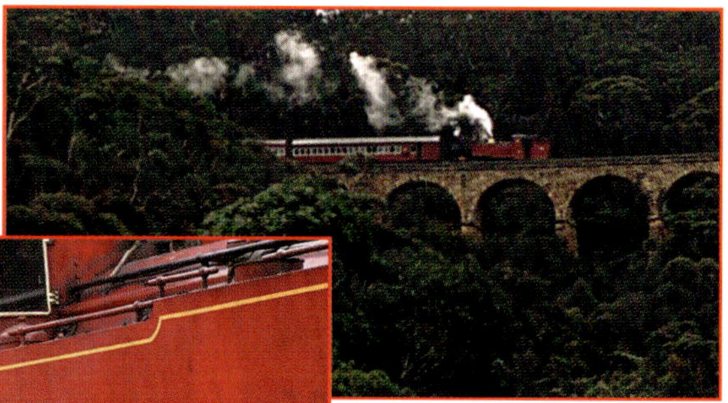

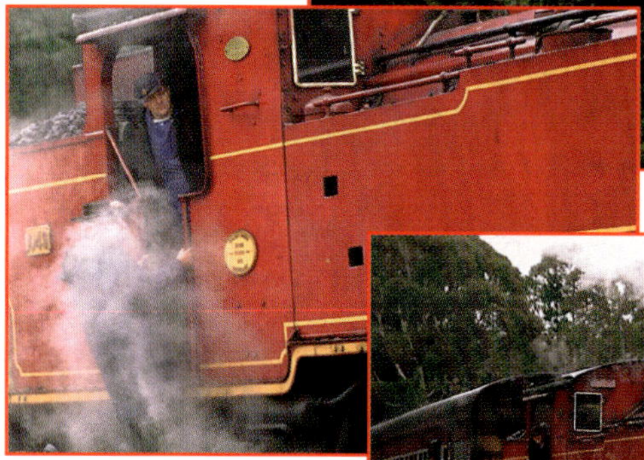

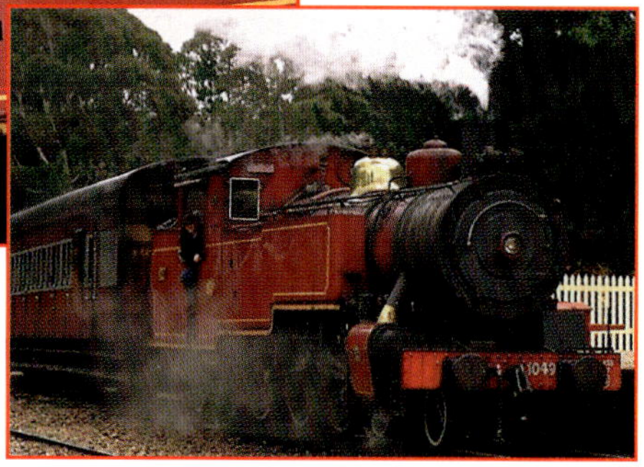

Sandstone and Steam: A tourist railway operates now the historic Zig Zag line.

Nowadays, a chain of Blue Mountains townships, Glenbrook, Valley Heights, Springwood, Faulconbridge, Hazelbrook and the rest all the way to the top of the range west of Mount Victoria, are extensions of Sydney's residential area. They had their beginnings as weekend and holiday destinations for city people, prosperous people, who could afford the escape from the summer heat and humidity of the coastal plain, and on both sides of the railway grand houses, evidence of times past, hide behind trees and hedges.

Commuter trains carry mountain residents to and from jobs in the city, and at weekends the Blue Mountains gain an extra population of tourists, drawn by the climate and the spectacular scenery which have brought people since the railway first made travel possible for anyone who sought it.

The economies forced on John Whitton as he built his way over the mountains have never been fully eased and, though the route is electrified now, the tunnels widened and the track doubled all the way to Lithgow, the Blue Mountains railway still has the sharpest curves and steepest grades anywhere between Sydney and Perth. It's

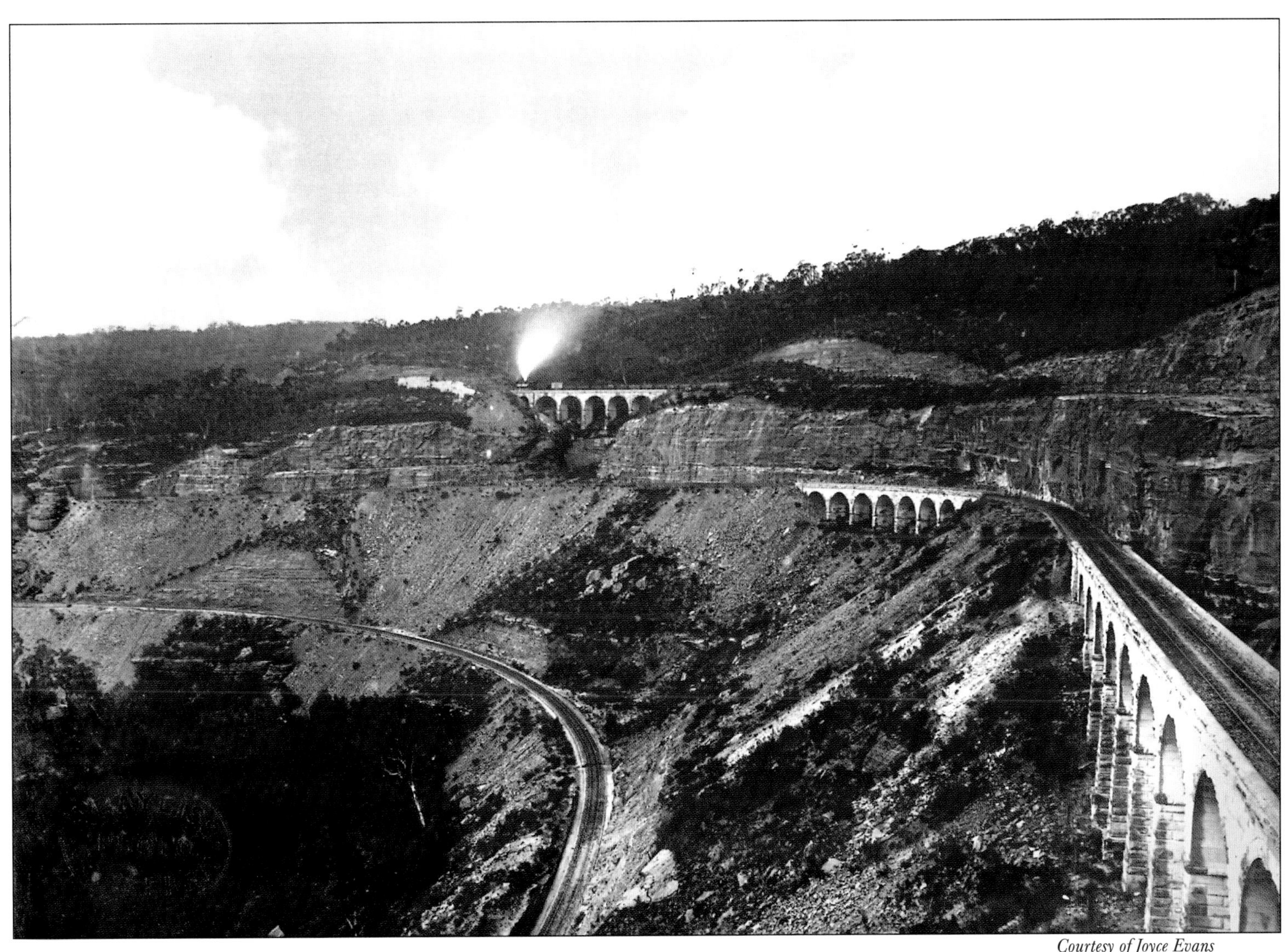

Courtesy of Joyce Evans

The Zig Zag in its original form.
Photographed by one of Australia's earliest landscape photographers, Charles Bayliss.

the sharpness of the curves that limit the speed of the Indian Pacific through the mountains. Trackside signs tell drivers the maximum speeds allowed on each section, and train controllers right along the way from Sydney to Perth and back have the east and westbound trains slotted into elaborate traffic plans.

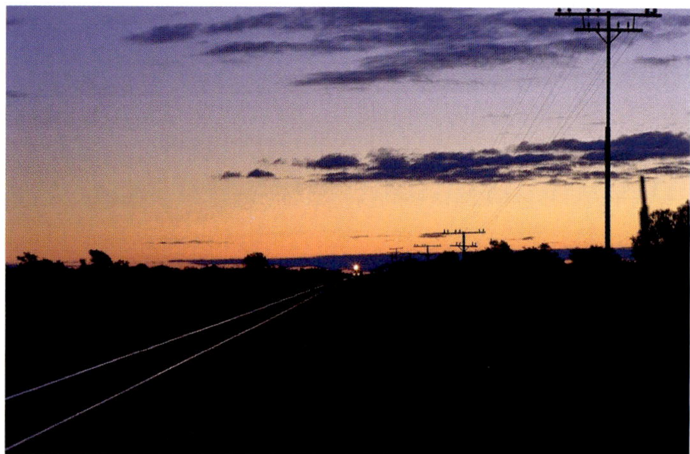

Western NSW, a link in the trans-continental chain ...

The passenger trains have their places in an intricate pattern of time and movement that will take them across the continent with minimum delays and few stops, and arrivals on time almost four and a half thousand kilometres later.

West of the Blue Mountains, the double track main line is reduced to single track almost all the way to Perth. This demands an exact choreography of rolling masses weighing perhaps six thousand tonnes and moving in opposite directions at a hundred and ten kilometres an hour and more. Passing loops make it possible, and because this is primarily a working railway and freight trains are its profit-makers, the freighters have right of way. That is why the Indian-Pacific will stop sometimes in the middle of nowhere, for no reason apparent until a coast to coast super-freighter howls past at the full power of two, three or four locomotives. The speed of the things, their relative silence until a short distance away, and their absolute unstoppability in less than a couple of kilometres, are the reasons the Indian-Pacific's doors remain resolutely locked at these passing loops. Some passengers complain it's officialdom being unnecessarily officious. The railways know that passengers sometimes do silly things, and that wandering about night or day around a passing loop is likely to damage the wanderer more than the train that runs him over. So the doors stay shut and locked, except for station stops along the way.

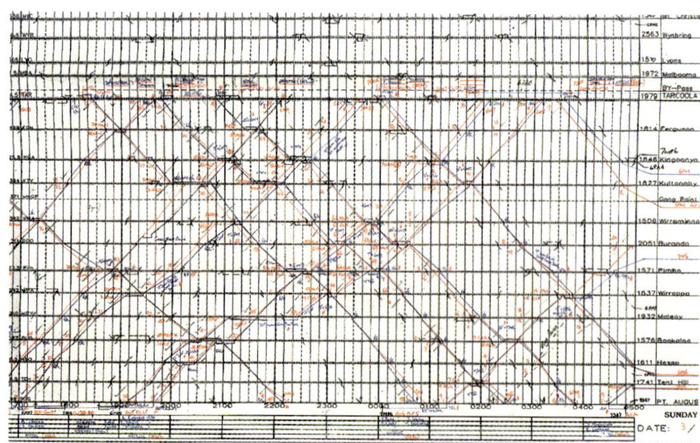

... and how it is managed.
Train movements diagram, train control, Pt. Augusta, SA.

Beyond the Mountains

The Indian Pacific, both west and eastbound, travels effortlessly over grades that made the working lives of early railwaymen hard and dangerous. For most of the steam age, engine men rode machines that gave them little protection from wind, rain and cold, and the furnaces which burned fiercely very close to them would overheat one side of a man while the mountain winds chilled the other. Nostalgia for the steam age is seldom shared by the men who worked steam over the Blue Mountains, and few railwaymen in Australia more welcomed the coming of diesel and electric locomotives.

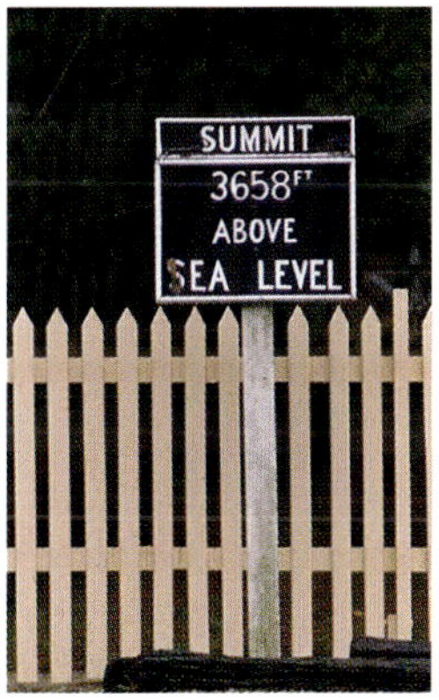

As well as the sheer hard work of constantly stoking the fire – only three classes of NSW locomotives were mechanically fired – the ten tunnels which replaced the Great Zig Zag were places of overpowering heat and dense, choking smoke. The railways provided respirators, which didn't work very well, and – never generous employers – made engine men pay for their own protective goggles. Makeshift protection from the heat and fumes of the ten tunnels provided some bizarre sights: Engine men would have hoods made from canvas or hessian bagging, soak them in cold water and with head and shoulders covered, save for a slit for their goggled eyes, steam at full power into the tunnels. The risk of stalling, or losing traction and coming to a halt inside a tunnel, brought the real fear of asphyxiation. Nor did the end of the tunnels and the top of the climb bring total relief: Certainly, it was easier going downhill but at the price of possible loss of control and the potential disaster of a runaway.

Most traffic over the mountain grades now is hauled by electric locomotives. As they run downhill, their traction motors become electric generators and act as brakes. The electricity they produce is fed back into the overhead wires and helps power another train working uphill. The CLP diesel-electrics which haul the Indian Pacific have a similar facility, but the electricity from their motors-turned-generators is fed to radiators in the roof and dissipated as heat by a system of fans.

At 1,067 metres of altitude, the train tops the Blue Mountains, having covered in an hour and 20 minutes country that defied early settlers for more than thirty years, and passes in a few seconds the unmarked site of another engineering triumph. The place was once called Newnes Junction, and it was the starting point for one of the most remarkable railways ever built in Australia. The man who masterminded its construction, the British engineer Henry Deane, went on to plan and build the Trans-Australian Railway which takes the Indian Pacific from Port Augusta across the Nullarbor Plain to Kalgoorlie. Deane's brilliance and foresight appears again later in this book.

First though, his impossible railway to the Wolgan Valley.

The Wolgan River carved over measureless time a deep valley in the sandstone of the Blue Mountains, and in this hidden valley, known in the late 19th century only to cattle thieves who grazed their stolen herds on its green river flats, early prospectors found signs of coal and oil

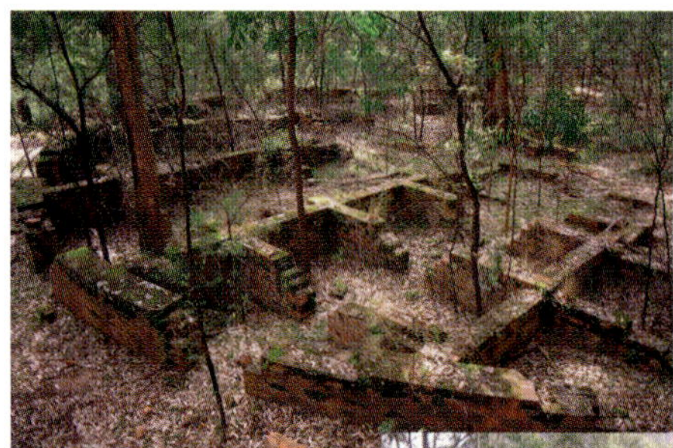

Archaeology of the Industrial Age: Newnes Oil Works, NSW.

shale. Shale is a soft rock that hides within its structure oil that can be coaxed out by heating in closed retorts. Further treatment could extract kerosene, and that was the product the colony needed: It was literally the difference between darkness and light in the age before electricity.

To mine and refine the shale of the Wolgan Valley, a company was formed in London. Its chairman was the knighted publisher George Newnes, and the mine site was named in his honour. But between the mine and the main line railway to markets was some of the roughest country Australia had to offer.

In little more than a year, the Engineer Henry Deane, his surveyors, engineers, tradesmen and labourers built an "impossible" railway: Fifty kilometres long, more than thirty miles; so steep that only special engines could climb it; built with little power other than the muscle of men and horses; tracks carved into sheer cliffs by men who worked at times hanging from ropes tied to trees above; shot holes gouged by hammer and bar, filled with blasting powder and fired by men who sometimes failed to haul themselves to safety in time and were blown apart together with the rock.

These men built a railway in less time than would be taken today by the environmental impact study. It was a triumph of man over environment. The track-builders did their work well; the Shay locomotives Henry Deane brought from the Lima Company in the United States hauled coal, coke, shale and oil trains up the savage inclines and through the tight curves they were designed for; the products of the mines, coke ovens and extraction retorts which grew on the floor of the Wolgan Valley were delivered by rail to market. But it was all in vain. The market could buy cheaper elsewhere. In the United States, Drake's first oil well promised an unlimited flow of oil at the price of drilling a hole in the earth, and the market for petroleum products, drawn, unwillingly and expensively, from shale rock, declined and failed. Oil cartels were forming. No local effort could compete with cut price imports. The Wolgan Valley project struggled on in fits and starts. There were disputes and strikes. The mine, the oil works, the railway, closed. The people moved away. The town died. Today, few traces remain of the industry and the thriving township it supported. The beautiful brickwork of the beehive coke ovens is falling apart, though enough remains to be identified. The railway platform is still there, but its buildings, and even its rails, are long gone. The track formation which railwaymen call the permanent way lives up to its name and can be traced still, by a determined walker, all fifty kilometres from the mine and works site up to the unmarked junction point on the path of the Indian Pacific, now over the dividing range and heading down to the Lithgow Valley.

Gold, Silver, Bronze

For a century, coal has been the treasure of the Lithgow Valley. A dozen mines export coal to world markets, and fuel two electricity generating stations.

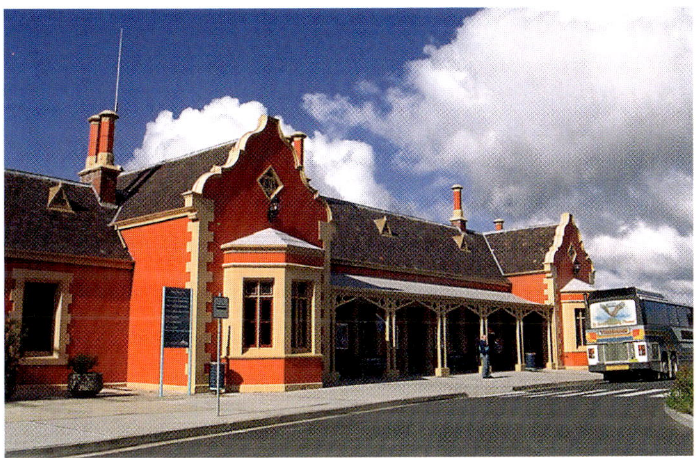

Bathurst railway station. The cosy feeling of NSW railway stations is unmatched elsewhere in the country.

For more than twenty years after the inaugural Indian-Pacific, Lithgow was a regular stop. The train would halt in Lithgow's sprawling railway yard, and while passengers ate dinner those in the know could detect from a shimmer in the soup plate or wine glass the bump as new locomotives eased in against the buffers at the front of the train. Lithgow was, and is, the western end of the electrified railway system of New South Wales, and from Lithgow on to Broken Hill the Indian-Pacific was powered by diesel-electric locomotives of the NSW Railways. That system of operation ended in the 1990s when Australian National took over management of the train from coast to coast. The same pair of CLP diesel-electrics which begin the journey in Sydney, now haul the train through to Adelaide.

West of Lithgow, a branch line heads off to Mudgee. Ahead, on the track west, is the city of Bathurst, and nearby at a place then called Summerhill Creek (and later named Ophir, after the Biblical city of gold) the first gold strike in Australia was made: February 12, 1851. The date was two years after the American gold rush, the Forty-nine, which began the rise of the state of California.

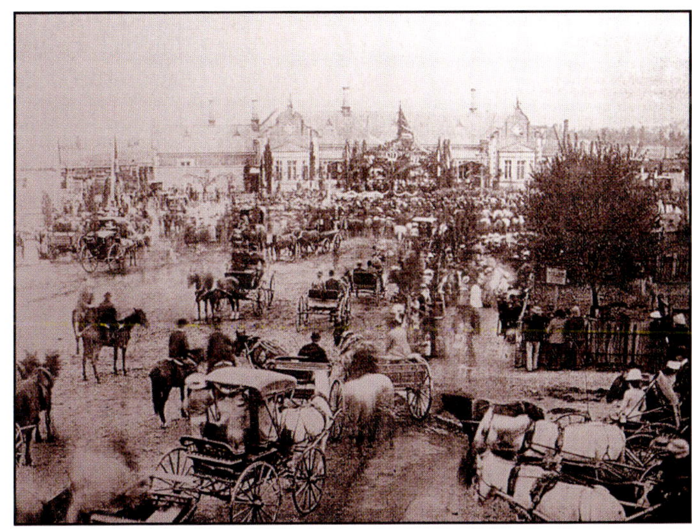

Historic Bathurst railway station: where horse met horse power, the result was inevitable.

The connection between California '49 and Bathurst '51 was a gold seeker named Edward Hargraves. He'd dug the dirt of California in '49, though pay-dirt seemed to elude him, and around Bathurst two years later he saw streams and land forms that resembled the American bonanza. With two companions he began panning Summerhill Creek. Hargraves was credited, and well rewarded by the government, as the discoverer of Australia's first gold, but as with the honour of the first crossing of the Blue Mountains, subsequent study suggests the two young men working with, or for, him should have the credit. Hargraves, these studies claim, was somewhere else at the time the wondrous metal first gleamed in the pans of the Summerhill prospectors.

The gold seekers came in their thousands: Diggers, they were called, and that was the name later generations of Australians gave the soldiers they sent to foreign battlefields. The trenches, the shafts and the drives the original diggers picked and shovelled were themselves a kind of battlefield: The natural peace of the bush was lost. Isolated groups of tents became brawling townships, and the tent towns came and went with new finds or rumours of finds of gold: Turon River, Hill End, Tambaroora. Bathurst had five thousand people and fifty hotels. Drunkenness was the major social problem of the time.

Cobb & Co., the coach line, moved its headquarters from Victoria and made Bathurst the hub of its network.

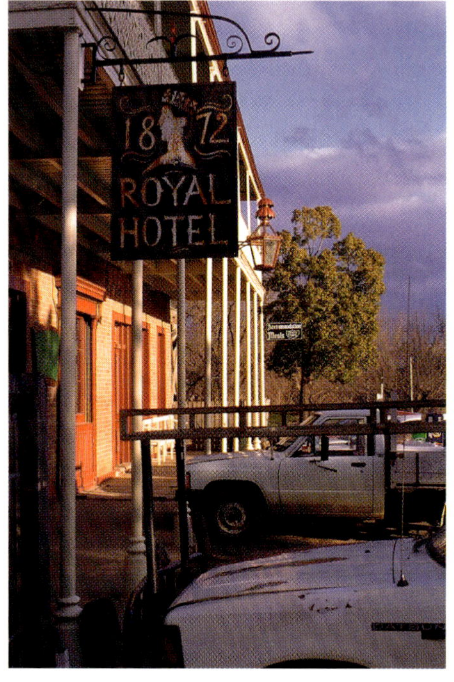

Old gold towns draw people with a sense of history: Sofala.

Gold...coaches...long hauls from isolated diggings to the city over the mountains. This was the formula, the story line, for the Time of the Outlaw in Australian history. We called them Bushrangers, and in a society not long released from convict status, where the police and the forces of law were largely despised, these men had plenty of friends as they ranged the goldfields and the bush.

From Bathurst westward to Parkes the goldfields stretched and the bushrangers prowled: Ben Hall and his gang rode boldly into Bathurst one Saturday afternoon in 1863, inspected the stock of a gunsmith, robbed a jeweller and went on for refreshments to the Sportsmens Arms Hotel. They took the place over, and ordered free drinks for everyone. Then left at their leisure with the Law nowhere in sight.

Two days later the Hall gang raided Canowindra. As masters of the little western town, they declared a holiday and organised a carnival. It was the most impudent challenge to the police in the history of Australian bushranging, and added to the status of Ben Hall as a hero of the bush. But a year and a half later Hall was betrayed by a one time friend into a police ambush, and he was shot dead at Forbes. He was twenty-seven.

Few of the diggers left marks more permanent than the traces of their scratchings along the creeks of the goldfields. But to the goldfields of Hill End came in 1861

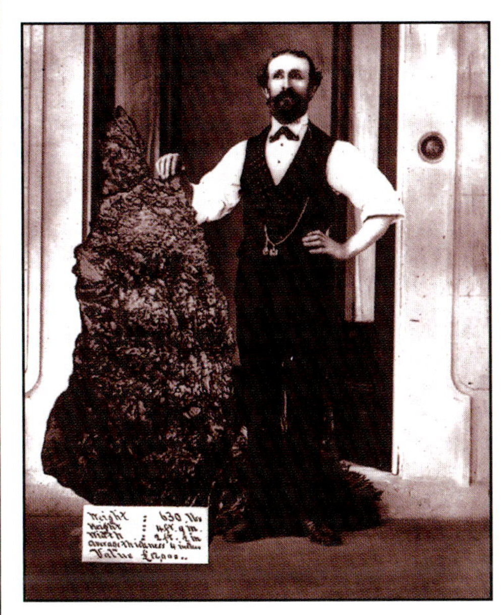

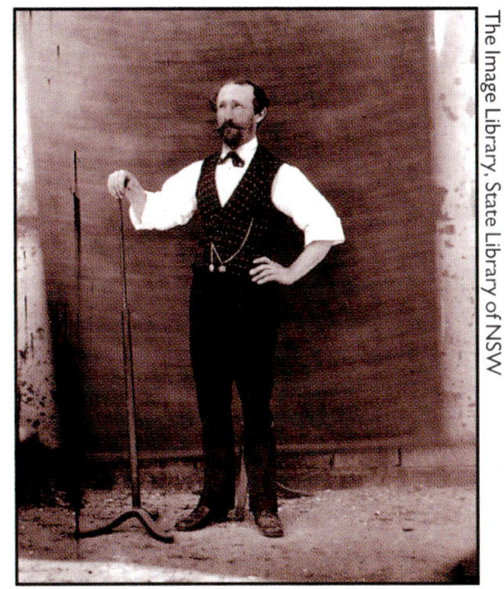

The Image Library, State Library of NSW

The famous image of Holtermann with the giant nugget is actually a photo montage. Executed by Charles Bayliss one year after the nugget was found, Holtermann was photographed in several positions with a hat holder (to keep still). The image of the nugget was copied into the picture, however, the size relationship seems to be correct. The resulting image was used for the production of a stained glass window.

one Bernhard Otto Holtermann. He acquired a share in a mine named, optimistically, The Star of Hope.

For six years, the claim seemed better named The Star of No Hope, but in 1867, Holtermann and his partners made a major strike, enough gold to allow Holtermann to diversify from the risky business of gold into the more certain earner of the liquor trade: He built the All Nations Hotel in Hill End. But the lure of gold seems to have drawn him more than the hotel trade. He sold up and put the money back into mining, into two failed ventures. The Star of Hope he made a company, and sold shares to keep it going until in October 1872 the mine discovered two new seams of gold. In the same week, the Star of Hope produced the biggest single lump of gold ever won, the fabulous Holtermann Nugget, three thousand ounces of pure gold.

Holtermann's place in the history of Australian gold was assured not so much by the discovery of the nugget as by the presence of a photographer to record it. Holtermann had encouraged the work of the pioneer cameramen Henry Beaufoy-Merlin, and he assembled some of the earliest photographic records of Australia in an exhibition which came to

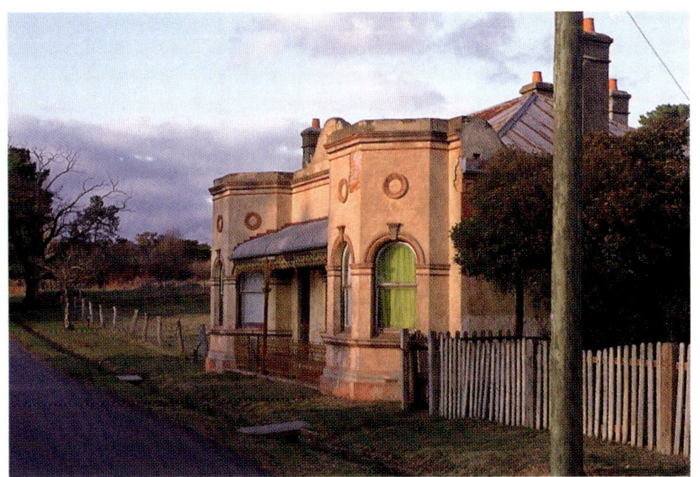

Hill End - some struck it rich

be known as the Holtermann collection. Holtermann built on high ground at St Leonards in Sydney a house which incorporated a tower designed as a camera and darkroom in one to photograph panoramas of the growing city. Beaufoy-Merlin was training an assistant, a young man named Charlie Bayliss. When Merlin died suddenly in 1876, Bayliss took over his work, and the famous Sydney panoramas were photographed by Bayliss and Holtermann.

Consisting of three negatives and measuring 14'6" by 3'2" their panoramas were the largest in the world. These pictures, and others made about the same time in Melbourne, Holtermann took around the world, and won a Bronze medal at the Philadelphia Centennial Exhibition of 1876. But his lasting fame, and that of Beaufoy-Merlin, is in the simple, telling pictures of life on a gold field, the Hill End Collection.

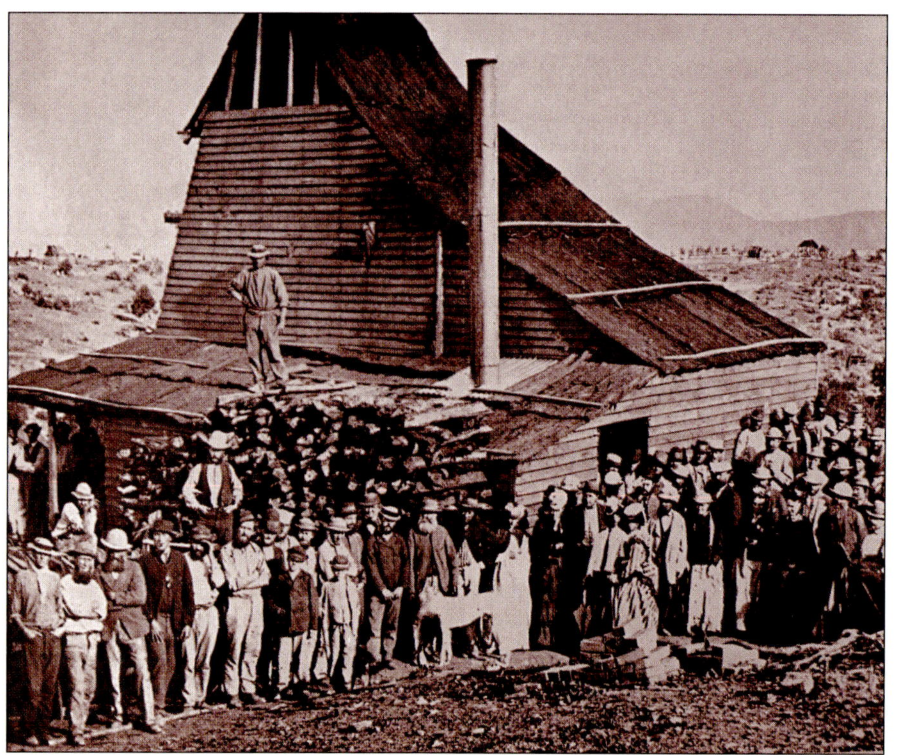

Shaft, outbuildings, miners, and members of the syndicate of the Star of Hope mine. Photographed by Henry Beaufoy-Merlin

Hill End still exists, and today's people search for gold in its creeks and gullies. Fossicking is an established tourist attraction here and around Gulgong and Mudgee, and it's little different from the way the pioneers searched for gold a century and a half ago: Some dirt from the creek bed in the pan, the patient swirling of water to separate out the lighter mud; the residue of little stones in the bottom of the pan... and amongst it, if you're skilled and lucky, the 'show,' the gleam of gold.

The faith of every prospector is that there's more gold in the ground than's ever been found, and someone's bound to find it, one day.

To keep alive this faith, they recall that as recently as 1979, near Orange, two local fossickers found a gold nugget of 160 ounces (gold is always measured in the old Imperial measure) and their afternoon's work gained them $100,000.

The Prime Minister from the Footplate

In time, a city grew on the site of the brawling gold town, Bathurst. Before the gold, the explorer George Evans had been the first European to walk this valley of the Macquarie River and assess its potential for farming and grazing, and as early as 1815 it was declared the site for the first inland town in the colony. The railway came in 1876, along the same route the Indian-Pacific follows 120 years later. The demands for fuel, water and maintenance of steam engines made it a railway town on the western line, and in 1885, the year Bathurst was optimistically declared a city, the wife of a town blacksmith gave birth, in a humble house across the road from the railway yards, to a baby boy destined to become one of the greatest men of his time, or any time, in Australian history. Patrick Chifley, first generation Australian born of parents from Tipperary, Ireland, named his newborn son Joseph Benedict.

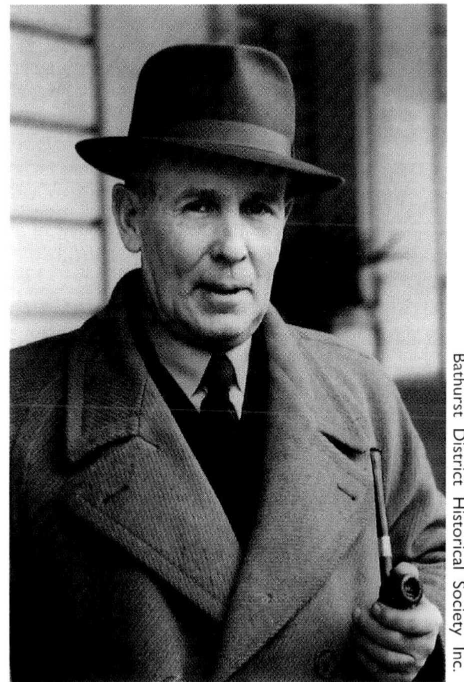
Bathurst District Historical Society Inc.

Ben Chifley

For nine of his boyhood years, Ben Chifley worked for his farming grandfather, and in 1903 he went to work for the railways as a shop-boy at the Bathurst locomotive shed. In the hierarchy of the railways, no job was more humble. The career path ahead of him was Cleaner, Acting Fireman, Fireman, Acting Driver, Driver. He didn't know, that day he joined the railways in 1903, that his career path would end as perhaps the greatest, most honourable Prime Minister Australia would know.

Ben Chifley, deprived by economics and family circumstance of formal education, began a lifelong program of self-education at the Bathurst Workers' Education Association, the Technical School and the Railways Institute. Four nights a week for fifteen years he studied. In 1914, he gained the coveted rank of Driver. That meant the end of days and nights hurling coal from a slim shovel into the fireboxes of steam locomotives on the main western line east and west of Bathurst. His association with the Railways Institute continued, and so good a student was he that he was appointed a part-time instructor.

Three years a driver, handling 2-8-0 goods engines and the swift passenger 4-6-0 *P* Class, Chifley found himself part of the railways strike of 1917. The issue was nothing to do with Chifley, or with Bathurst, or with the railways. It had begun at the Tramways Workshop at Randwick, Sydney, over a work-recording card the Union said was a version of an infamous work control system Henry Ford had introduced to his car factories in America. Union solidarity brought the strike to Bathurst Loco. On August 6, 1917, 400 loco crews, Chifley included, joined the strike. On September 17, Chifley was sacked for 'active participation in the strike.' He was later re-employed, but reduced in status to fireman. He was prominent in the formation of the new and industrially radical Federated Union of Locomotive Enginemen and became a Union Advocate. The blows of perceived unfairness forged the potential politician and set Ben Chifley on the path to Canberra.

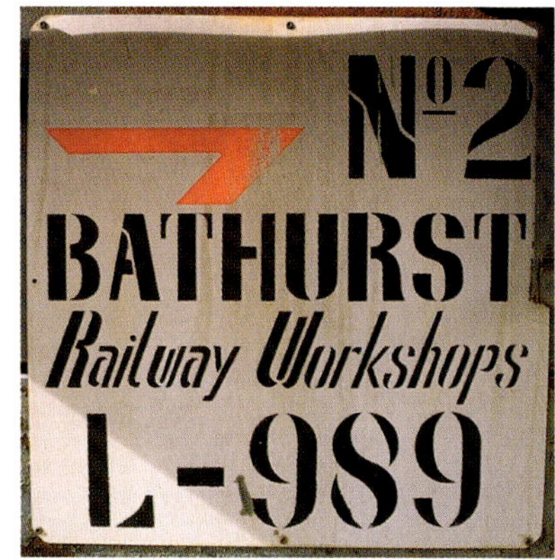

Nothing in Chifley's life came easy: His first political bids, for state office, failed, as did his first try for the Federal Parliament. He went to Canberra first as a new Member of the House of Representatives in 1928, and was Minister for Defence in 1931 when Labour lost office. Nine years in the political outback, he returned to Canberra in 1940, and took up residence in a room of a Canberra hotel in which he spent his political life. When a squabbling conservative government fell apart in October 1941, Chifley, as Treasurer, and his Leader Curtin found themselves running a country which had declared itself at war with faraway Germany. Two months later, the Japanese attacked Pearl Harbor. For the first time since the British took Australia from its Aboriginal inhabitants, there was the real threat of invasion. Curtin and Chifley were the wartime leaders. Curtin died only a month before the atom bombs ended the Pacific war. Chifley, the Prime Minister from the Footplate, began his time of power.

He put it to good use: No Prime Minister, before or since, has left such a mark on the country. He nationalised the one-time outback airline Qantas and set it on a path to international fame. He formed a Government-owned internal airline, TAA, and re-established the Commonwealth Shipping Line. He made possible the aluminium industry. He launched the Snowy Mountains Hydro-Electricity Scheme. He facilitated formation of the ABC News Service. He allowed the formation of the Australian Security Intelligence Organisation, the less-than-famous ASIO. He had a pivotal role in General Motors' decision to build the Holden car.

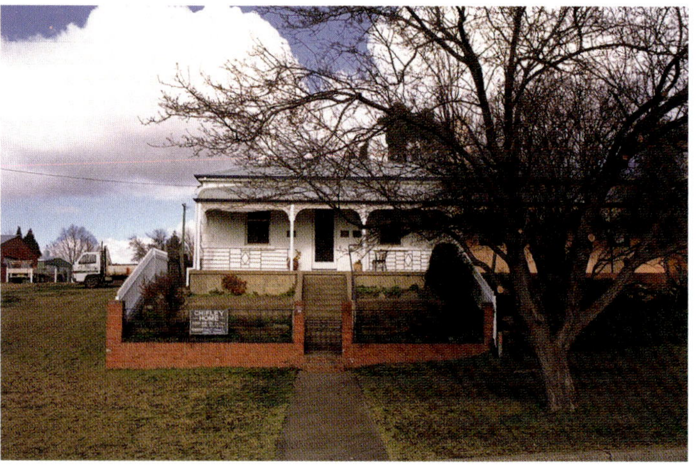

The Prime Minister's home in Bathurst. This, and a Canberra hotel room were where he spent his political life.

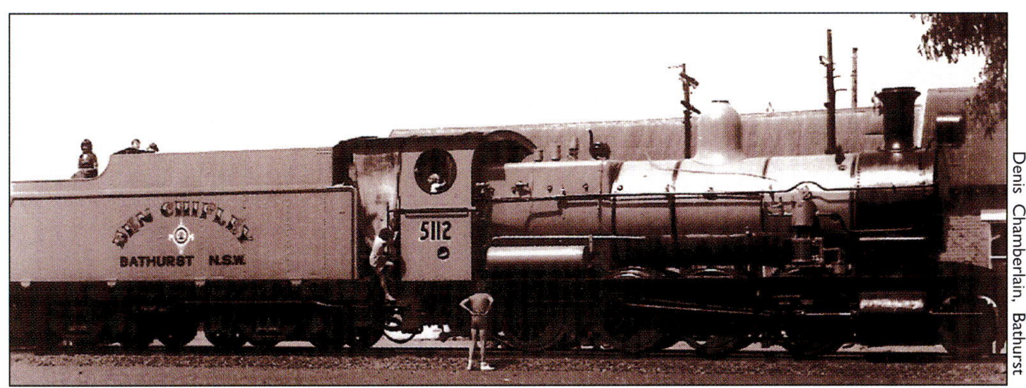

Denis Chamberlain, Bathurst

A locomotive named Chifley: 5112 was on of the locomotives Ben Chifley drove East and West of Bathurst. The decorated tender is a later addition.

In a statement of personal goals, Chifley said: "I shall not do anything which has not the mark of common sense upon it."

He fought the communist infiltration of Australian unions. In the disastrous coal mines' strike of June to August 1949, which left cities and towns in darkness and cold, stopped trains and trams and put 500,000 out of work, Chifley sent in the Army to work open-cut mines. He outraged some sections of the union movement. There were many people in Australia who still regarded the Russian dictator Stalin as the hero wartime propaganda had made of him. Chifley saw Stalin in another role, the mastermind of an international conspiracy to manipulate the strength of the trade union movement against governments unsympathetic to communism. Chifley, a union man to the core, faced the bitter necessity to break a union. But the country applauded him and the communist party never regained the influence Chifley had cost it.

Chifley, in turn, lost when he challenged the banks and proposed to nationalise their Australian operations. He was defeated in the election of 1949, and died two years later.

His memorial is hard to identify: The humble home he maintained in Bathurst is one; one of the locomotives he drove is preserved as another. But his words are the most powerful monument he left, and it would do no harm to carve them on the desks of subsequent, lesser politicians:

"I have never made rosy promises which I knew were not true or could not be given effect to.....I will never make an election promise unless I am already sure that it can be carried out."

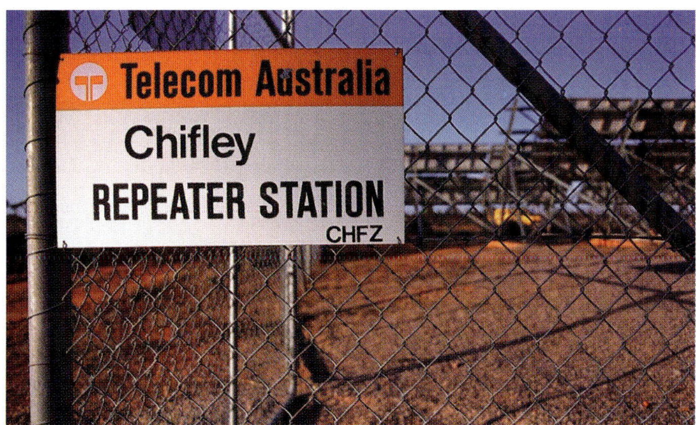

Chifley repeater – but could there ever be another?

Top Soil

As the glamour of gold faded from the Bathurst district, agriculture was there as a more permanent source of wealth. Land grants were the basis for big grazing properties that made wealthy men of those lucky, or influential, enough to benefit from a land allocation system which carefully preserved privilege. Elaborate homesteads in the country between Bathurst and Orange, the district called the Central West, recall the boom times of the nineteenth century, when the better off land owners built grand houses and surrounded them with gardens and trees in the style of English country estates. They were Englishmen, and naturally they set out to create an image of Home. Many Australian place names reflect the homesickness of these people. So do the trees they planted, the houses they built, and – sadly for the fragile soils of Australia – the farming methods, the farming machines, they brought with them.

Australia's first farmers were accustomed to the deep top soils of British farmland. And they had worked within a climate they could depend on for regular seasons, reliable rain. But the soils of Australia were old, shallow and fragile. It took more than a hundred years for the basic facts of life in rural Australia to be generally recognised: Over-

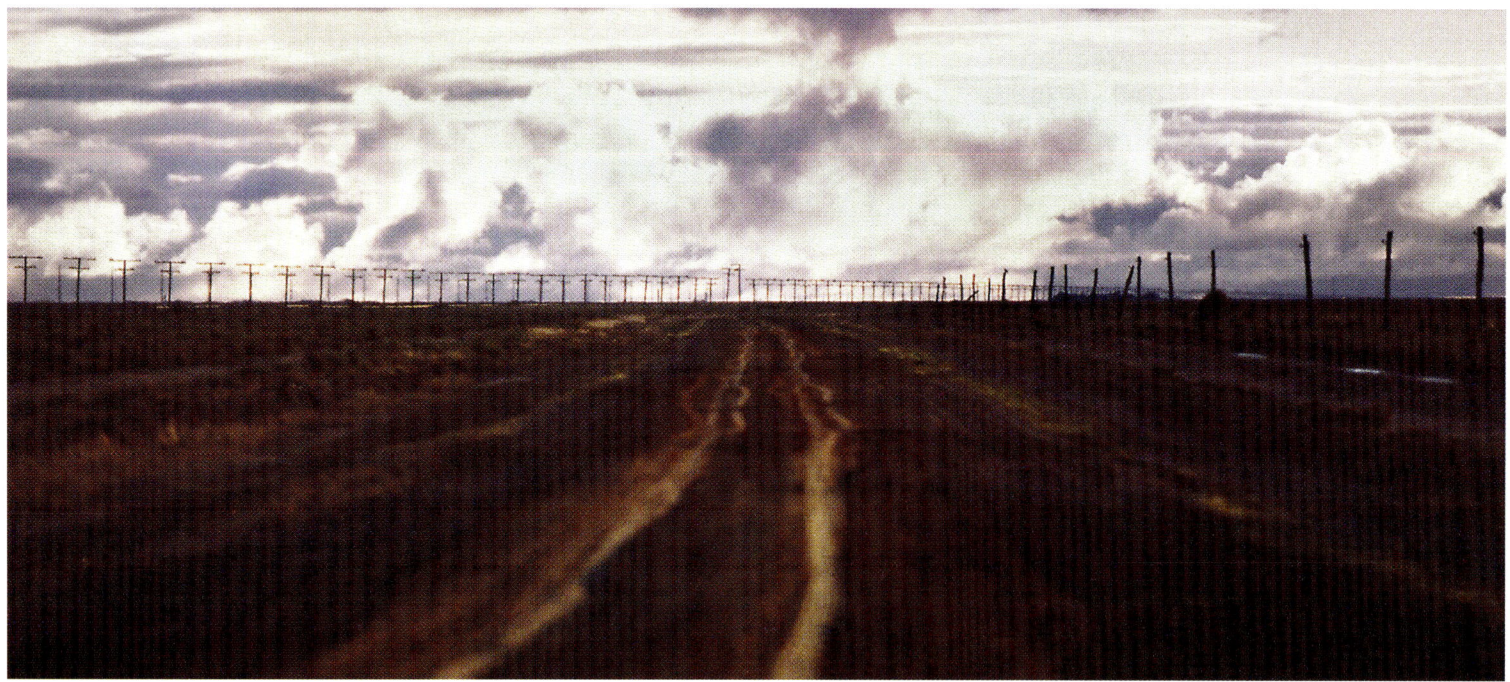

Wet season in outback NSW.

working destroys the soil. A clean ploughed and harrowed paddock might look good, but every breeze will blow away, every storm wash away, this thin and irreplacable layer of topsoil, where all the crops are grown and where all the wealth is. Drought is not a freak of Australian nature: It is a regular feature.

Good seasons, generous rain, are the natural freaks, and farming planned around them will inevitably fail.

In recent years there's been at last a general realisation that traditional ways were wrong ways. A nationwide movement called Landcare has brought to the notice of Australians everywhere, and especially those who have custody of the land, that unless things change, quickly and drastically, Australia's future as a producer of food and fibre will be at serious risk.

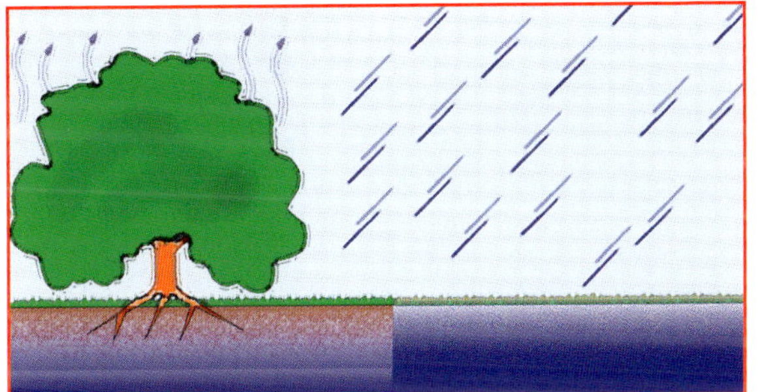

Deep rooted trees keep the water table low: Salt stays well below the surface. On cleared land rainfall and irrigation make the water table rise. Salt is transported to the surface and non-salt-resistant plants die.

Along the route of the Indian-Pacific in New South Wales, South and Western Australia, the signs of damaged, even destroyed, land are clear to see. Soil erosion is the most obvious: Gully erosion where water moving along a channel as innocuous as a sheep track will, over time, gouge out a gully a metre, two metres, deep. And the more insidious sheet erosion where wind and rain have stripped bare the topsoil and revealed bald clay in which nothing will grow.

Worst of all, salination, where the mindless over-clearing of trees, often at Government direction and financed by Government subsidy, has taken away the natural pumps which control the underground water table, and water, carrying destructive loads of natural salt, has come to the surface and the land is destroyed, forever.

In only two hundred years of farming widespread areas of serious damage have developed. In some places, notably the wheat belt of Western Australia, land has been damaged beyond economic repair in just one generation. It is that phrase 'beyond economic repair' that so concerns soil scientists.

It means that while much of the eroded or salted land could be returned to production, it could never grow enough to pay the price of its repair. So it's lost, forever, to Australian farming, to world food production, to Earth itself.

In the apportionment of blame for this agricultural catastrophe, the farmer is the obvious culprit. But it's unfair to blame this generation of farmers, or their fathers, or even their grandfathers, because they all worked as well as they knew how and often followed the recommendations, even the regulations, of Government land authorities, who were more often wrong than right. In Western Australia, just one generation ago, the first clearing of bush took place in the northern wheat belt. The land was surveyed and divided into blocks which took no account of land forms, paid no heed to the paths of creeks and storm waters, ignored totally the level of ground water and the

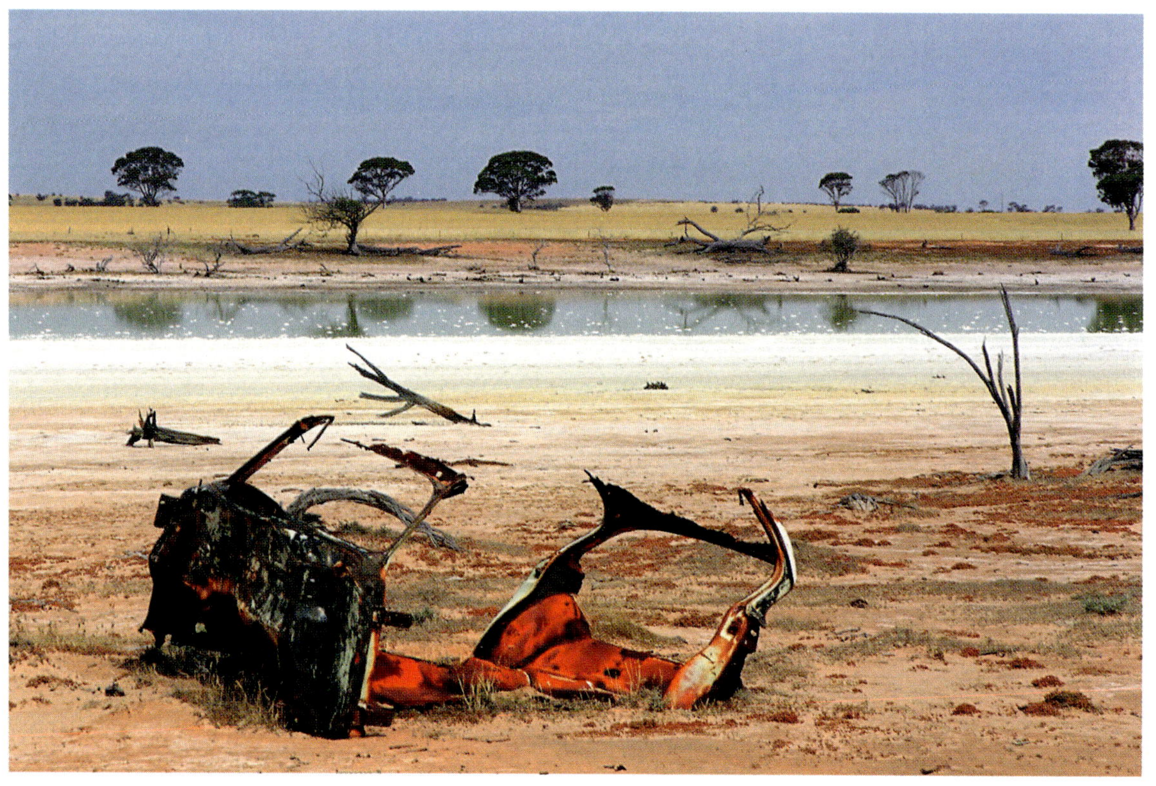

Ruined land, 1996, Southern Cross, WA: Beyond economic repair.

It's not too late, the optimists say. But history is against them.

It is another tragedy of the land in Australia that the realisation of the damage we have done has come at about the same time as yet another financial crisis for the land. Since earliest times, Australian primary producers have had to accept what the buyers of the world have been prepared to offer. There has never been a serious or successful attempt to control markets. Always, we have obeyed them. And in the last quarter of the 20th Century, when predatory market manipulators, either political or financial, in other countries have managed world farm trade as part of the broader picture of politics, Australian producers have suffered.

Wool is the perfect example: Australia has warehouses full of the stuff, unsold, while the international buyers, sellers, re-buyers, re-sellers, manufacturers, wholesalers and retailers manipulate the market and decide between themselves how many thousands of percent of profit will be added between the fleece shorn, say, in a shed

effect upon it of the mass removal of trees. Blocks that looked equal, neat and symmetrical on the walls of a departmental office in the capital, Perth, were an exact plan for the salination disaster that would strike the area only a quarter of a century later.

Despite this and other disasters of land clearing, natural Australia is still under assault in the name of development. After two hundred years of farming the place, we should have learned better. We are all, it seems, slow learners.

alongside the Indian-Pacific track west of Orange, and the 'all wool' suit on sale in London. There is a modern Australian legend of a wool grower, shopping for a suit in a fashionable Sydney establishment, raising his eyebrows at the price of the suit the salesman suggests. "But sir," the salesman urges, "it's pure wool. And do you know the price of wool these days?"

"Listen, son," says the wool man, "they paid me around two dollars eighty last year for enough wool to make that suit. You want eight hundred for it. Swap you jobs, son."

As the 21st Century looms, a process nearly two centuries overdue is just beginning in Australia: Specialist mills are processing the best of wool into the best of cloth. The Colonial Governor Phillip Gidley King proposed something similar late in the eighteenth century: The establishment in the Colony he governed of a high quality wool industry.

Squawks of alarm resulted from London. King was instructed that Australian wool could be processed locally only into convict clothing and blankets. Quality material would continue to be woven in British mills, to be re-exported to Australia if desired and afforded, and his job was to ensure an on-going supply of quality raw material.

Subsequent Australian governments, for more than a hundred years, loyally accepted that role whileever Prime Ministers saw themselves as elected Colonial Governors. While in Europe, Italy and Japan, Australian wool was crafted by skilled, but entirely mechanical processes, into the finest fabric ever made.

The woman who began the Australian wool industry, Elizabeth Macarthur, would have been proud of the small farmer couples who are developing new, small scale fibre industries in modern Australia.

Elizabeth developed the breeding program which produced the famous Australian Merino sheep while her more lauded husband, John, was off playing politics in England.

Along the railway almost from the edge of Sydney to the beginning of the inland's arid zone, around every town are the small holdings, hobby farms they're called, of five to fifty acres and supporting rural enterprises that either drain or supplement the town incomes of their owners. They grow wine grapes, or graze angora goats. The elegant alpacas from South America look curiously at passing trains. The brown and back sheep, genetic throwbacks long despised as polluters of good white fleece, are bred for the handicraft markets.

The 'five-acre farmers' have long been derided in country Australia. Until people, particularly businesses and local governments, began to do their sums and realised the hobby farmers were making unprecedented injections of developmental money into local economies. Around them had grown small service industries, providing skills from fencing to bulldozing, and the goods and services demands of these five-acre newcomers were bringing a new and often previously unthought of level of variety and choice in everything from hardware shops to supermarkets.

Rails West

Orange, the next stop on the westbound path of the Indian-Pacific, was founded on gold, but it's the centre now of one of the food bowls of Australia, famous for food crops and orchards, though fruit has nothing to do with its name: Orange was named, for some inexplicable reason, for a member of minor European royalty, the Prince of Orange, who became king of Holland.

At the centre of the Orange landscape is Mount Canobolas, all that remains of the last active volcano in this region.

At 1,395 metres, Canobolas is not much as mountains go, yet it's the highest point of land between Sydney and Perth. Around Canobolas is a significant wildlife sanctuary, where a census of the animal population found thirteen native species, from brush tail possums to black snakes. There are resident native bird colonies, and migratory species visit the mountain to breed.

Australia generally has a poor record for preserving native species both animal and plant. Its record of extinction of mammal species in the world's worst, and of some 22,000 native plant species, a quarter are at risk.

Orange is the site of the Australian National Field Days, a yearly exposition of farm machinery and farming techniques, which has earned an international reputation. Anyone with a new machine, or a new idea, can show it at the field days and judge from the reaction of thousands of potential users if it's likely to succeed.

The grazing zones of the Central West merge into the grain belt of the western plains, and beyond the plains into the Arid Zone. The train visits, like a spirit of the night, the sleeping little towns that serve the bush. But it seldom stops, and the traveller's impression is of a vast blackness relieved occasionally by a patch of lights, a glimpse of an empty main street, a moment of activity at a railway station.

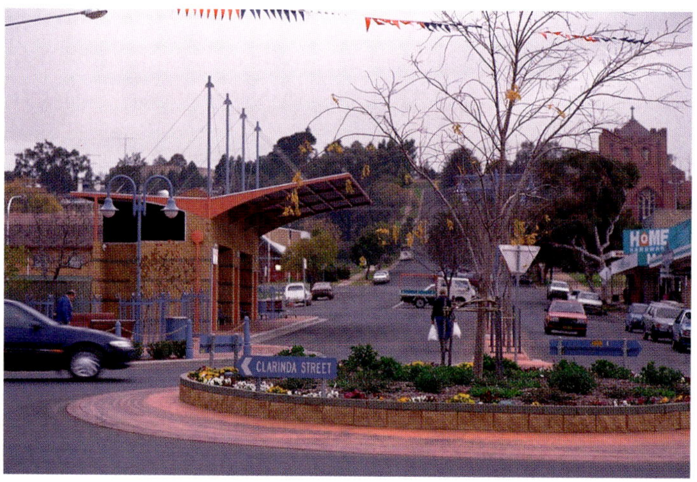

A quiet country town, a centre of world science: Parkes, NSW.

Parkes is a necessary stop for another change of locomotive crew, and one of the diesels can be shut down here and towed all the way to Adelaide, for there's hardly a hill worthy of two locomotives from Parkes all the way to Perth.

You'd never know, from the sleepy station and the view from the train, that this pleasant little town is a centre of world science: In the midst of wheat fields a few kilometres out of town is an instrument which seeks to link us with the stars: One of the great radio-telescopes of international astronomy.

Built and operated by the CSIRO, the Australian national scientific and industrial research organisation, the Parkes radio-telescope listens with a great electronic ear to the sounds of the universe, receiving and decoding the

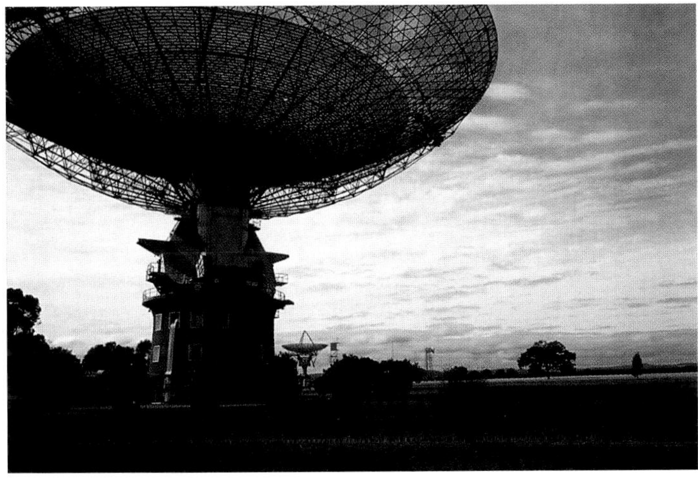

Listening to the sounds of the Universe: Radio telescope, Parkes NSW.

signals of the galaxies, natural radio emissions that have travelled through space for thousands of years.

Many discoveries in astronomy are credited to the scientists and the giant instrument at Parkes: They have watched the birth of stars; Quasars, the most luminous known objects of the universe, were identified from Parkes; there has been notable work on the mysterious deep space sources of regular signals called Pulsars.

West of Parkes, near the wheat town, Condobolin, the train crosses the Lachlan River, and after the Lachlan there's only one more river to cross all the way across Australia, and that's the great Darling.

The River Darling is part of the Murray-Darling system, Australia's biggest. It stretches from southern Queensland and the Snowy Mountains of New South Wales west almost as far as Adelaide. Water from the Murray-Darling irrigates huge areas of intensive agriculture and is the water supply for scores of towns and even for the city of Adelaide.

But the system is also used as a drain: The effluent of river bank towns flows into it. The runoff from irrigation carries in a destructive load of agricultural chemicals. The river system shows signs of serious overload. Growths of poisonous algae have contaminated reaches of the Darling: 2,000 kilometres of the river once turned bright green from its spread, and in 1996 1,000 kilometres of the Darling's banks collapsed.

Along the Murray irrigation has upset the natural water table and salt, normally at a safe depth underground, is rising dangerously close to the soil surface and threatening the farming future of as much as 200,000 hectares of the Murray-Darling basin.

The solution? Trees, lots of trees. Trees by the million to replace those destroyed by farmers and graziers who saw trees as competitors against their crops and stock for the nutrients of the soil, and by government land and agricultural experts who regarded only cleared

Permanent water vanished, and with it the wildlife and vegetation. The people moved, and kept moving following the rain, the food animals, the seasons. Proof of their passing, and their pauses, they left in rock paintings and carvings which endure still in the nearby Mootwingee National Park.

The Indian-Pacific at Menindee.

The Europeans who brought their sheep this far west in the 1850s came in a season of rare plenty. They brought too many sheep, but prospered and made money until the weather cycle changed and a run of drought years turned their pastures into dust. This was part of the process of learning about this new country, that it could not be farmed, as Europe and England were farmed, and grazed at so many sheep to the acre of hectare. Here, it would be many acres for each sheep, so the properties had to be of enormous areas: Today, 7,000 to 40,000 hectares is about the range, for every sheep needs up to five hectares of grazing to sustain it.

Such properties, or 'stations' as they came to be called, made nonsense of the old ways of caring for sheep. This was no place for shepherds. A new breed of man developed to control a new breed of sheep. These men rode on horseback around the limits, the boundaries, of the stations and tried to keep enormous flocks of sheep contained and controlled. They were called boundary riders. One of them was a man named Charlie Rasp, and riding his boundary one day in 1883 he noticed something odd about the surface rock outcrops at a place called the Broken Hill.

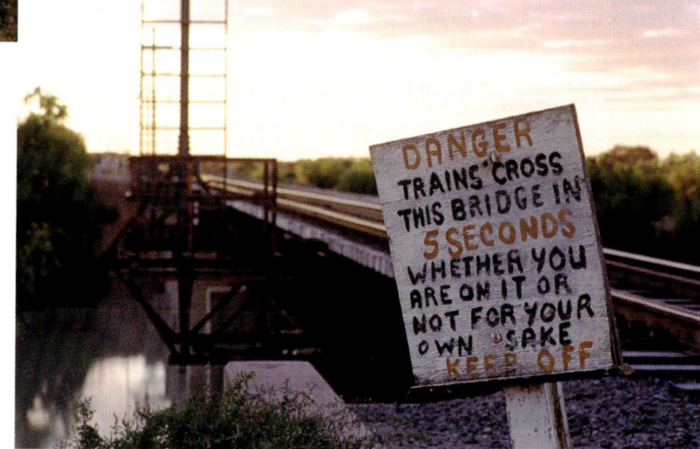

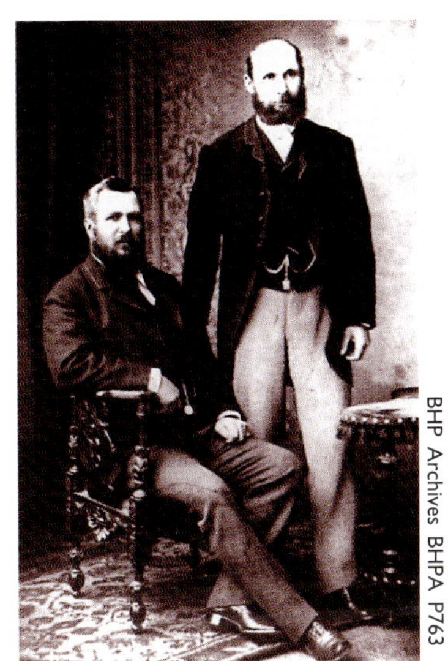

George McCulloch (l) and Charles Rasp (r).

To a knowing eye, the surface traces of mineral were as effective as a sign saying 'Dig Here.' And when dug, these hard old hills revealed one of the richest mines the world has ever seen; a mine that would last a hundred years and more; that would not only create a city around it but would become the stuff of national legend, the origin of social change and political development. This was not the flash in the pan wealth of gold. The wealth of Broken Hill was, and is, in industrial metals, lead and zinc, and the sterling metal, silver. Together, the rich ores of Broken Hill would finance the beginning of industrial Australia.

Rasp, the discoverer of the Broken Hill mineral field, was anything but a simple stockman. Accounts of his origins are many and varied, but it's known, from his own account, that he was German born, near Stuttgart, in 1846. He claimed to have been a food chemist, but historical research suggests that Rasp was a military deserter, a former officer of the 12th Corps of the Prussian Army, who'd sensibly vanished during the Franco-German war of 1870, and surfaced in Melbourne, under the name von Hengel in 1871. He worked in vineyards, and dug for gold in Victoria's high country. He went to the deep bush, working along the Murray River and north to Mount Gipps station, where the boundary he was assigned to ride included the broken hill where the black oxides of tin stained the brown and yellow earth.

With two associates he pegged the first claim on the Barrier Range, and with them and his boss, the station manager McCulloch, the overseer, the storekeeper and a station hand he formed a syndicate which eventually became the Broken Hill Proprietary Company, BHP.

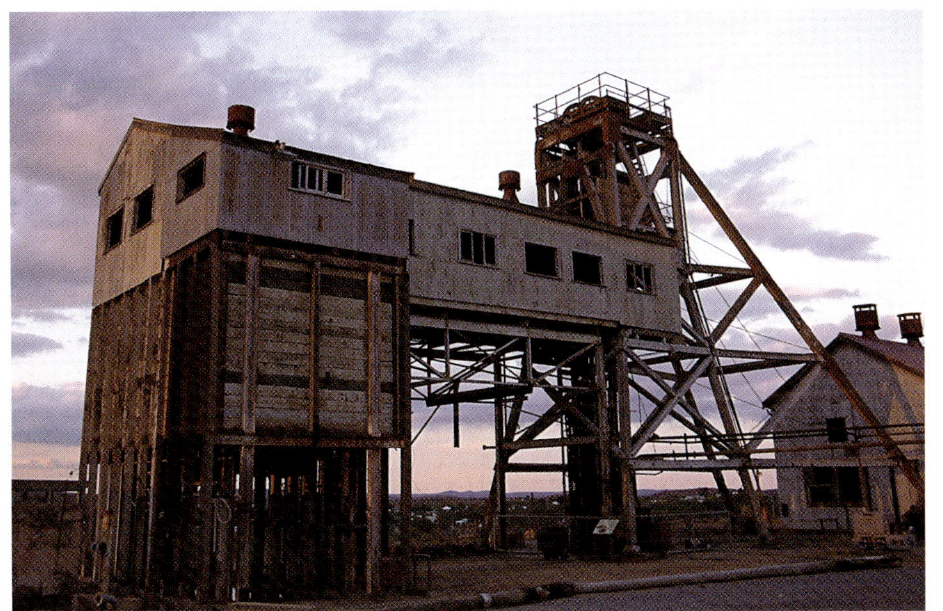

Old Junction Mine, Broken Hill.

The miners came and the tent town typical of a

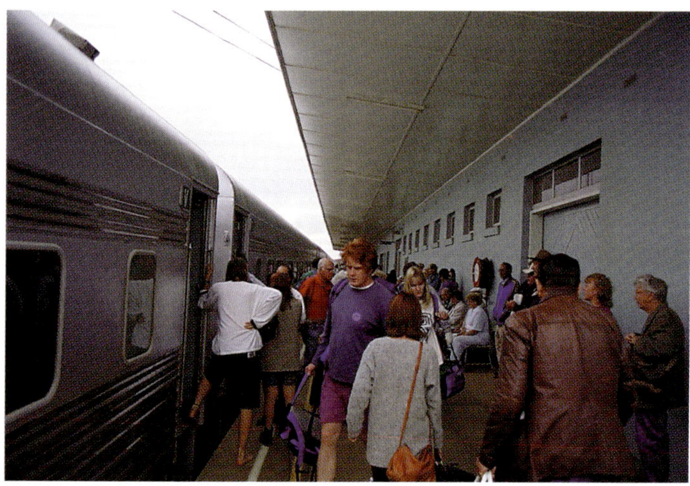

Broken Hill railway station.

new minefield grew around Broken Hill. In the way of Australian mining, the richest lodes lay in the harshest country, and the Barrier Range, almost on the western border of New South Wales, was harsh indeed.

There was absolutely no permanent water, a miserly rainfall, and summer temperatures above 40 degrees Celsius – or 110 in the shade as they measured it then, but there was no shade. Tin shacks joined the tents as more miners came. Everything was temporary, as in all mining towns of the time, because miners knew from sad experience that few mines lasted long.

The landscape, bare already, was scarred by smelting and waste dumping. Accidents scarred and killed miners. The diseases of dust from work underground in primitive conditions crippled them; plagues like typhoid and scarlet fever threatened their families. The miners' determination that there had to be a better way to work and live began a social and industrial reassessment that would spread nationwide.

Trade Union power in Australia did not originate at Broken Hill. That happened in Queensland, in the shearing sheds, where in the 1890s for the second and last time in Australian history the military waved its guns in the faces of its own people (The first flourish of arms against civilians was at the Eureka stockade, on the Victorian goldfields, forty years earlier).

The revolution at Broken Hill was a long and determined campaign, never a violent uprising. The miners saw the level of profit their work was returning the Company's shareholders, and they wanted better working conditions and safety underground. They won, on both issues, and along the way established in Broken Hill a tradition of union dominance that continues to this day. There is an organisation called the Barrier Industrial Council, a Union of Unions, and it is the real Government of Broken Hill.

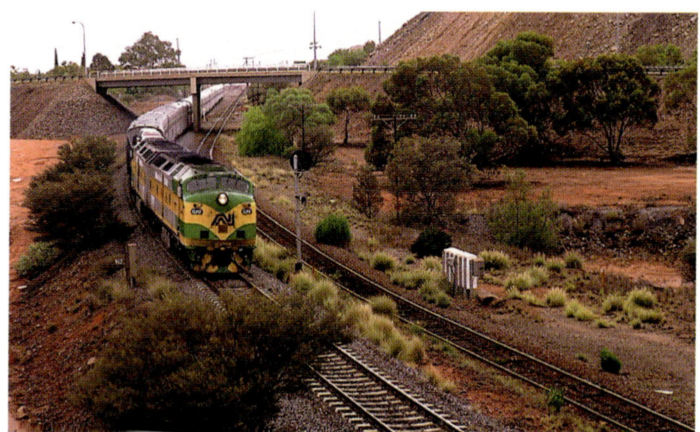

The Indian-Pacific amid the man-made mesas of Broken Hill.

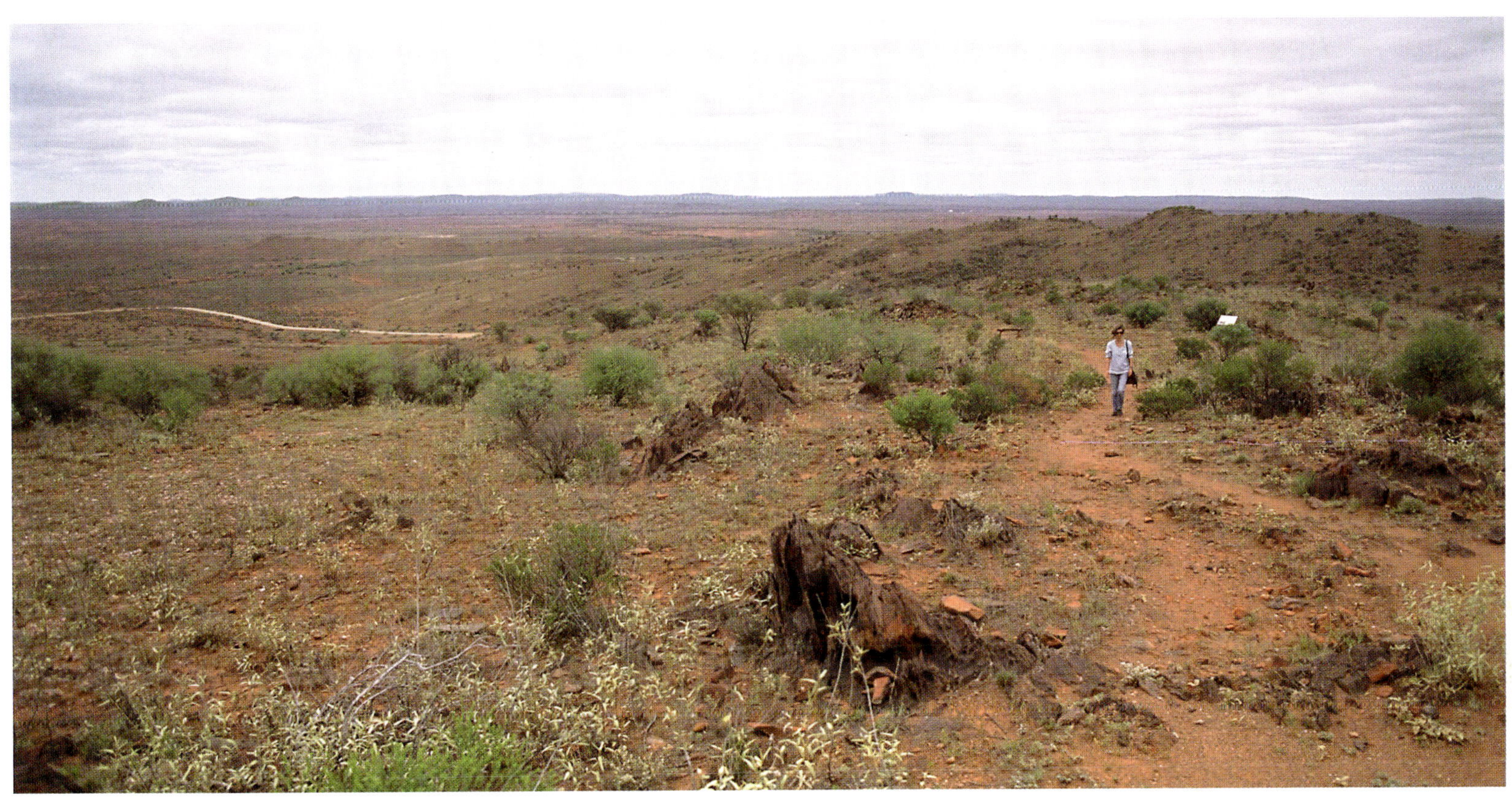

One of the oldest landforms in the world:
The Living Desert, Broken Hill, NSW.

From the windows of the Indian-Pacific, the first sight of Broken Hill is an array of grey and flat-topped man-made mountains: mullock heaps, in miners' language. They're the result of the earth turned inside out, the rock in them has come from deep underground. Mullock is the rubbish of mining, the rock that lay between the miners and ore seams, blasted out and lifted to the surface. It does little for the Broken Hill landscape, but it's the price of more than a century of prosperity for a city which otherwise could not exist.

A Tram to Silverton?

As the wealth of Broken Hill's mines became apparent, refining and smelting on the coast was the next step in development of a metals industry based on the Hill's lodes.

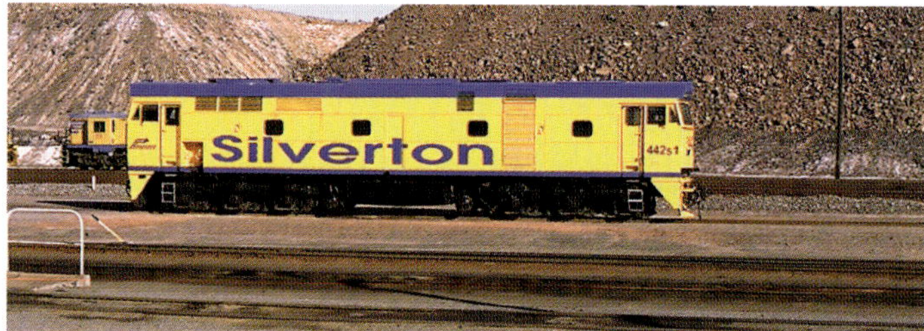

Silverton 'tram'.

Port Pirie, in South Australia, was the nearest practical seaport, but an almost impenetrable barrier existed between the mines and the port: It was the state border between New South Wales and South Australia, and to the government of NSW it was unthinkable that the products of mines in that state should go to another for processing. Never mind that Port Pirie was less than half the distance from Broken Hill to Sydney. State honour, not to mention state revenues, were at stake.

South Australia had built a narrow gauge (3'6") which ended at Cockburn, 53 kilometres west of Broken Hill. New South Wales would not permit extension of this line to the mines across its border.

Years before Rasp discovered Broken Hill, a rich silver strike was made at a place that came to be called Silverton, some 20 km to the west of the Barrier Range. So rich were its mines, and so prosperous its people, that in 1886 a company was formed in the town to build a railway connection across the border to the South Australian railhead, Cockburn. Governments considered railways to be their monopoly, so the new company called its iron road a Tramway, the Silverton Tramway, and to this day it owns and operates the yellow diesel-electrics, painted bright yellow and boldly lettered 'Silverton' that work around the Broken Hill railway yards.

The company has contracts to shunt and assemble the trains, sixty wagons long and weighing up to 5,000 tonnes that the National Rail Corporation hauls to the Port Pirie Smelters.

Though limited now to the shunting yards, the Silverton Tramway was Broken Hill's rail connection with the coast for more than eighty years. Its passenger trains connected with the South Australian system at Cockburn, and until the NSW Railways eventually crossed the Darling and reached Broken Hill in 1927, the Silverton Tramway's Sulphide Street station was Broken Hill's only gateway to a big city. It helped form a bond between Broken Hill and Adelaide, and for generations Broken Hill people on holiday went automatically to Adelaide, the nearest city, the nearest coast and beach. Their link with NSW was merely political.

The trains of the Silverton Tramway ran on their narrow gauge tracks until 1970, when the standard gauge went through from Broken Hill to Port Pirie. Signs of the Silverton's path are still clear to see as the Indian-Pacific from Broken Hill heads into South Australia.

The World beyond the Streetlights

The emptiness of inland Australia seems to begin at the last street light of Broken Hill, so suddenly do the signs of settlement end. For Broken Hill is an oasis, a place that, but for its mines, would have no right nor reason to exist.

Three of its institutions are signs of the extraordinarily diverse community its 23,000 people have built. One is a thriving colony of artists – they've become known across Australia and beyond as the Brushmen of the Bush, and one of their number, the celebrated artist Pro Hart, has on show in Broken Hill one of the finest private collections of paintings in Australia.

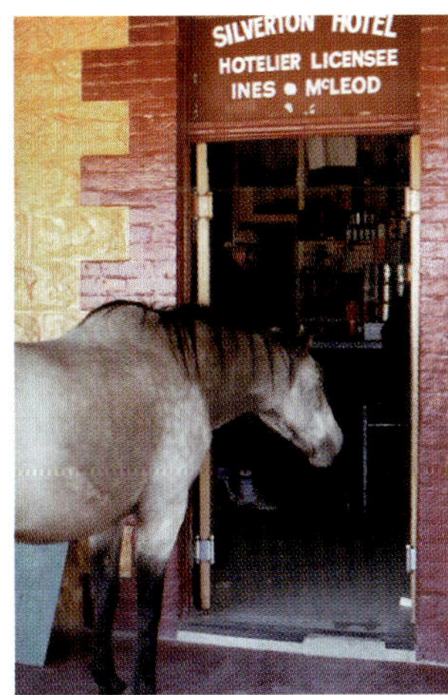

The pub in Silverton.

A second Broken Hill institution (though part of an Australia-wide network) is the Flying Doctor. From a base at Broken Hill's airport, the Flying Doctor spreads a corner of the 'Mantle of Safety' promised to the outback by the founder of the service, John Flynn, a Presbyterian Minister, when with one doctor, one pilot, one aeroplane, he first brought together the power and the promise of medicine and aviation.

More than any other factor, the Flying Doctor, and the communications network the service developed, have made outback life tolerable for families. From its twelve bases around the outback's borders, it covers 80% of the area of Australia, and no matter how remote the station, the mining camp, the township, emergency medical treatment and transport is never more than a few hours away. The Flying Doctor Service has nearly forty aeroplanes. In a typical year, its doctors see more than 150,000 people.

It flies 10,000 medical evacuations a year, and along the track of the Indian-Pacific from bases at Broken Hill, Port Augusta and Kalgoorlie the Mantle of Safety covers every passenger on the train. The cover has been put to the test more than once: When the train has stopped alongside a landing strip, marked only by a windsock, for a seriously ill passenger to be transferred to a Flying Doctor aeroplane.

For the Flying Doctor to be effective, a reliable system of communication was essential: A tall order in the early days of radio, when electricity was unavailable, more often than not, in the outback. An Adelaide radio enthusiast (radio was called wireless at the time) named Alf Traeger invented for the Flying Doctor a remarkable piece of technology: The Pedal Wireless, a radio transmitter-receiver whose power came from a generator turned by pedals. Imagine an exercise bike, no handbars, with a small generator in place of the flywheel, a box of valves and wires and mysteries the user didn't need to understand, a microphone to talk into and headphones to listen to. It was simple, reliable and relatively cheap, and it changed the lives of the people of the outback.

As radios improved – few technologies have ever progressed at the rate of electronics – and as electricity became more available, the pedal wireless became a museum piece. But the communications system it began made possible in later years another of the institutions of outback Australia: The School of the Air.

Working from Flying Doctor radio bases, teachers trained in distant education operate two-way classrooms that may cover an area the size of England. The quality of education they offer children is deservedly famous, and rated as probably better than in a city school room.

One of the things they may learn, in History, is that during the First World War, the only enemy shots fired in Australia were fired at Broken Hill. It happened like this....

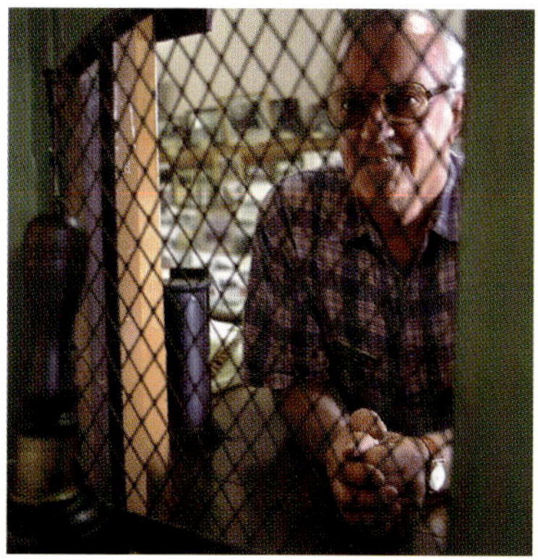

Broken Hill railway museum where the story of the Battle of Broken Hill is told.

On New Year's Day, 1915, the war in Europe was five months old. A new and terrible weapon had appeared, the U-boat, the submarine, and something even more terrible, aerial bombardment of civilian cities from the great airships called, after their designer, the Zeppelins, was only three weeks in the future. The first use of poison gas in war was being prepared by the German conquerors of France, and the dreadful blooding of Australian soldiers in the botched invasion of Gallipoli, in Turkey, was to come in only four months.

At Broken Hill, it was Miners' Picnic Day, and on a special train twelve hundred people riding in open goods wagons were off to the picnic grounds. Just out of town, on a hill overlooking the railway, was a horse-drawn ice-cream cart. The picnickers knew it well, it was a Broken Hill institution, the ice-cream cart and its proprietors, a couple of odd foreigners. Mohammedans. And in the Australia of 1915, any foreigner, especially a Mohammedan, was very odd indeed.

But today, the ice-cream cart was flying a flag, a Turkish flag, if anyone had recognised it, and it was a flag of war.

The ice-cream men, neither of them Turks, had declared their own war, and with a pair of ancient rifles, opened fire on the holiday crowd. Six people died that day in the Battle of Broken Hill: The two self-appointed soldiers of the Sultan of Turkey who thought they'd be heroes of a holy war, and four people of Broken Hill who thought they were going on a picnic.

Half an hour out of Broken Hill, the Indian-Pacific crosses the border of South Australia, which is only a line on a map drawn for no better reason than the convenience of the Colonial Office in London. The border causes no great change in the world as seen from the train. One discernible difference since leaving Broken Hill is the smoothness of the ride, because from Broken Hill through to Adelaide the train is on a new track, built to the highest standards of railway construction, with welded rail on concrete sleepers, completed in 1969. This is part of the rehabilitation of railways in this region since management of all long distance trains in South Australia became the responsibility of the now sadly depleted Australian National.

The first township inside South Australia, Cockburn, has been mentioned before as the meeting point of the South Australian narrow gauge with the privately built Silverton Tramway, and now a relic of past Australian railway follies.

This region is one of the haunts of the great wedge-tail eagle, the aristocrat of Australian birds and the symbol chosen as the logo for the Indian-Pacific. From Cockburn, on to Olary, wedge tails can be seen flying their high, distant, lazy circles and searching the ground for food. Small animals, lizards, anything that moves will trigger a swift and accurate dive, a flash of beak and talons, and there's lunch.

In flight or at rest, this is a magnificent bird: Soaring on up-currents of air rising from the baking earth, the wedge-tail is the essence of the freedom of flight, trim feathers on the ends of its two-metre wingspan, and the changing angle between wings and body, the only visible movements to sustain flight. And on the ground, it is an arrogant, imperious being which seems to look down its noble beak at any human creature that may come, slowly and carefully, close.

As mining wealth built and sustains Broken Hill, the promise of minerals also brought people to this dry and desolate country. Australia's first discovery of uranium was made here. The mine was called Radium Hill. Mining in Australia is big business, big, big business. Mining company spokesmen are often heard to say they're all that keeps the country going, and they quote the huge value of their investments in exploration and development. All very true. But few of the majors make much of the fact that almost all of the major mineral discoveries of Australia, from the first gold at Bathurst to the mountains of iron in the Western Australian Kimberleys, have been made not by big mining companies with all their science and resources but by individual prospectors, with hammers, curiosity and dreams:

Hargraves (or his associates) at Bathurst, Rasp at Broken Hill, Hannan at Kalgoorlie, Campbell Miles at Mount Isa, Walton and McConachy's uranium at Mary Kathleen near Cloncurry, Lang Hancock and the iron of the Pilbara.

And in areas like this empty land west of Cockburn, individual prospectors can still be found searching, or one or two people living from a small lode of an unusual ore that's not worth the investment of a big operation.

For every Broken Hill, a long-term mining town, Australian history offers a dozen of the opposite: Places of brief glory that died, vanished even, when the ore lode was mined out. There's no mining to be seen at Silverton these days, nor at Burra, South Australia. But Burra, dying late last century as its copper mine was closing, was the scene of a mass migration never known before or since in Australian history. There was no future in Burra, for anyone. So virtually the whole town packed up and set off for the new mines of Broken Hill 350 km away. There was no railway, there were barely roads. Few of the impoverished miners owned horses. Their only transport was their own two feet. Some had wheelbarrows, and wheeling or carrying everything they owned, the men, women and children of Burra walked to Broken Hill.

Occasionally nowadays, to raise money for charities, there's a wheelbarrow race over the same course, Burra to Broken Hill.

But there are support vehicles, portable fridges, cold beer on demand, and it's all great fun. It's also, in its own irreverent way, a kind of tribute to the courage of desperate people of a hundred years ago.

Much more recently, two hundred passengers on a westbound Indian-Pacific found themselves walking, too, but only a hundred metres or so, through mud, from their stranded train to rescue buses. The train which had left Sydney on February 6, 1997, was blocked by flash flooding near Olary, South Australia, the next afternoon. Further flooding washed out the track behind it. Adelaide, home base and main supply point for the train, was only hours ahead, and provisions were low. For the first time in its history, the Indian Pacific evacuated its passengers, and the train sat marooned on a patch of high ground until the tracks were rebuilt. It was an incident reminiscent of the infamous old Ghan train of Central Australia, which once sat for weeks marooned by floods, and the driver shot wild goats to feed his passengers.

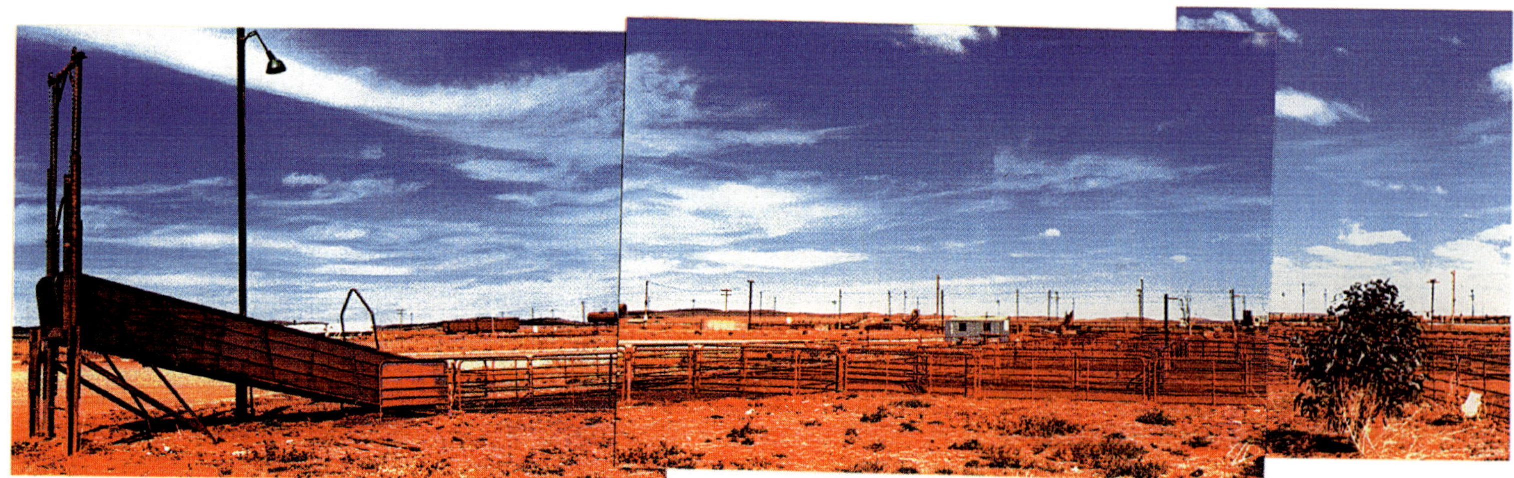

Stockyard at Oodla Wirra.
Photographic collage by Joyce Evans.

A Colony of Free Settlers

The railways, like mining, created new towns, and these towns prospered with the railways and declined with them. The standard gauge line the Indian-Pacific follows from Broken Hill to Adelaide follows quite closely the route of the original narrow gauge from Cockburn to Gladstone – the original surveyors got it exactly right – and today's trains pass swiftly the remains of little towns which once served the railway: To water the iron horse and fuel it, and rest its tired riders. When steam went, replaced by diesel-electrics, the need for the little service towns went too, and then within a decade the narrow gauge closed altogether. That left even the bigger towns, Peterborough is one, with the urgent to need to create new reasons for being.

Peterborough was originally Petersburg, but the name had a Germanic sound harsh to the ears of the patriotic zealots who went a little overboard in Australia during the war with the Kaiser. Burg or Borough, Petersplace in its railway days was the prime example of the silliness of Australian railway planning, for there, three railway gauges met: Standard, broad and narrow. That confusion has been gone for many years, the broad and narrow gauge tracks torn up except for the tourist line operated from a base at Peterborough by the SteamTown railway museum. Its narrow gauge steamers run on weekends and holidays to Orroroo or Eurilia, and the locomotive roundhouse is being restored as a tourist draw.

At Jamestown, the next station west, the elegant old railway station is a museum of district history, and its future care and preservation is guaranteed as part of the National Trust.

West again, to Gladstone, another of those names of long-gone English politicians in the Australian bush. Gladstone was the trans-shipment point made necessary by the South Australian mix of gauges, and everything sent on this line from Adelaide had to be transferred from broad gauge vehicles to narrow: everything, from fuel to fertiliser to groceries, and people.

All that ended when the standard gauge went through. Most of the railway jobs went too, and a town created by the confusion of bad planning had its future cut short by good planning.

In earlier years of the Indian Pacific, the train did not visit Adelaide. East and westbound trains met at Gladstone and stopped with their service doors opposite each other. Cooks, waiters, conductors of the New South Wales Railways would climb down from the westbound train and board the eastbound back to Sydney. Crews of the then Commonwealth Railways would make the opposite change. In those days, the character of the train would change at Gladstone, the free and easy nature of the Sydney crews replaced by dour and distant C.R. men under orders from their administration not to fraternise with passengers. It was, indeed, a strange way to run a railway, especially a train so dependent on the tourist trade.

With the formation of Australian National, and establishment of its headquarters in Adelaide, the route of the Indian-Pacific changed to include a call at AN's base station, Keswick terminal in Adelaide's former Mile End freight yards. For Perth-bound passengers, it's a 400 km diversion, but allows a run through country which was once the heartland of Australian farming.

The change from the arid zone to farmland occurs at Peterborough, and the landscape changes as suddenly as if a line is drawn on the map from dry, bare and largely empty country to productive crop land. There is such a line, and it was drawn on the map of South Australia last century by a prescient man who said farming could not succeed north and east of his line.

Though visionary, the man who drew the line for South Australian farming was no clairvoyant: He was a Surveyor, the Surveyor-General of the state in fact, George Goyder, and the line he drew to define the limits of possible farming is still called the Goyder Line. He used no crystal ball, studied no stars or planets. He studied only rainfall records, and he realised something no-one else had noticed. South and west of an almost exact line on his survey maps the rainfall suddenly increased, and there would be rain enough in an average year to support farming, grain growing. East and north, farming would be risky, and bound, in the long term, to fail.

It was, of course, held to be nonsense by some, particularly those who wanted 'progress' at any price, or who had something to gain. But those who tried farming in defiance of Goyder's Line found to their cost the Surveyor-General was right.

At a township named Crystal Brook, the Indian-Pacific takes the left leg of a Y-junction and turns south for Adelaide, through intensive farming country to the Adelaide plains.

Although Australia's first successful wheat was grown just west of Sydney, it was on these plains north of Adelaide that the commercial production of wheat began, and for years, this was the granary of Australia. Tall, white grain silos mark the line of the former broad-gauge railway, long abandoned. These days, the silos taste new crops introduced to bridge the uncertainty of the international wheat market.

South Australia had its beginnings as a colony of free settlers in 1836. There were no convicts brought here, and in earlier times when such things mattered and convict ancestry, convict history, were things of shame rather than the pride of today, some South Australians were inclined to boast they were descendents of better people, people who came because they wanted to come, and worked for their own gain rather than the threat of the lash.

Hard headed farmers settled South Australia. Some refugees from religious persecution came from Germany, bringing their taste for wine and their skills in making it.

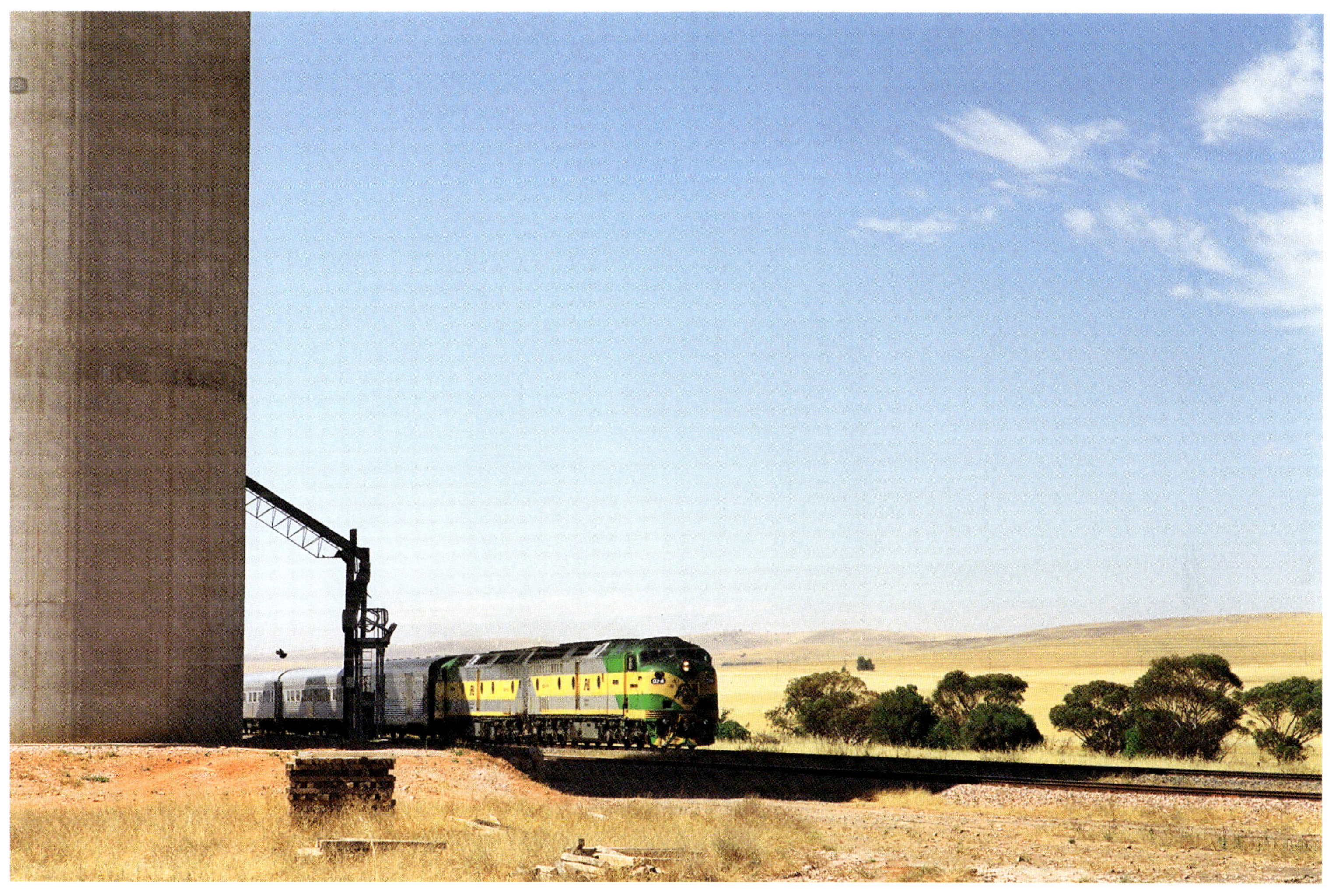

The Indian-Pacific at Redhill south of Crystal Brook, SA.

As the settlement of Adelaide grew, people came who knew how to grow food crops, and the Adelaide plains became an enormous farm garden. Fruit and vegetables from here are sent all over Australia, and vineyards and gardens line the way of the Indian-Pacific into the centre of a city that sees itself as the most liveable of all Australia's capitals, Adelaide.

Adelaide

Alone among Australia's state capitals, Adelaide was built to a master plan devised a hundred and fifty years ago. As the South Australian colony, free of the excesses of the convict system, thought about where to site its centre a British Army Surveyor, William Light, was commissioned to prepare a design for a city.

His plan placed the business core centrally, with parkland on all four sides and residential suburbs beyond the parks. Further out again he provided for industrial areas, then the farms and gardens to produce the city's food. For good reason, modern Adelaide honours Colonel Light, and his statue surveys his creation from a vantage point called Light's Vision.

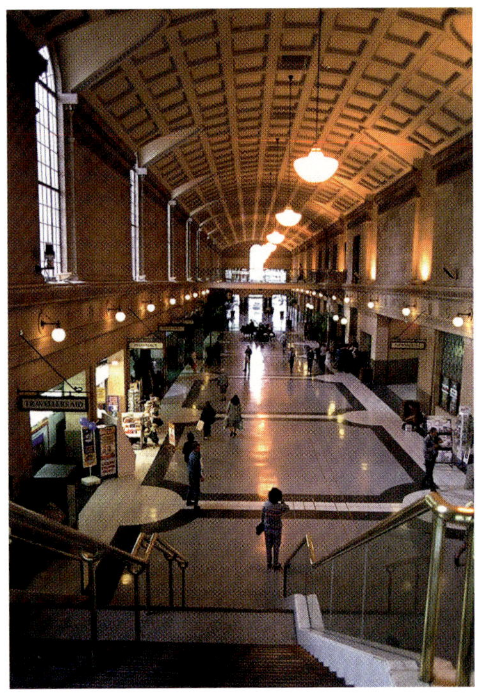

Adelaide's Central station, nowadays a gambling casino. The Indian-Pacific gives it a miss.

Adelaide's principal streets follow a geometric grid pattern, wide enough, legend says, to U-turn a bullock team. Unlike Sydney, built around its vast harbour, or Brisbane, bisected by its river, the site of Adelaide presented few planning problems. It had two significant lacks: There was no river of substance, and no reliable water supply. The river problem was easily solved: A scrubby creek was dammed, its banks decorated with parks and gardens, and named the River Torrens. With a background of city high-rise, and as foreground the spectacular buildings of the Festival Centre, the Torrens looks lovely. Best not ask about the water quality, though: Long known to be too polluted to swim in, its reputation was more damaged when rowers were advised for a time not even to put their boats in the Torrens' water.

As with a river made where only a creek existed, so with industry. The rapid process of industrialisation, which changed the South Australian economy from dependence on the land to a base of manufacturing industry, began at the end of the second world war.

South Australians had elected as state Premier, the year before the war, a skilled and determined politician and ex fruit farmer named Tom Playford. He was Premier for nearly three decades, and the South Australia, the Adelaide, that gave him the top job in November, 1938, was unrecognisable by the time he retired in July 1966. He attracted industry as a magnet attracts iron, an apt simile, because the manipulation of iron and steel into manufactured goods for mass markets became the strength of South Australia. Playford courted the industrial magnates of England and especially America. More than one industrial mogul, visiting Australia to look at expansion prospects, was surprised and flattered to be met at Sydney airport by the 'Top Banana' of a distant state

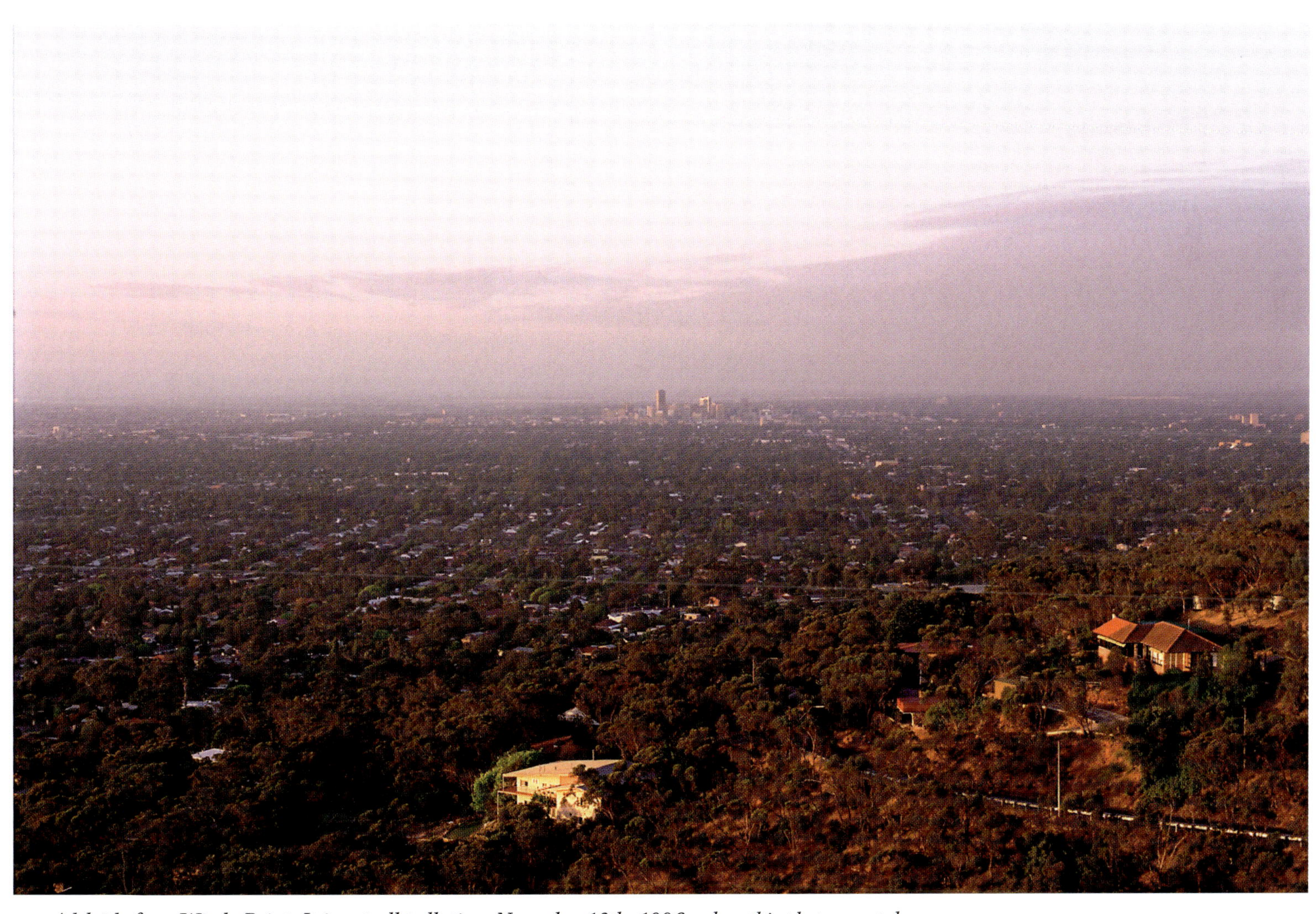

Adelaide from Windy Point. It is not all pollution: November 13th, 1996, when this photo was taken, the old News building made the news and was burnt out.

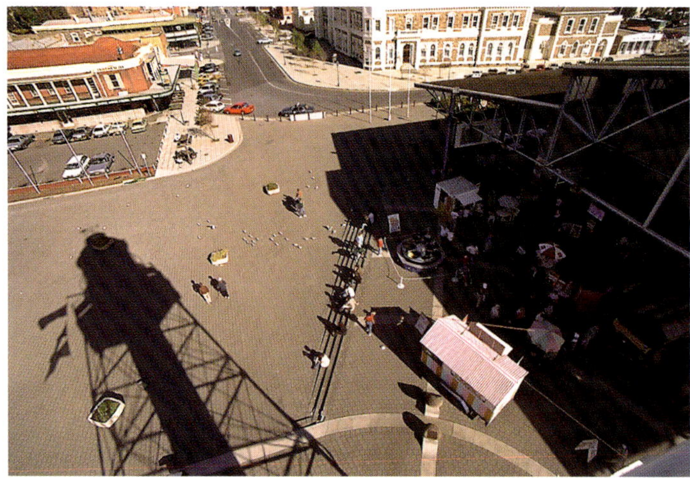

Port Adelaide

bearing offers of industrial sites at bedrock prices, tax benefits, energy concessions, even the provision of Government housing for the workers the new enterprise would attract. And, he'd find the workers, too, if need be. Thus Playford brought to South Australia, principally, but not exclusively, to Adelaide, motor car factories, the makers of washing machines, stoves and refrigerators, the providers of many of the consumer goods newly prosperous Australia was demanding.

To man the factories, Playford attracted immigrants from England. His Government built new suburbs, even a new satellite city, for them to live in. He named it Elizabeth, in honour of the British Queen, and was there when she opened and named it. General Motors came to a new factory in the new city. The Chrysler Corporation set up works on the other side of Adelaide. South Australia had been working iron ore mines at Iron Knob on Eyre Peninsula since the 1890s, but the ore was shipped to NSW for smelting. In 1939, the Broken Hill Proprietary Company, inheritors of the wealth found by Charlie Rasp, opened a smelter at nearby Whyalla to make pig iron.

Twenty years later the fine hand of Tom Playford could be detected in the decision by BHP to expand the smelter and make steel at Whyalla. Housing needed? Electricity? Water? The Government could provide all, through the Housing Trust, The Electricity Trust, the Engineering and Water Supply Department, Tom Playford's tools for the future of his state.

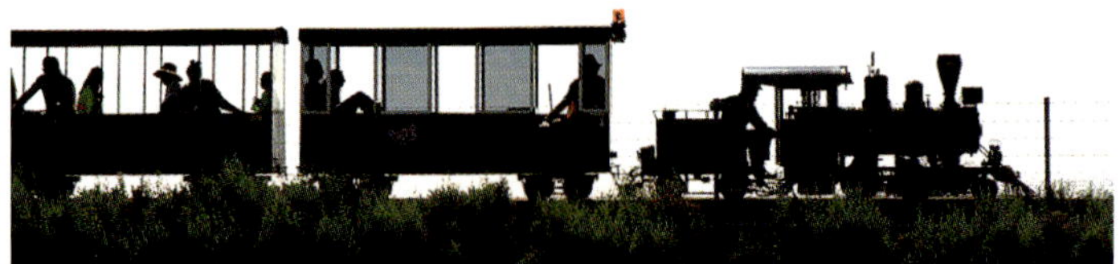

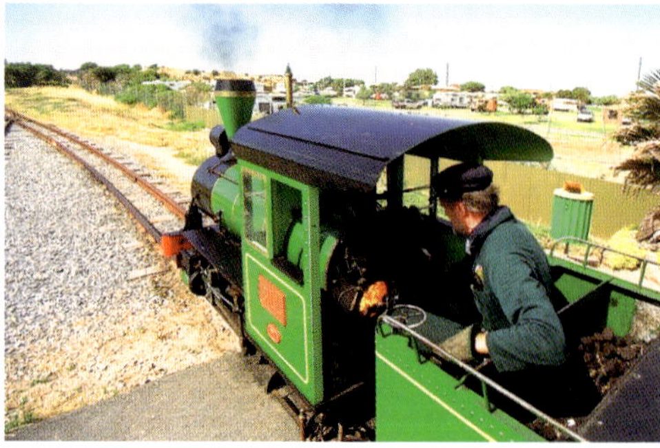

Locomotive 'Bill': Built by Willis of Western Australia, this little train is operated by Adelaide's Port Dock Station Railway Museum at Semaphore.

Playford was a determined Conservative, as was his grandfather, an earlier South Australian Premier. Yet, to develop his state, he created a regime more socialist than anything ever achieved by the most rabid of socialists.

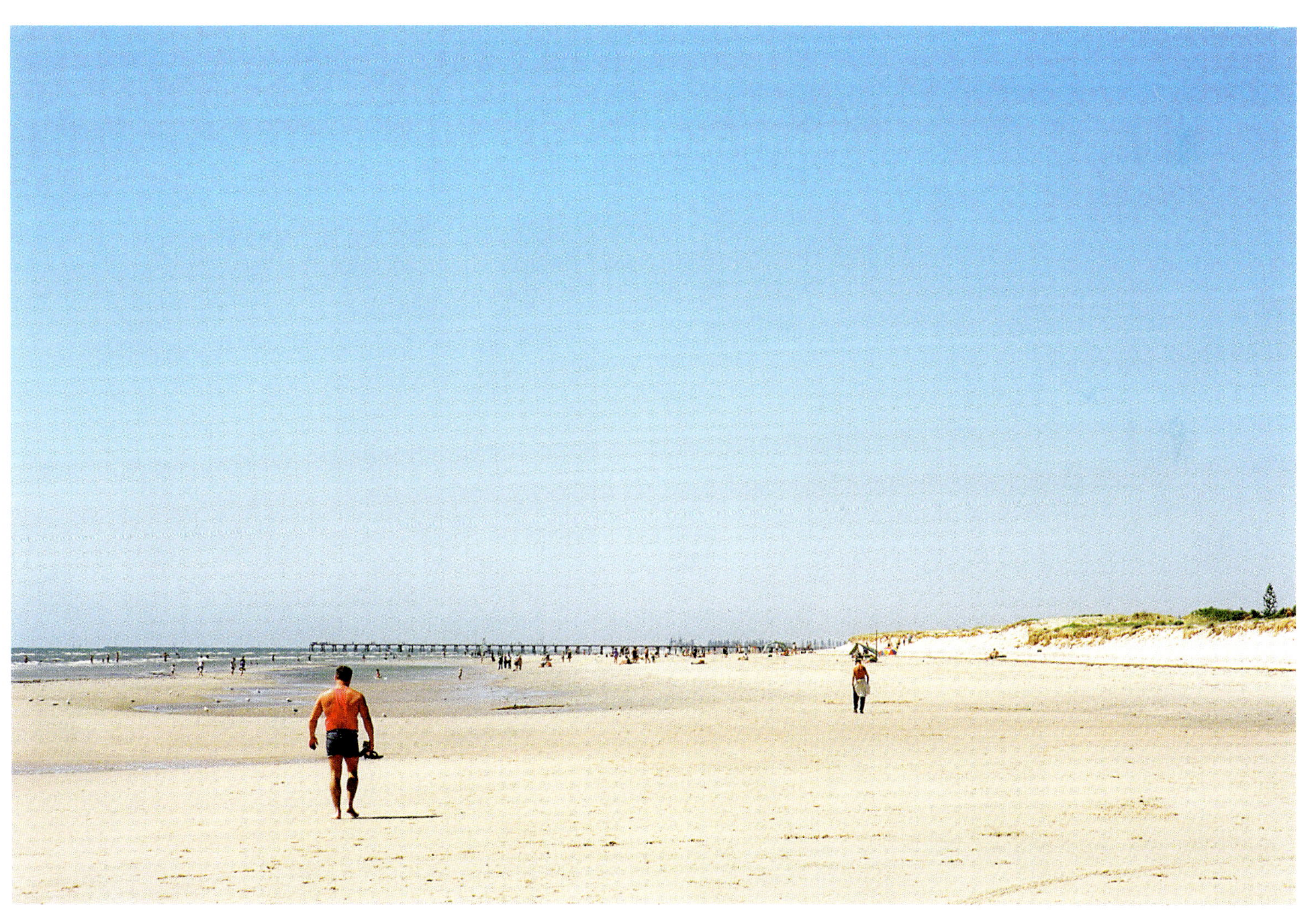

Semaphore beach, Adelaide, SA.

Land of Wine and Mine

From Keswick Terminal, the Indian-Pacific edges cautiously through a complex layout of tracks, with the Adelaide suburban system, still running on 5'3" broad gauge, parallel to the main line north:

Past the old Islington railway workshops which built some of the steam giants of the former South Australian Railways, and their first main-line diesels. Later, Australian National used the design and construction skills of Islington to produce innovative freight wagons for the trans-Australia line to Perth; past the One-Stop Shop wagon repair centre where Australian National, for the first time in Australia, brought multi-skilling to railways maintenance and broke through some of the union demarcation silliness which has long bedevilled Australian industry; past the AN Motive Power Centre where thediesel-electrics of three rail systems are serviced; and through the great freight yards at Dry Creek where the place of railways in the national transportation system is displayed.

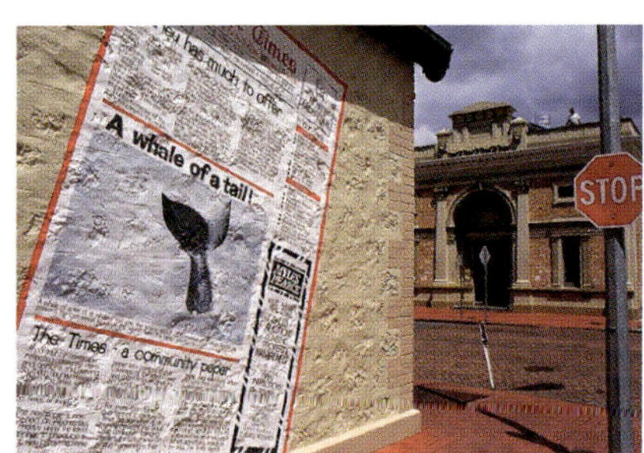

Victor Harbour, a favourite destination for Adelaide people on holiday.

On the right of the northbound train, the hangars and runways of Edinburgh air base, headquarters of the Air Force's long range ocean reconnaissance Orion aircraft. The Orions, and the men who fly them, won plaudits from around the world when they found, and guided rescue ships, to sailors in distress in two solo round the world races in recent years.

Over the low hills beyond the airfield is the most famous of Australia's wine provinces, the Barossa Valley.

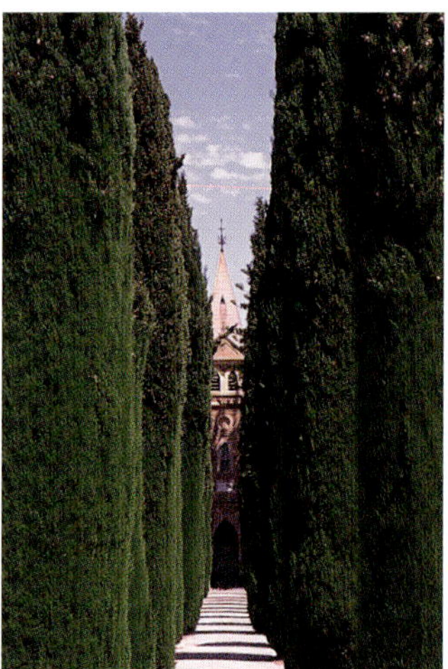
Lutheran Church, Langmeil, Barossa Valley.

South Australia's renowned wine industry is a monument to the German settlers who brought the first vines here in the 1830s. For more than a hundred years, the wines of the Barossa were a private treasure, because past generations of Australians were not much interested in wine: Beer and spirits were the vehicles for the drug alcohol, rum especially had been historically significant as a medium of trade and the currency of the first recorded official corruption in the colonies.

But in one generation a change, more a revolution, in tastes and social patterns occurred. Australians discovered what others had known for thousands of years: Wine.

There came the sudden realisation that here, on their own doorstep, they had a national treasure. Vineyards expanded as never before, far beyond the Barossa, far beyond South Australia, and now every state claims a wine industry. South Australia, though, has a store of wine making experience that's hard to match, and the leading scientific centres of grape growing and wine making are in or near Adelaide.

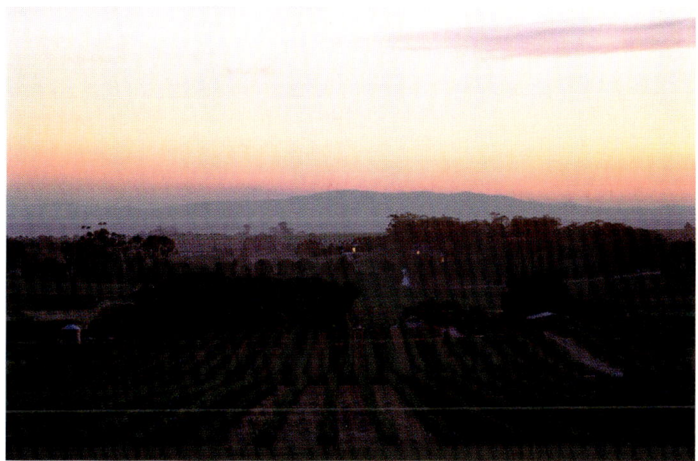

Vineyards in the Barossa valley.

In exquisite old buildings of crafted stone, in caves and tunnels, and in air-conditioned, controlled-atmosphere wine making laboratories, the industry pursues ways, old and new, of drawing the magic of wine from the juice of the grape. Its success is best judged from the stream of Australian wine pouring to markets in America, Europe and Asia: Supplying the taste for luxuries as once wheat from hereabouts made the basic bread for Britain and Europe.

The growth of Adelaide, the spread of industry over the Adelaide plains and the need for intensive growing of food crops, pushed broad-acre farming ever further out. Elsewhere in Australia sheep and cattle grazing were dominant rural industries, but here in South Australia, on the rich flat lands inland from St Vincent's Gulf, the wealth was in wheat. To this granary came the clipper ships to take its crops to the world.

The second half of the 19th century was an optimistic time for South Australia, there seemed no limit to its potential for growth and riches. Sites for a hundred towns and villages were declared and pegged out, and along the coasts of the two gulfs named Spencer and St Vincent, twenty new ports were declared. Few ports ever got past the paper stage, and even fewer survive. Most of the villages have gone too, because changes in farming here have taken away their reason for being.

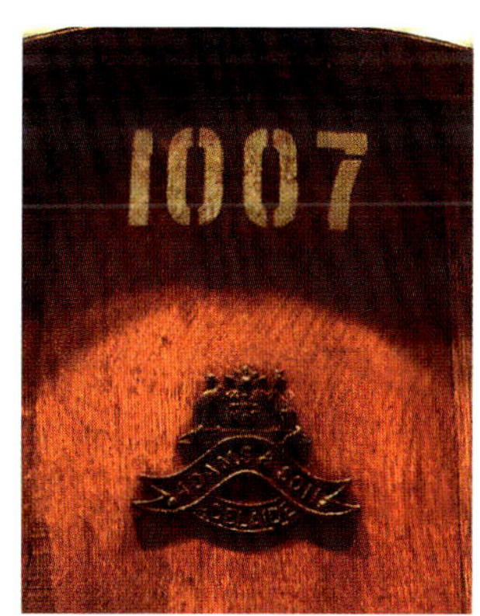

The small farmers who brought new settlements, new villages, into being have long gone, their holdings brought together to form bigger farms to meet the economic demands of the times and to make better use of the advanced machinery almost everyone uses these days.

People don't need to live on the farm any more: They've gone to the towns on the nearby coast, where life's easier and amenities better, and they go to the farm most days to work, as a city worker goes to office or factory. The old farmhouses are abandoned in the midst of grain fields, fine old stone houses, some of them, that elsewhere would be bought for fortunes and lovingly and expensively restored.

One of the twenty port sites that not only survived but went on to unimaginable prosperity is Port Pirie, on the eastern shore of Spencer Gulf and on the left of the railway. Port Pirie flies a banner of smoke from a stack that soars like a flagpole 205 metres high above the biggest smelter of its type in the western world. Port Pirie, it could be said, married well: Its union with the mines of Broken Hill was formalised with the formation of a company called Broken Hill Associated Smelters, and the decision to site its works at the seaport nearest to the mines.

Every day, trains of 6,000 tonnes of concentrated ore arrive from Broken Hill. At Port Pirie, masterful processes of chemistry and mechanics extract its treasure: Lead mainly, and zinc, but also profitable quantities of metals from antimony through silver to gold. They refine knowledge here, too, and metal smelting and refining techniques developed at Port Pirie are used, under licence, all over the world.

Port Pirie has assured prosperity as long lasting as the mines of Broken Hill. But it is something of a Faustian bargain, for the city is the subject of frequent concerns about the pollution of its air and the lead contamination of its earth.

Powerful and persuasive arguments are periodically mounted on either side, without resolution.

The Indian Pacific no longer calls at Port Pirie, whose former broad-gauge Victorian Pavilion railway station in the main street is now a National Trust Museum, part of a complex that brings together the Ellen Street railway station, the old Customs House and the original Police Station.

The standard gauge track, these days the main line to Perth, has a passenger pick-up point at a place on the edge of Port Pirie called Conamia (pronounced Coona-myer). Though passenger trains pass it by, Port Pirie is firmly established in the area of railway operations where the profits are: As well as its daily ore trains, the port handles every year a quarter of a million tonnes of export grain, because geography has placed it at about the northern limit of reliable farming. Only 14 km to the north, an abandoned port lies on the other side of that limit. It was named long ago, in the optimistic times, Port Germein.

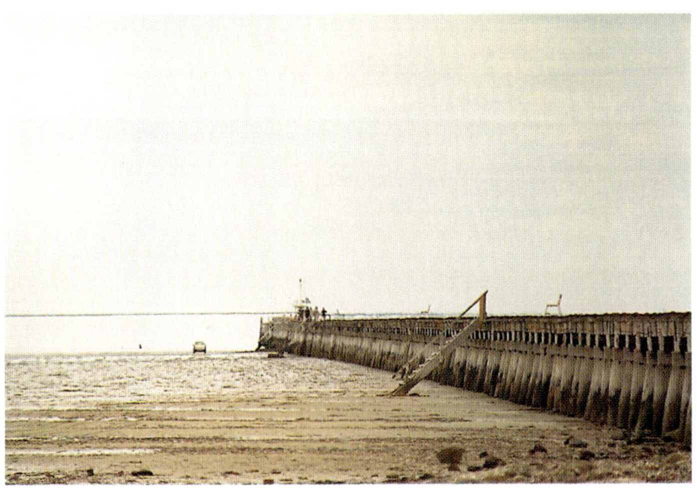

Port Germein jetty.

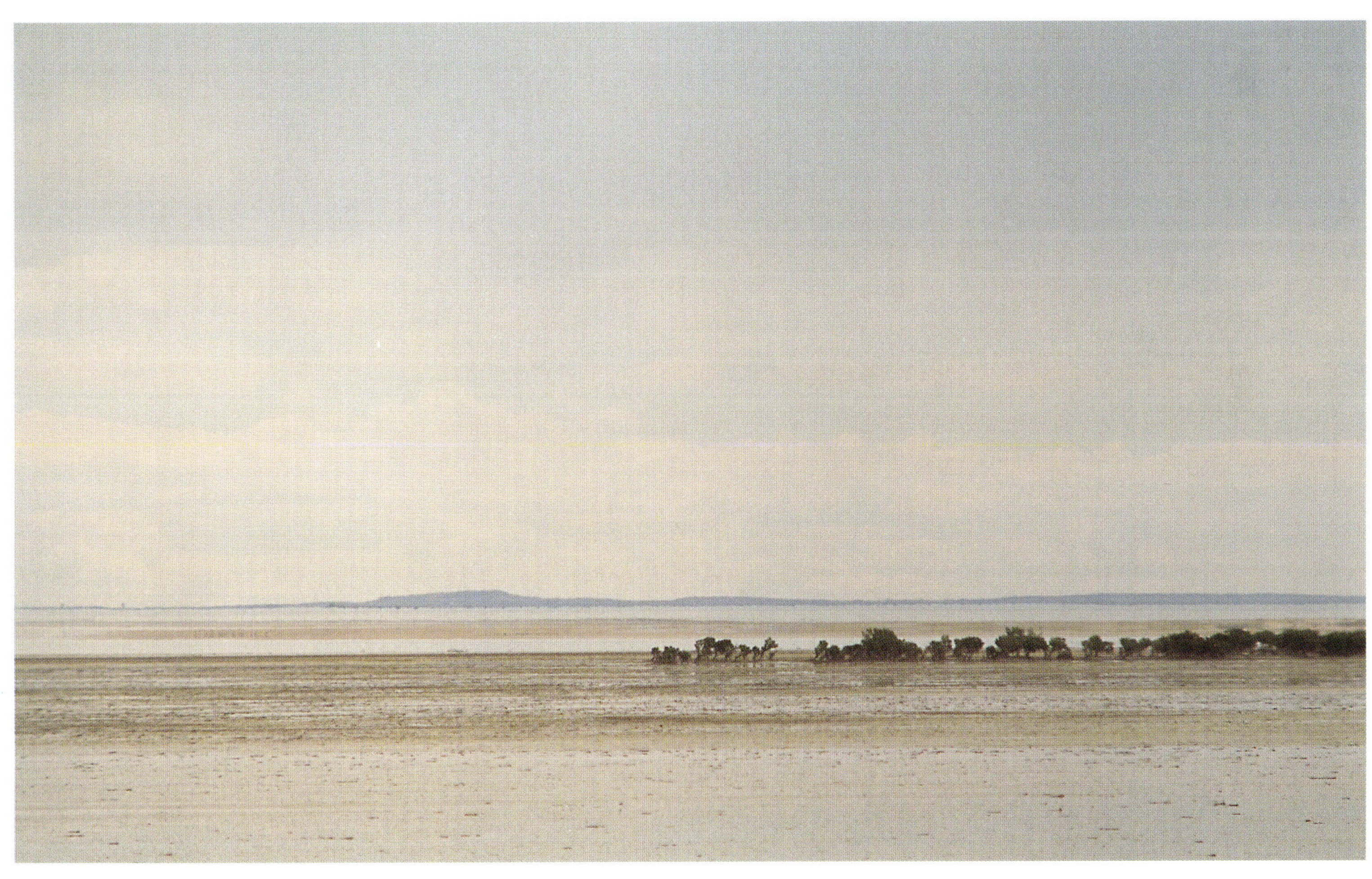

Mangroves at Port Germein.

Spencer Gulf

Port Germein died with the hopes of the farmers whose gateway to the world it was intended to be. The town is on the left hand side of the northbound Indian-Pacific, but it's not the town that first catches the eye of the traveller: It's the enormous jetty, thrusting out into the Gulf and vanishing sometimes in the mist a kilometre and a half out to sea.

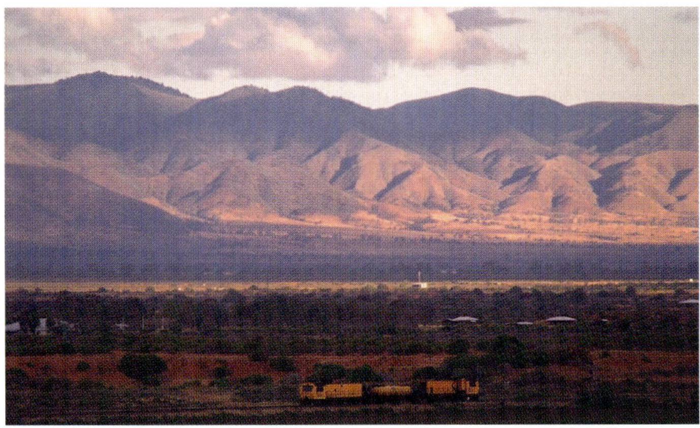

View from Matthew Flinders Lookout, Pt. Augusta.

That enormous jetty was built out to deep water, water deep enough to clear the keels of the square rigged clipper ships like Cutty Sark and Thermopolae that would be drawn here, so the hopers hoped, by the wealth of grain and wool coming down to the coast through the pass in the Flinders Ranges a generous nature had provided close to the site of Port Germein. It was another of those 'Best laid plans of mice and man that aft gang awry,' because farming failed on the northern side of the Flinders Ranges.

A pipeline parallels the railway from Port Pirie through to Port Augusta. Like the pipeline from the Darling River to Broken Hill, the pipe from the Murray River at Mannum to the three cities of South Australia's Iron Triangle, Port Pirie, Whyalla and Port Augusta, is the lifeline that makes possible these cities and this whole rich industrial province.

They have no sufficient rainfall, no permanent watercourses. Without water from the distant River Murray, the three cities whose business is minerals and energy could not exist: Port Pirie and its metals refining, Whyalla the steel town, and Port Augusta whose power stations keep lights burning and machines turning over most of South Australia.

Whyalla's iron comes from the long established mines of Iron Knob, Port Pirie's concentrates from the Barrier Range at Broken Hill, Port Augusta's coal from seams laid down at Leigh Creek between 200 and 240 million years ago. All of them assurances of a measure of long term prosperity, but Port Augusta, at the head of Spencer Gulf, has its future as a railway town under threat as a result of the dismemberment of Australian National Railways. The major AN workshops and the freight yards are to be phased out as national railway managements, now centred on the east coast, pursue what they call 'rationalisation' of rail services.

Port Augusta's history has been tied to transport since the days of horse teams and camel trains. The nearby pass through the Flinders Ranges called Pichi Richi has connected the coast and the hinterland for travellers since Aboriginal times, and when the railway came, the Pichi

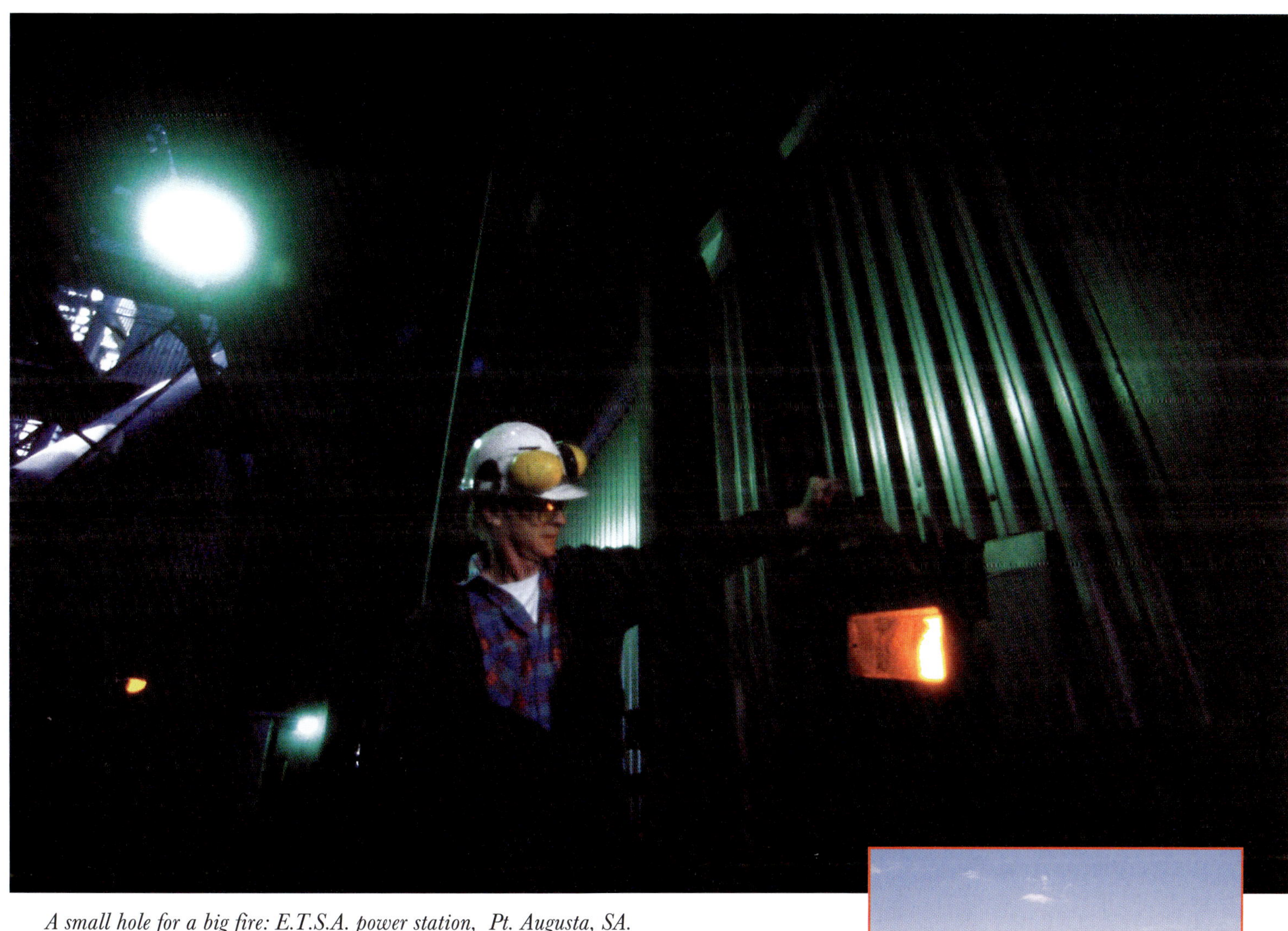

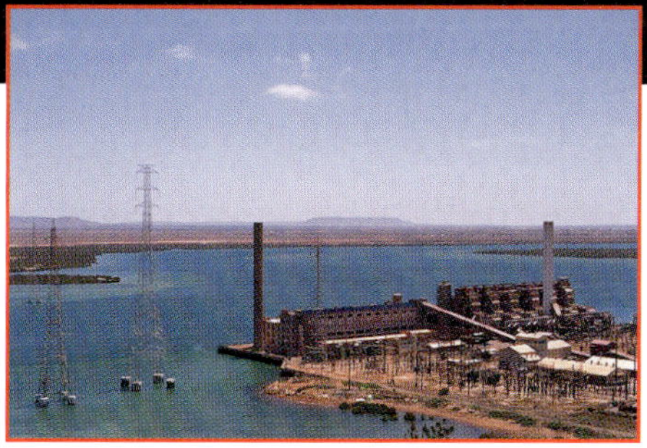

A small hole for a big fire: E.T.S.A. power station, Pt. Augusta, SA.

Richi pass offered the best route north. The original railway to Central Australia, the Ghan Line, ran from Port Augusta via the Pichi Richi to Quorn, Hawker, Maree and Oodnadatta, across the Finke River, the oldest known waterway on earth, and on to Alice Springs.

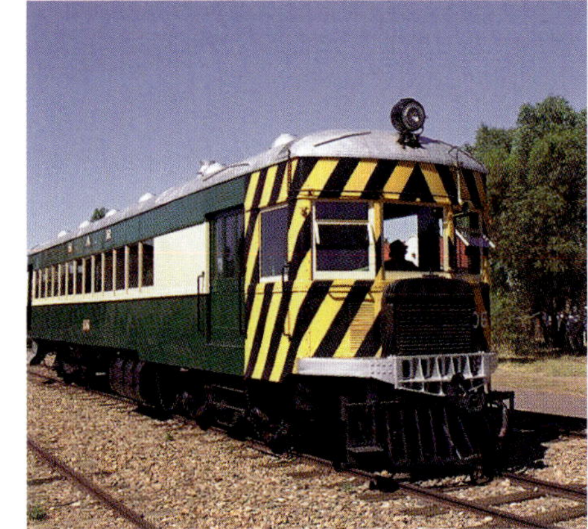

Railcar at Quorn.

It was to have been the south-north railway, the link from Adelaide to Darwin. The old line has been replaced as far as the Alice by a first class standard gauge track built as part of the Australian National system, but the line to Darwin, a political promise almost a century old, remains just a promise.

By all the rules, the old Ghan line should be no more, its narrow gauge tracks, locomotives and wagons melted down as scrap. Much of it has been, but part of the line remains as a working railway, kept alive by volunteers, railway enthusiasts, who've restored a section of the line as far north as the old town of Quorn. It runs tourist trains which draw enthusiasts from around the world, and naturally it's called the Pichi Richi Railway.

In the years before farming failed in the country beyond the Flinders Ranges, horse and camel teams brought wheat and wool to the wharves of Port Augusta and great sailing ships queued in the roads at the top of Spencer Gulf waiting for places at its crowded jetties. Some of the famous grain races began here: Clipper ships racing to load their new season's wheat and be first off from the port, first down the length of Spencer Gulf and south to catch the windstream called the Roaring Forties to carry them half way round the world by the shortest, swiftest track round Cape Horn and to throw them, like stones from a slingshot, into the two Atlantics, South and North, for the honour, and the commercial advantage, of being first home to England. The last race, marking the end of the era of the sailing ship, left Port Augusta just before the start of the second world war.

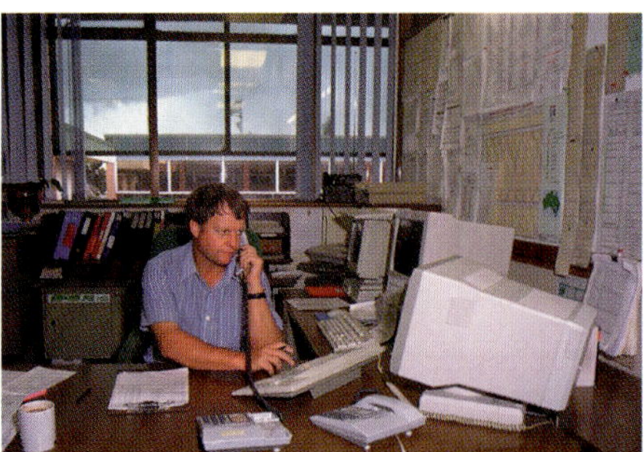

Train Control, Pt. Augusta.

As the port declined, its hinterland turning to desert, its wool and wheat trade gone and the metals business dominated by its bustling neighbour Port Pirie, Port Augusta's railway industry became even more important to the economy of this isolated town. Early in the 20th Century, a piece of political bribery, noble in intent and nationally beneficial in outcome, gave Port Augusta a railway future that would last for nearly a hundred years. It was the promise, by the then embryonic Federal Government of Australia, to build a railway across the continent, with Port Augusta at its eastern end.

A Breeze of Eyre

The desert journey of the Indian-Pacific begins, as the original railway began, at Port Augusta, and as the train heads northwest out of town, it approaches the edge of the main populated areas of South Australia. No-one's ever defined the boundaries of Outback Australia. The Outback's so big, so varied, so distributed between the states, that any boundary line drawn on any map would never be agreed upon. In South Australia, though, along the track of the Indian-Pacific, it's reasonable to say the Outback begins about half an hour northwest of Port Augusta, where the train crosses the map-maker's 32nd parallel of latitude. South of the 32nd live 99 percent of South Australia's population.

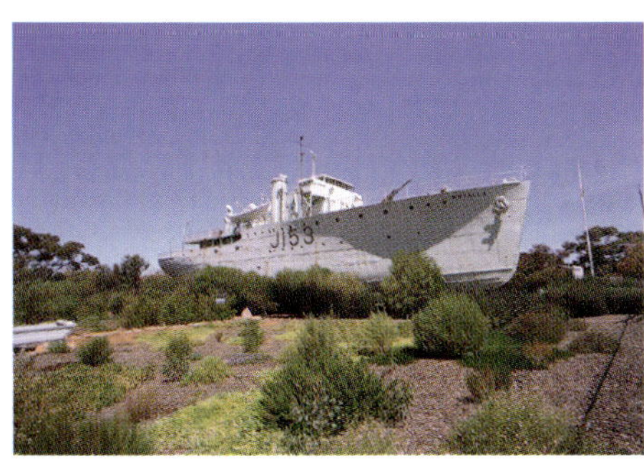

HMAS Whyalla memorial, Whyalla, SA.

To the left of the railway, stretching 300 km southwest, the bulk of Eyre Peninsula shelters Spencer Gulf from the winds and seas of the weather cauldron called the Great Australian Bight. Eyre Peninsula grows grain, wool and beef. It has iron ore mines, and a smelter and mill at Whyalla make steel. Whyalla had a history of shipbuilding, but its shipyards were an early casualty of the same worldwide shipbuilding upset which closed the yards of Britain, Germany and Scandinavia. A World War II light warship, built at Whyalla and named for the city, stands high and dry in a Whyalla Park as a monument to both a war and an industry.

Some 100 km along the cost, southwest from Whyalla, the Cowell district offers another example of the infinite variety of Australia: In an area of 9 square km., there are more than one hundred outcrops of nephrite jade, including the rare and beautiful black jade. A local farmer made the first find in 1965 – he'd been using lumps of the strange, tough rock to hold down sections of his rabbit-proof fence – and since then a small industry, deliberately kept in low profile, has developed around this exquisite stone. The Cowell Jade Province, declared by the state Mines Department, brings gemmologists and geologists from many countries and the finished product, carved, polished and fashioned into jewellery, is a tourist draw.

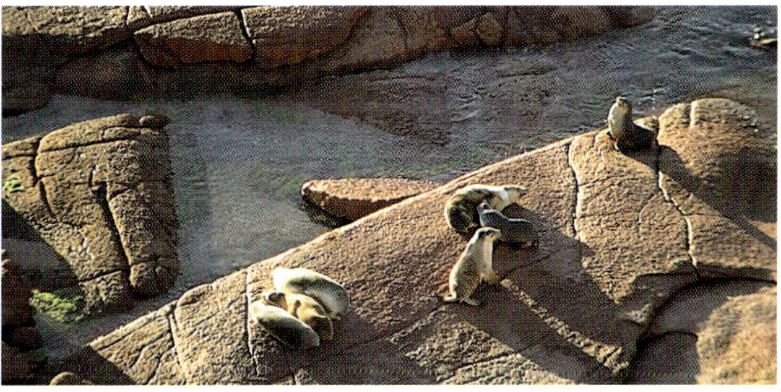

A colony of sea-lions at Pt. Labatt, Eyre Peninsula, SA.

South again, along the eastern coast of Eyre Peninsula, is another of the successful 'port' towns of South Australia, Port Lincoln. It's a major wheat port, but its attraction for most of its visitors is the fishing: From whiting to the great white shark, the waters off Port Lincoln, beyond Boston Bay and Boston Island (named by the whalers from America's New England) are one of Australia's great fishing grounds.

The Port Lincoln fishing fleet brings in blue fin and striped tuna (much in demand in the sushi restaurants of Japan and worth sometimes thousands of dollars per fish), rock lobsters, king prawns, garfish, snapper and salmon. Oysters, abalone and scallops are commercially fished along this coast.

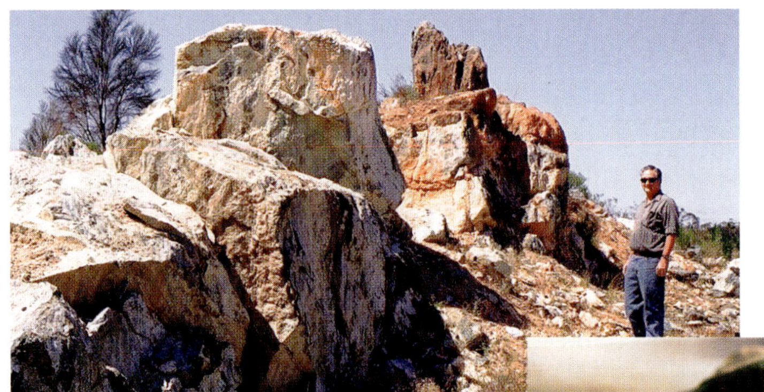

Outcrops of black jade, cutter, and cut jade.

At the foot of Eyre Peninsula, around Cape Catastrophe and the twin capes Wiles and Carnot, there begins one of the most spectacular coastlines of all Australia, the west coast of Eyre Peninsula, where the Southern Ocean's eternal attack on the Australian coast has created cliffs, bays and beaches amid magnificent isolation. And to the northwest, beyond the town of Ceduna, nature has created a favoured breeding ground for one of the most magnificent of all its creatures, the Southern Right Whale.

Now, where the whalers of the world once sailed to find and slaughter these gentle sea animals, the Government of South Australia has declared a permanent sanctuary for the Southern Rights, a place they can come to mate and calve in safety, little disturbed by the 10,000 tourists who come each year to watch and photograph them. Above all, they are safe here from the commercial savages who still hunt them in defiance of world opinion, and disguise their greed by such words as 'research.' There are said to be only some 3,000 Southern Right Whales surviving in all the world's seas, and 700 of them use these South Australian waters as their breeding ground, this area called the Head of the Bight, the eastern end of the Great Australian Bight. Ceduna is the nearest town of any size, and it's at Ceduna that the Eyre Highway from Port Augusta joins again with the coastal National Highway One and heads northwest towards the Nullarbor. While to the north, the path of the Indian-Pacific gently swings westward. The vegetation thins. Commercial animals are fewer, and soon vanish. The end of the grazing land comes at the end of the saltbush.

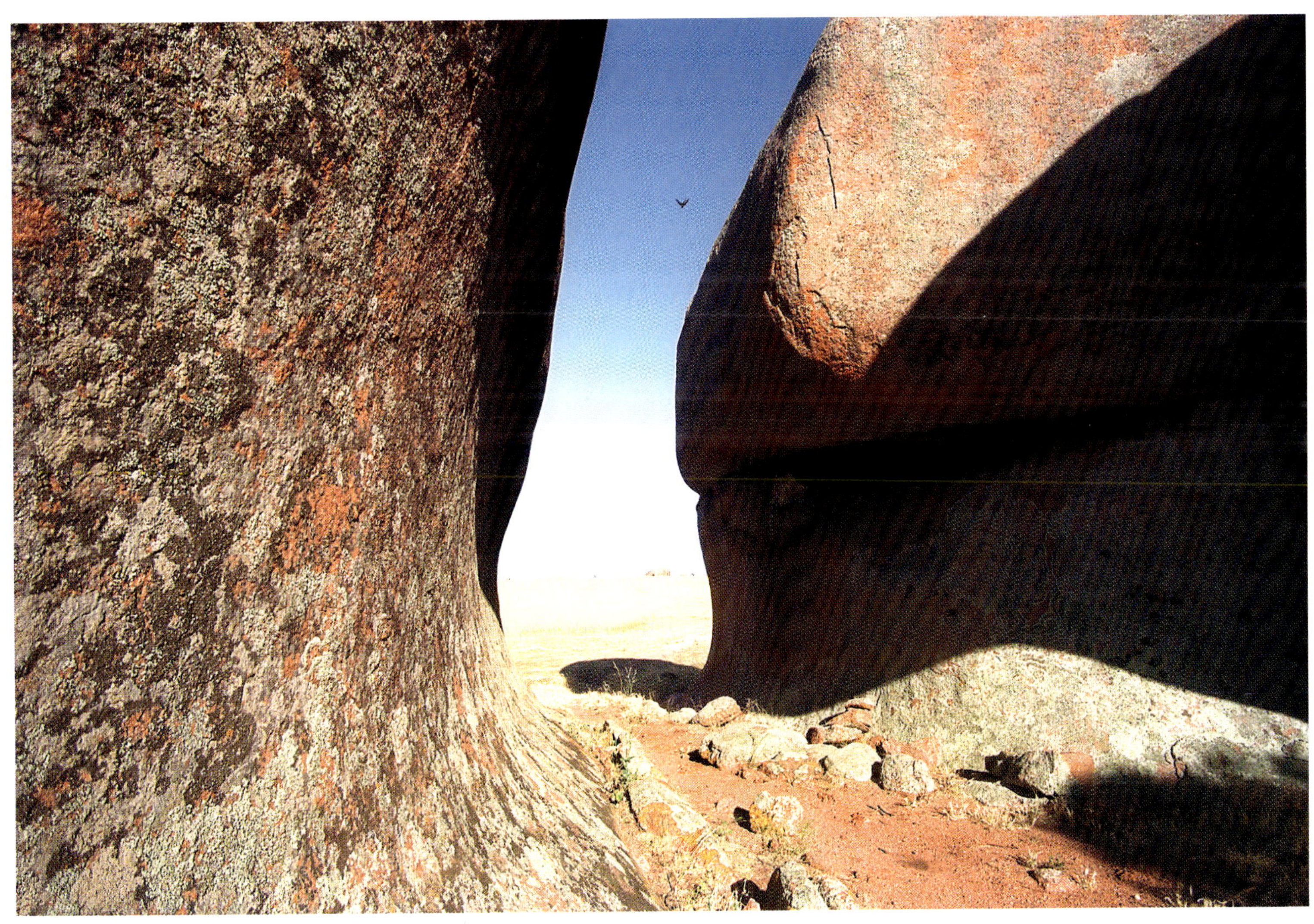

Murphy's Haystacks, Eyre Peninsula, SA.

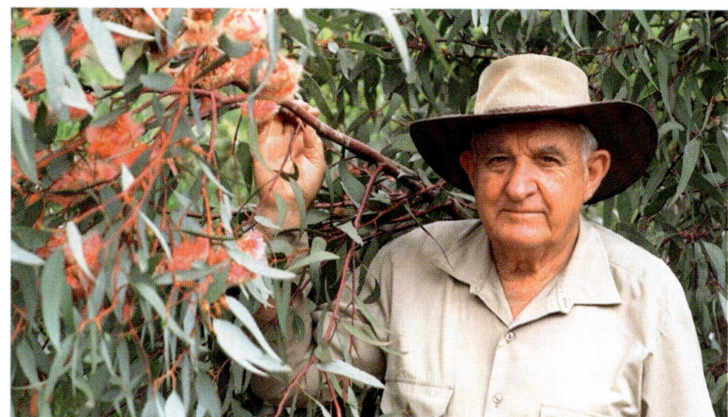

Brian Powell irrigates his salt tolerant gardens with salty bore water.

That's no coincidence: It's the saltbush that makes grazing possible far into the desert, because this low, grey-green shrub has the ability to draw its moisture from the air when the ground has none to give. The saltbush is a grazing marvel in arid Australia, and science is looking to it for clues to how other feed plants can be made to grow in country where the saltbush has evolved.

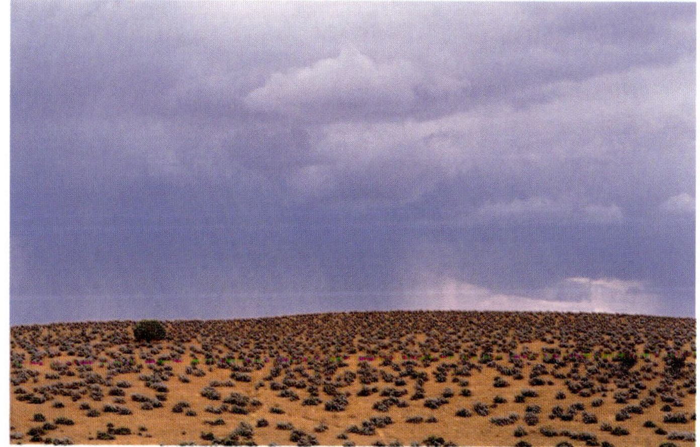

Saltbush vegetation near Pt. Augusta.

At Quorn, northeast of Port Augusta, Brian Powell, a former sheep station manager, has developed a garden and nursery of trees, shrubs and plants for the arid country. He began in 1974 on experimental work with food crops: Almonds, olives, carobs, pistachio nuts, figs and even grapes on salt-tolerant stock. There is an orchard of Quandongs, the Australian wild peach, which is believed to have a commercial future. Trees and shrubs of dual purpose – decorative in good times, cut back for stock feed in droughts –are among the hundreds of species of drought and salt tolerant native plants Brian Powell grows and gives away: 25,000 of them every year to outback stations and communities.

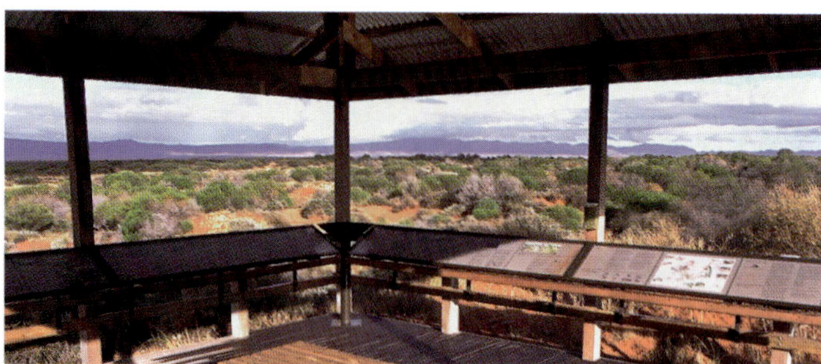

Arid Lands Botanic Garden, Pt. Augusta.

At Port Augusta, the City Council's Parks and Gardens staff is developing an arid lands botanic garden, one of only four in the world. Eventually, it will cover 200 hectares in 3,500 different species, with an adjoining 500 hectares reserved for an arid lands research centre whose goal will be finding farming solutions for land on the fringes of Australia's deserts, the recovery of fresh water from salt water and the utilisation of the one energy resource plentiful in outback Australia, the sun.

The Outback

The one percent of South Australians living north of the 32nd parallel – the outback border – are a hardy breed, and people of great variety. There are bushmen, of course, the stockmen and station hands who want no other life; there are prospectors, geologists, drilling teams and scientists looking for the treasures that almost certainly are there to be found. And occasionally, there are people whose work is so secret that few details of it are publicly available. Some such people live in a place called Nurrungar, close enough to the railway siding of Pimba for its lights to be visible on the right side of the westbound Indian-Pacific. It is an American military installation of some significance, built and operated during the Cold War by the Space Command of the U.S. Air Force. From this place in the Australian outback, kept secret by its isolation as much as by its chain-wire fences, surveillance satellites are controlled and monitored. Nurrungar was established as part of America's early warning system, able to detect and report ballistic missile launches. Its role since the Cold War simmered down is uncertain.

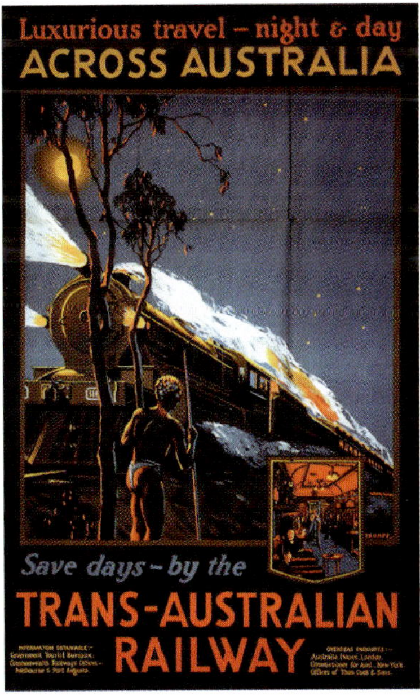

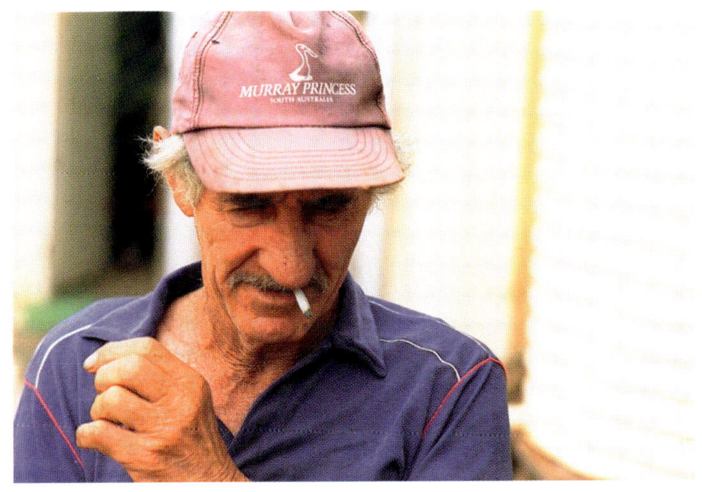

Also in the Pimba area is the former Woomera Rocket Range, where a village, a park and an open air museum are the only benefits from a monstrously expensive program of rocket trials carried out by the British from the 1950s. The 2,000 km of land to the northwest, the rocket range, made available by Australia to the British military, was deemed to be uninhabited, for in those days no-one paid much attention to the Aboriginal inhabitants.

As far as anyone knows, or is prepared to say, none of the nomadic Aborigines on the far end of the range got in the way of rocket fire. Perhaps that's because the rockets weren't very successful, and the target area was a safer place to be than the launching ramps where rockets with bold names like Blue Steel and Blue Streak too often provided spectacular, if unintended, local displays of fireworks.

Further west, an elaborate security fence alongside the railway line marks the southern boundary of another area of Anglo-British military activity. This was the area called Maralinga – a rough translation of the Aboriginal meaning is 'Place of Thunder', but the name was bestowed by Europeans not Aborigines – and it was here that the British fired off their experimental nuclear bombs. Again, the area was held by the authorities to be uninhabited, and again, they'd got it wrong. The subsequent claims by the resident Aboriginal people, for compensation and restoration, are so far only partly met.

The political and military disregard of the Aboriginal people of Australia continued in the 1950s and '60s a long established practice. When the explorer Forrest made the first crossing of the Nullarbor Plain he believed the Aborigines he encountered were cannibals, and this belief, without any surviving proof, was still common in the camps when the transcontinental railway was being built. It was part of the folk lore of the work gangs.

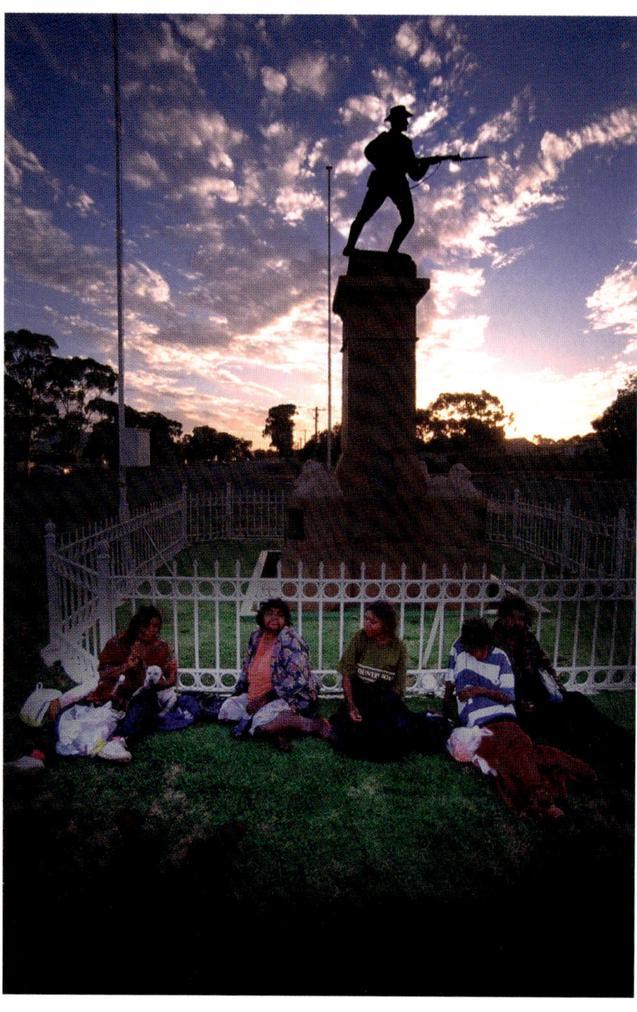

Kalgoorlie mob. Not far from Kalgoorlie railway station is the Belgian war memorial, a popular meeting point. Most Kalgoorlie Aborigines live in old miners' huts unbearably hot in summer. Elsewhere it would be called a slum, but in the gold town it is a heritage area. So the green cool reserve makes a better living room...

The desert Aborigines, drawn to the railway camps for the worst of reasons, were given the worst of treatment. Managers and workers alike saw them as nuisances. Except for the women, who were seen as something else.

The Aborigines for their part saw, and too often adopted, the worst of European ways, and as groups of them followed the construction camps their tight tribal structure broke down and unruly mobs resulted.

One woman, alone, took up their cause. Daisy Bates, born in Ireland in 1859, was at the time an infernal nuisance to politicians and the railway builders, but history reveals the rightness of her cause.

Daisy Bates saw problems ahead for the Aborigines even before the first railway sleeper was laid, unlike the planners, who simply regarded the area as uninhabited. Well before the railway began, Daisy Bates was writing to Premiers and Commissioners asking that all along the length of the transcontinental line, the railway be declared an area prohibited to

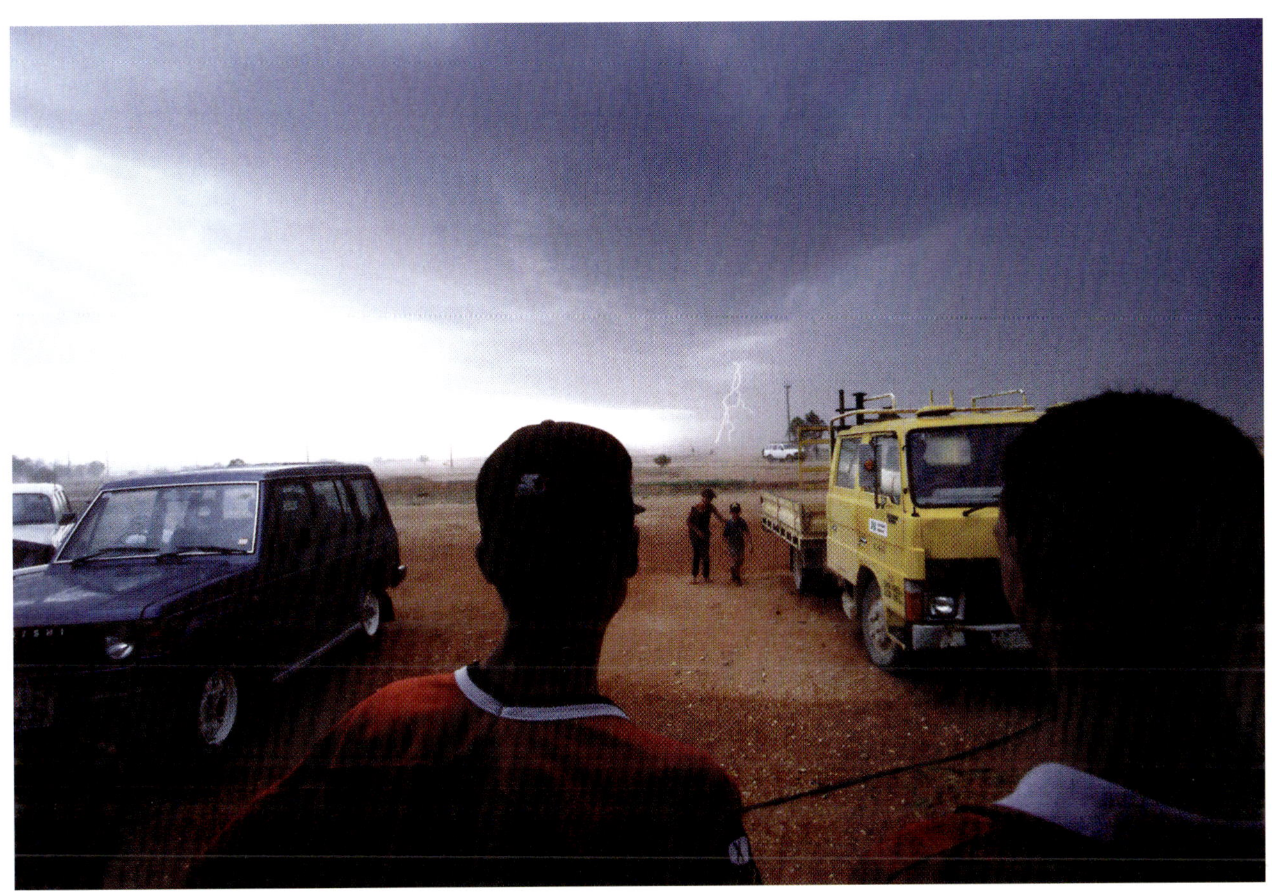

The day has been searingly hot, as an evening thunderstorm hits Cook.
The railways have certainly contributed to the decay of the traditional lifestyle of Aborigines, but at the other hand were the first to offer equal opportunity employment to Aborigines.

Aborigines. Her aim was not so much to keep the Aborigines out as to keep the whites, their appetites and their influences, in. If this were not done, her powerful letters said, if Aborigines were given free contact with the worst excesses of the railway camps, then the Aboriginal way of life would be lost and the people's extinction accelerated by generations.

In reply to the passionate and prescient letters of Daisy Bates, Government offered the usual soothing sounds, while ignoring the substance of her fears and warnings. Until her death in the 1940s, Daisy Bates stayed in the desert for most of her life, watching from around Ooldea water hole the decay of a lifestyle and a people she had predicted and fought to prevent.

Desert Life

Scientists argue about how long the Aboriginal people have lived in Australia: 40,000 to 50,000 years seems agreed as a minimum. For indigenous animals, the time frame is millions of years. In all these times, the destructive mark of man and animal was barely left on this old island, Australia. But in the two hundred years of European occupation, imported man and imported animals have had a devastating effect. Strangely, this is nowhere more apparent than in the arid country along the transcontinental railway.

For hundreds of kilometres west from Port Augusta, marginal sheep grazing country continues as far as the saltbush lasts. Bore water and saltbush is all life has to offer the outback sheep. But beyond the saltbush, life continues. In the apparently empty land just outside the train windows, a busy and perilous animal world exists.

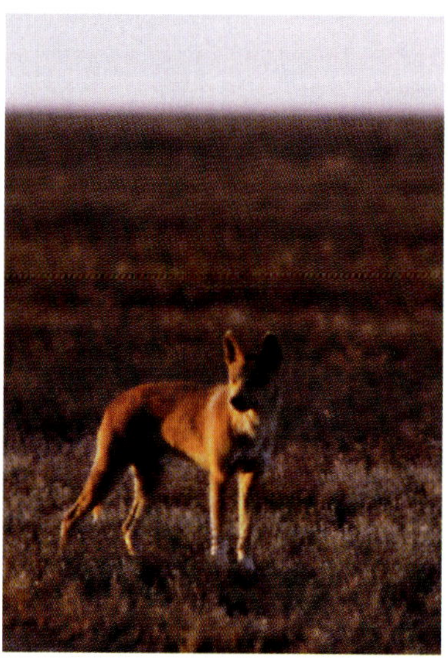

The dingo is a late migrant to Australia arriving some 8,000 years ago.

Much Australian wildlife is nocturnal, and every night in the cooling desert it seeks the food and moisture it must have to stay alive through the heat of tomorrow. Once the light and noise of the passing Indian-Pacific has gone, the endless struggle for survival resumes, for almost everything that moves is sought by something else as food. For measureless time, the balance between eater and eaten was maintained, but in just one century, new animals have so distorted the natural world that it will never recover. The intruders came with man, or because of him: They are the rabbit, the fox and the dreadful feral cat.

Naturalists who research these arid and desert regions are aghast at the environmental damage imported animals cause. No native creature in the Australian desert, or in the bush, was equipped by nature for defence against foreign predators and their numbers are seriously depleted. Whole species are under threat, some have already been wiped out.

Cats came to the desert as the camp pets of the railway builders. Their offspring, unwanted and abandoned, were left to run wild as the construction camps moved on, and by the process of evolution called Survival of the Fittest, a very tough breed of cat has developed. Or rather, perhaps, the cat has shed the trappings of a few thousand years of human indulgence and reverted to its natural state.

It's hard for fond owners of household cats to imagine the feral variety: So different are they from the purring pussy at home that perhaps they're not cats at all any longer, rather some new species between cat and leopard. They are big, twice the size of a domestic cat. They are fierce, and fearless, and to wildlife they are murderous.

Birds, small animals and the legions of lizard species that live here have no defence against so efficient a hunter.

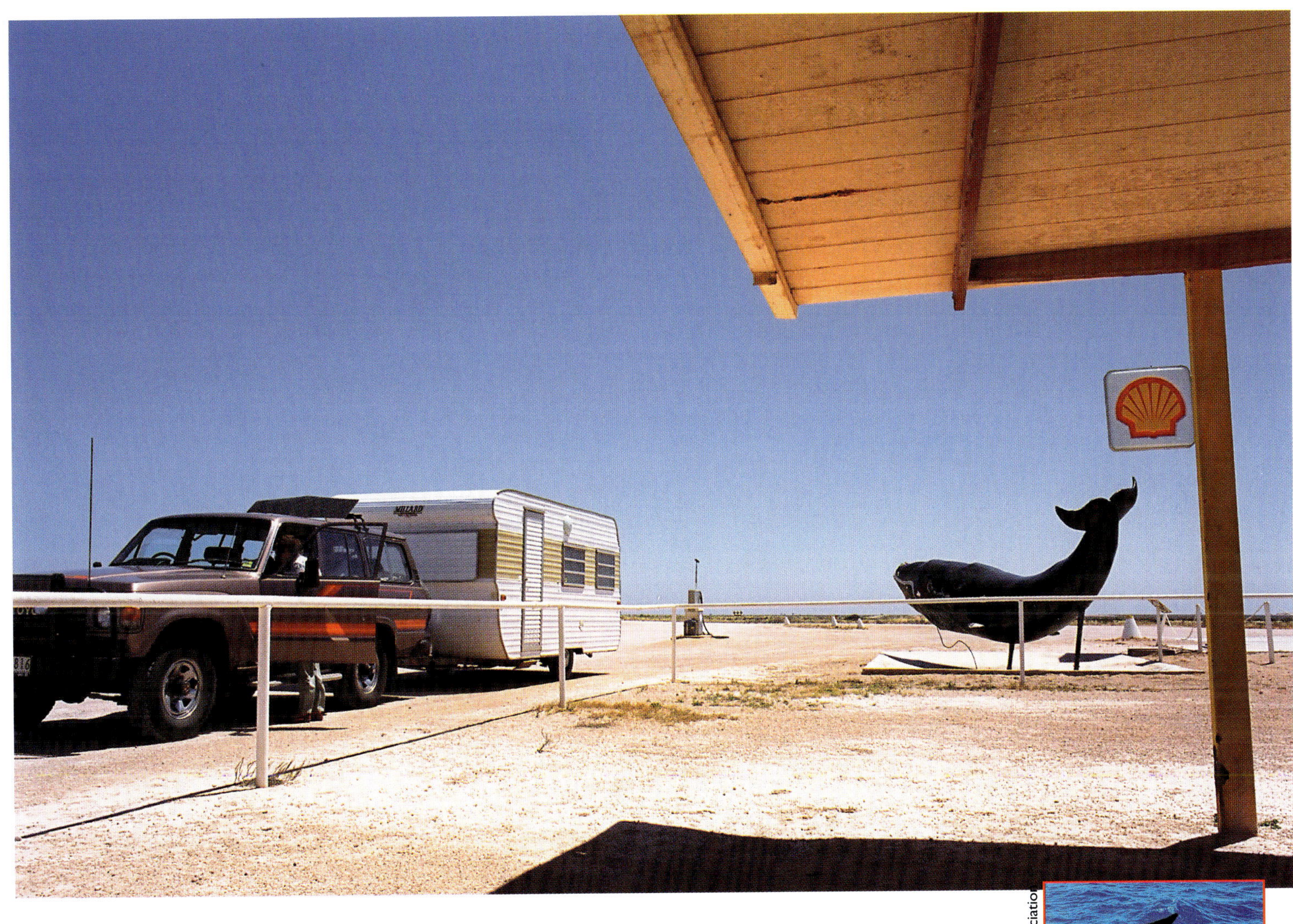

Eyre Peninsula Tourism Association

The threat of the rabbit is different. It eats only vegetation, but it eats so thoroughly that the vegetation is demolished rather than eaten down, and in a few generations rabbits can strip land bare of anything that grows.

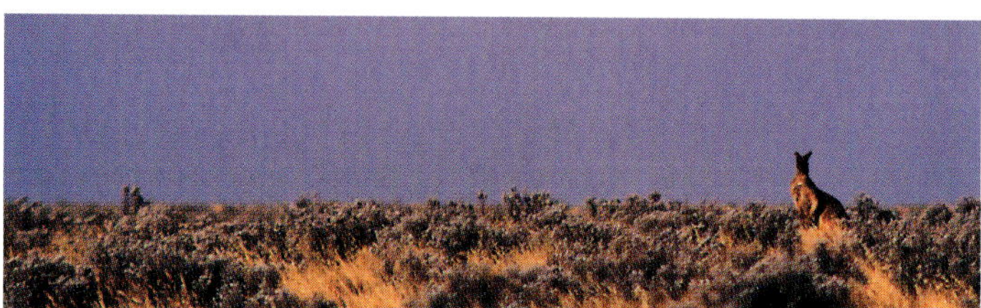

In the evening the Nullarbor comes alive.

Native grazing animals, kangaroos, wallabies and a myriad of smaller creatures find nothing is left for them when the rabbits arrive.

The rabbit population attracts its own predator, the fox, which sets up house close to rabbit warrens to ensure its food supply. But the fox has other tastes as well, and to vary its menu eats its way through native wildlife.

Australia has more than its fair share of the less lovable of Creatures Great and Small: Some of the world's most venomous snakes and poisonous spiders have Australian citizenship, but the creature most hated in bush Australia is the timid, furry rabbit: Hero of television cartoons; motif of nursery decoration and baby's food bowl; target of eradication campaigns so drastic that man uses them on no other species, other than himself: Germs, guns, gas, fire, explosives.

But the rabbit bounces back. In this land where survival is so hard, the rabbit, totally foreign to it, is a superb survivor. In good times, it breeds prolifically, a new generation every eight to ten weeks. Five hundred rabbits can come from one pair in one year. But when times are bad, as in drought, the rabbit shuts down its breeding through a fertility system that is environmentally controlled.

The rabbit was brought to Australia for sport. A gentleman-farmer who'd acquired some land near Geelong in Victoria thought it would be amusing to have some rabbits for himself and his guests to shoot.

The fox was imported for sport, too, by people trying to recreate in Australia some of the ways of the old world they had left, including dressing up in strange clothing and pursuing on horseback a pack of dogs set loose to find, chase and kill a fox, imported and released for the purpose. Fox hunting survives in only a few desperately nostalgic societies, but th depredations of the fox are measured each year by the naturalists who identify the damage it is doing to a fragile environment.

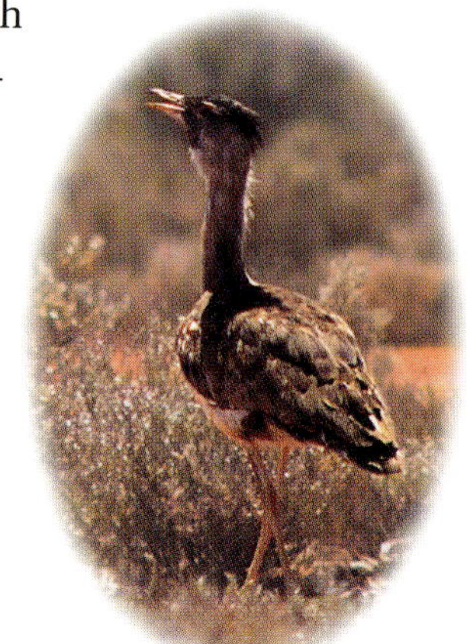

The Bustard from the Bush.

Perhaps there is a fourth predator in the Australian wilderness, and it is us. Man has been harsh on this environment, his piles of rubbish only too obvious along the railway, sometimes close to townships, sometimes in the middle of nowhere. Derelict cars, rusting or burnt out, litter the bush far from settlements, and it's sadly apparent that some of the people who've come this way have shown little regard for those who'll come later.

Tarcoola

Nowhere but in Australia would be found a town named after a racehorse. It would be either a mining town or a railway town, and Tarcoola is both.

It existed before the railway, the site of an intense but short lived gold rush, and when the railway builders reached it on the way west from Port Augusta, it was a town on the way out. Tarcoola was named in honour of the winning horse in the Melbourne Cup in the year of the gold rush. Its population, as the railway pushed out towards the Nullarbor, was made up of miners and prospectors who'd stayed on when the gold reef ran out and the newcoming railwaymen. A lively mixture, and not – as Daisy Bates had so accurately predicted – the kind of European influence that would advance the quality of Aboriginal life.

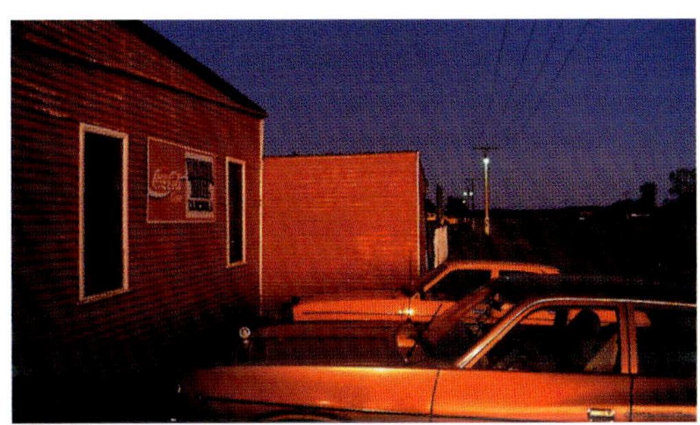

The Tarcoola pub.

The railway guaranteed the dying little mining town a future as a railway town. From a construction base it became a key water and fuelling point when the line opened in 1917. It was at a convenient distance from Port Augusta in an operating system whose limits were dictated by the demands of steam locomotives for coal, water and service. It was a crew change point also, for human endurance on the footplate of steam engines had a limit as well. And the engines of the Trans-Australia Railway, mainly adaptations of the *T*, *P* and *C-36* classes of the New South Wales Railways, were little suited to desert conditions. The 412 km from Port Augusta to Tarcoola, a 10 hour run on a good day with no problems and no delayed crossings with trains bound in the opposite direction, was more than enough for driver and fireman. Tarcoola offered a break before the return journey, accommodation in what the railways called a 'barracks': Basic bed and no breakfast, cook for yourself, sleep on a mean mattress in a grimy room, and be shaken awake all too soon to work the eastbound back to Augusta.

Tarcoola also had a pub, and still does to this day, the last pub west to Kalgoorlie or north to Alice Springs. The future of both pub and town seemed bleak from the day in 1951 that Commonwealth Railways' first diesel-electric locomotive, GM-1, named Robert Gordon Menzies in honour of the reigning Prime Minister, growled into town on a trial train from Port Augusta to the west.

That locomotive, and those of the same and other classes that followed, proved the prescience of the long dead Engineer, Henry Deane, who had told his Government masters forty years before that the association between the steam locomotive and desert railway would be unhappy and expensive.

The diesels quickly pushed steam engines into the scrap sidings, and Tarcoola seemed about to join them. Then, a railways decision was made to rebuild the line to

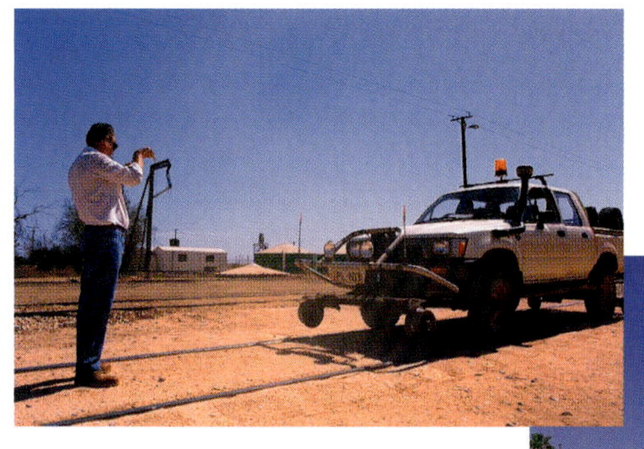

Workgang with Hi-rail at Rawlinna.

Central Australia, the old Ghan Line, which had made its legendary, unreliable, way north through the Flinders Ranges. The new line would be a standard gauge, concrete sleepered, welded railed road to the centre and perhaps on to Darwin, the railway promised decades before but as elusive politically as the inland sea had been physically to earlier generations.

Significantly for Tarcoola, the new railway to the north would join the trans-Australia line there, and the little town rose again from the threatened ashes of oblivion. Then, a new generation of gold seekers came to Tarcoola, and brought with them new ideas, new machinery, to sift through the waste, the mullock heaps, left by the miners of three generations before and to recover payable gold. Tarcoola lived yet again.

And in the middle of the decade of the '90s, a century after the brief golden glory of Tarcoola, the prospectors and claim peggers came again and marked out their exploratory blocks around the compass from Tarcoola: North, East, South, West, negotiating this time with Aboriginal land-holders for the right to seek and mine gold in land called the Maralinga and Gawler Tenements.

West of Tarcoola, the railway villages began. They're mostly in the past tense now, because they existed only to serve the one-time needs of the railway, and their reason for existence has gone. Of some, only a railway signpost remains. Others still have a house or two yet to be demolished, others again are barely marks on the ground or the scars of fires where railway houses were deliberately burned down by the railways, a drastic action, but judged preferable to their inevitable attack by vandals.

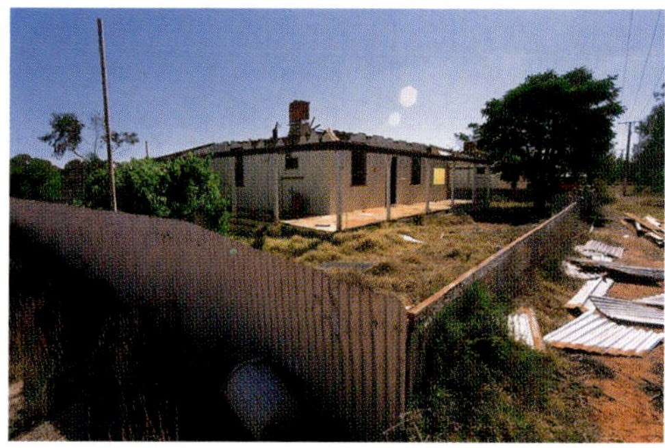

Abandoned railway houses, Zanthus, WA. The Railways will burn down the village when a fire ban is lifted.

The railway villages were the 'permanent' settlements left in the wake of the transcontinental railway builders. As the construction gangs moved on, maintenance men and their families stayed behind, because the building of a railway in this hostile country was only the beginning of a work program that would never end. Maintenance was constant, the enemy was nature itself: Huge ranges in temperature, from below freezing to half way to boiling,

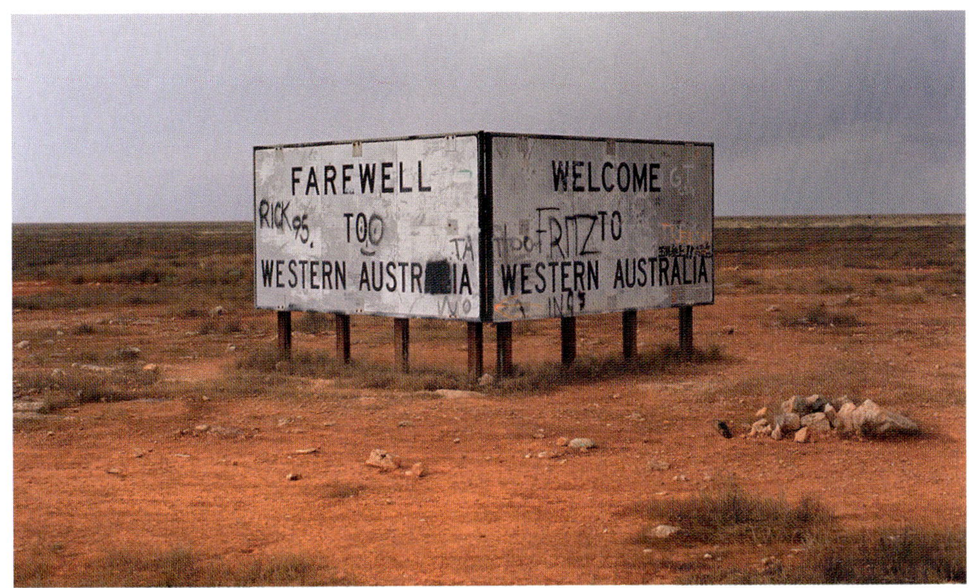

Borderline: A signboard in the desert marks the border between South Australia and Western Australia.

caused problems with the expansion and contraction of steel rails; there were washaways in the rare but sometimes savage local floods; the sleepers (called more accurately elsewhere 'cross-ties') were eaten by termites, which regarded any wooden structure as breakfast, lunch and dinner. Inspection of the line, from the petrol-powered three-wheel trolleys railwaymen called trikes, was a daily task. The entire transcontinental railway was divided into maintenance sections, and each section had its own work team: Gangs they were called, and the men in them were Fettlers. The boss was the Ganger. Every day, in the cold of the early morning, they hauled their little trolleys out of lineside sheds, loaded them with the tools and materials they'd need, checked that no unscheduled trains were on the line, and set off to work their sections.

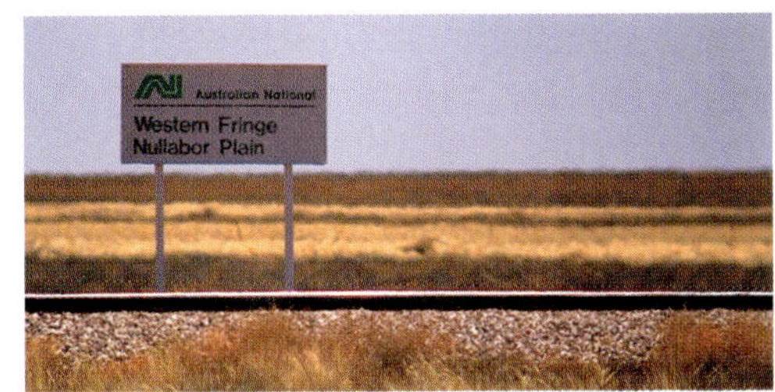

Nullarbor - official start.

The tents of the construction gangs became shacks, the shacks became houses grouped in tiny settlements strung out along the length of the railway and named mainly after prime ministers, politicians, soldiers: Barton, O'Malley, Cook, Denman, Hughes, Deakin, Haig, Kitchener, Chifley, Blamey, Curtin. Names of glory and inglory, triumph and disaster.

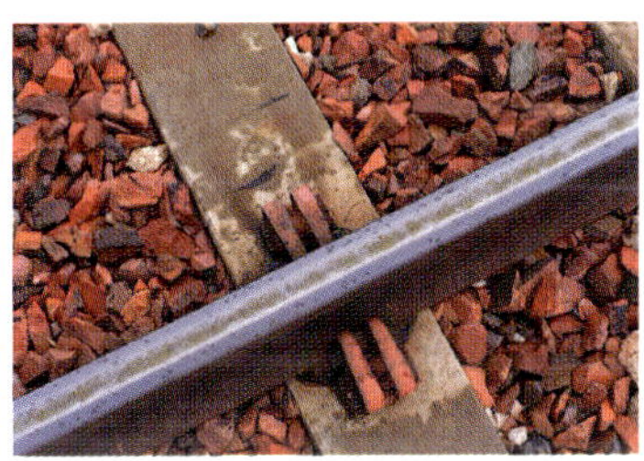

A small change in technology with an immense impact on infrastructure – concrete sleeper, rubber plate and bracket, instead of wooden sleeper and steel spikes.

Just names now, most of them, because the age of concrete sleepers and welded rails has done away with much of the maintenance task. A concrete sleeper lasts for 50 years at least, and machines the early fettlers could not have imagined are the new navvies of the Nullarbor.

Nulla Arbor

The Great Nullarbor Plain begins, for the sake of geographic convenience, at a dot on the map called Ooldea, once called Ooldea Soak, a water hole the Aborigines knew for millennia. At Ooldea, water from an underground river with origins in the Musgrave Ranges, far to the north, comes to the surface. It is the last natural surface water until the western side of the Nullarbor 676 km away.

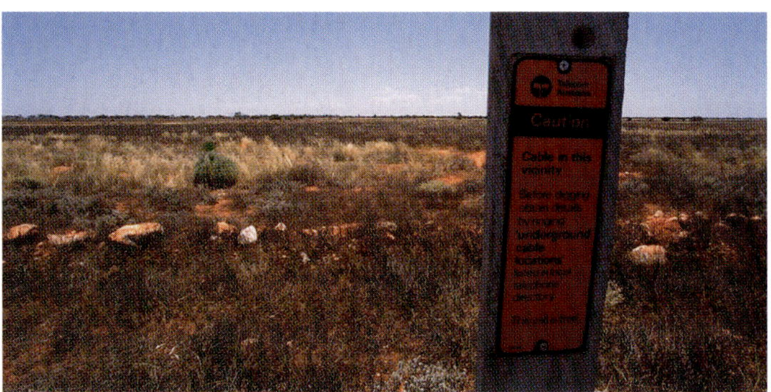

This call is free... Cheap advice with no telephone for 100 kilometres. Telecom fibre optic installation.

Zoologists might argue that the Nullarbor in fact starts somewhere other than Ooldea; Botanists somewhere else again; Geologists would disagree with both. What is certain though is that the railway crosses the true Nullarbor. Motorists using the east-west Eyre Highway along the coast do not, and the window stickers boasting 'We Crossed The Nullarbor' are not telling the precise truth, unless the cars were carried on the Indian-Pacific.

The Eyre Highway does offer endless views of a coastline so stark, so sharply defined, that it's easy to imagine it as the freshly broken edge where the Australian landmass broke away from the super-continent Gondwana and began its timeless journey north. Rough tracks connect some of the former railway villages with fishing spots on the coast. Train passengers see no other clues that from the heart of the Nullarbor, a day's ocean fishing is only a few hours' drive away.

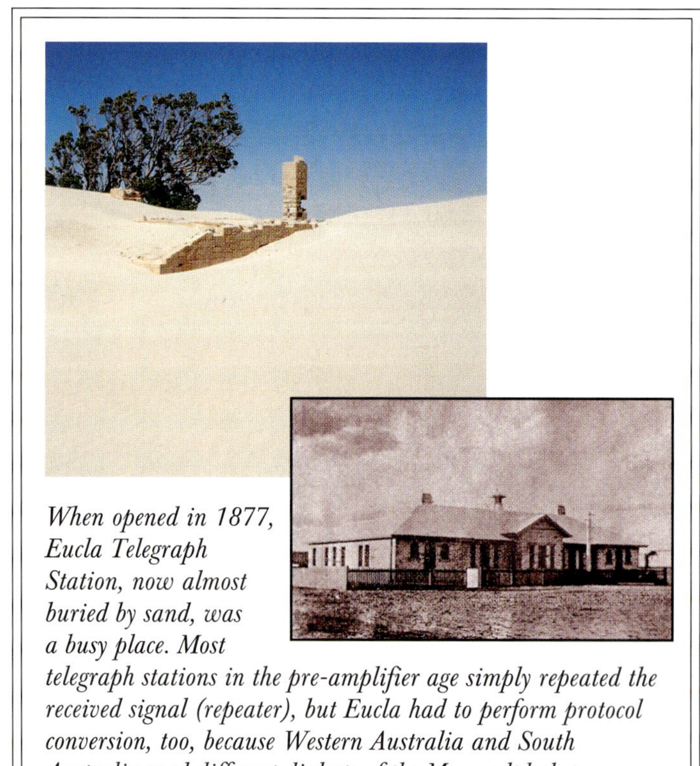

When opened in 1877, Eucla Telegraph Station, now almost buried by sand, was a busy place. Most telegraph stations in the pre-amplifier age simply repeated the received signal (repeater), but Eucla had to perform protocol conversion, too, because Western Australia and South Australia used different dialects of the Morse alphabet.

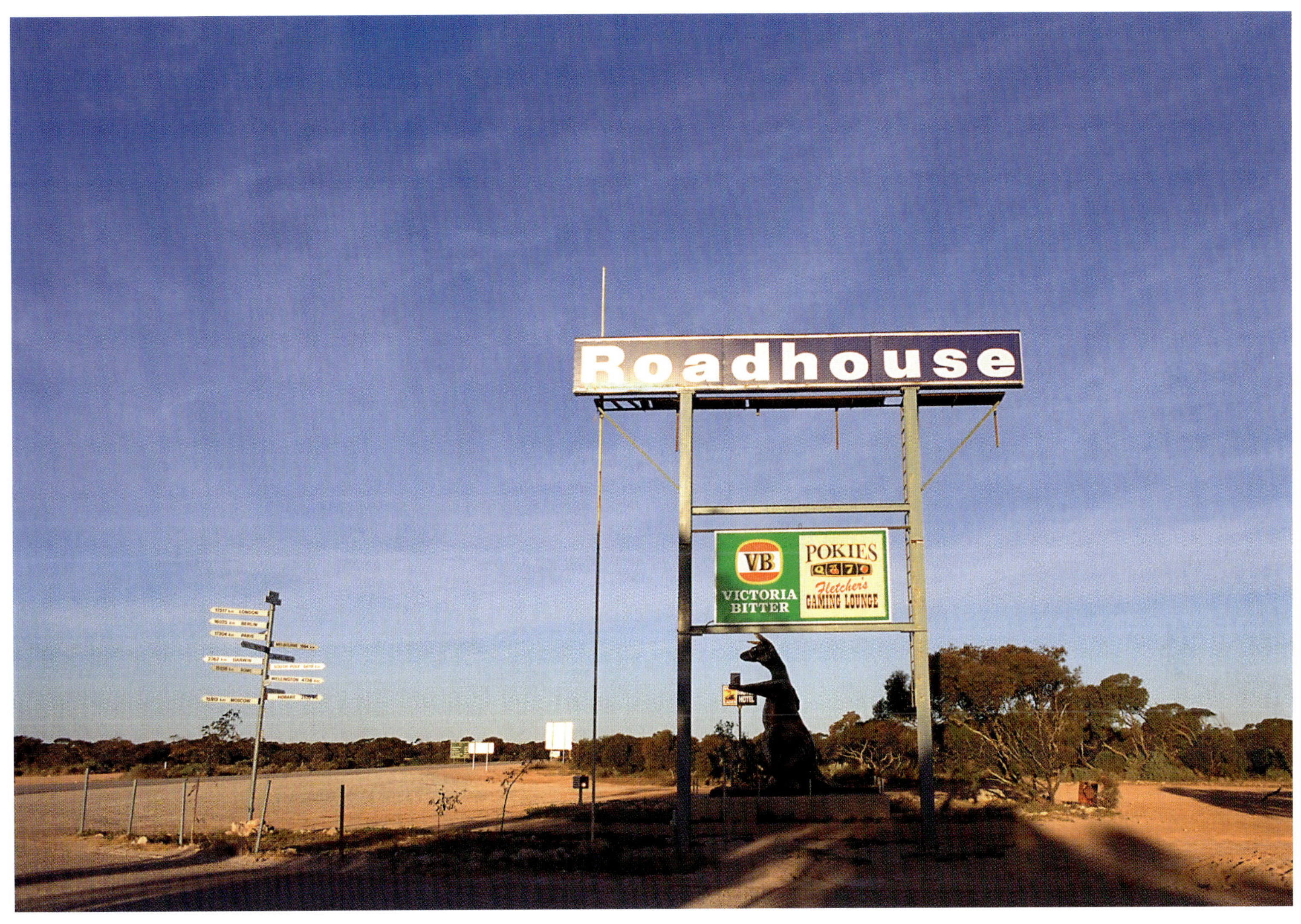

Border village on the Eyre Highway.
The border of Western Australia boasts the most rigorous quarantine controls.
Beer is not confiscated but virtually everything else is...

The Nullarbor was once the bed of the sea, thrust up in the convulsions of the separating Gondwana. Its structure is that of a vast limestone sponge, and its system of caves stretching far inland has been little explored. It's known, though, that caves exist big enough to house a jumbo jet, and cave systems can be traced as far as 100 km inland by the blowholes which bring the cool salt air of the coast into the dry desert. Railway workers built a crude structure of wooden sleepers over one blowhole, and used it as a kind of sauna in reverse: A cool room to escape the heat of the day.

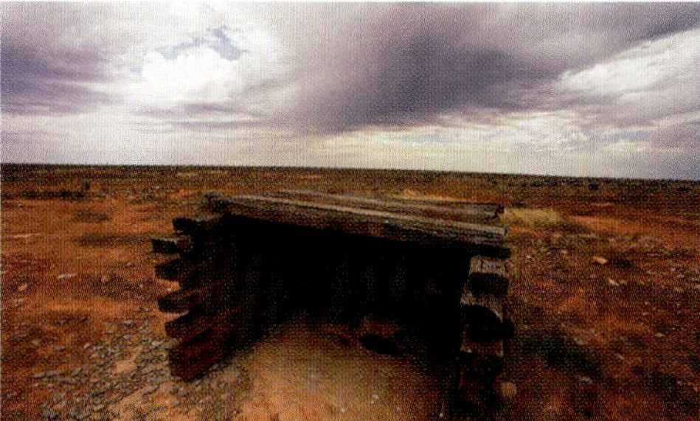

The reverse sauna.

Apart from the railway, there are few signs of human presence on the Nullarbor. Once, there was the 'pole line', the telephone line of copper wires on steel posts, shared by the railways and the telegraph authority. Built at the same time as the railway, it was the main east-west communications link until technical improvements in telecommunications made it obsolete, replaced first by a microwave system then by the fibre-optic cable buried a metre deep a hundred metres away from the railway line, its path marked by the occasional repeater stations whose solar arrays convert sunlight into the electricity which powers the system.

Towards the end of the old pole line's life, its copper wires carried traffic unimaginable at the time it was built: Traffic from the moon, collected from the Apollo space craft and transmitted by the pole line to eastern Australia and on to the United States.

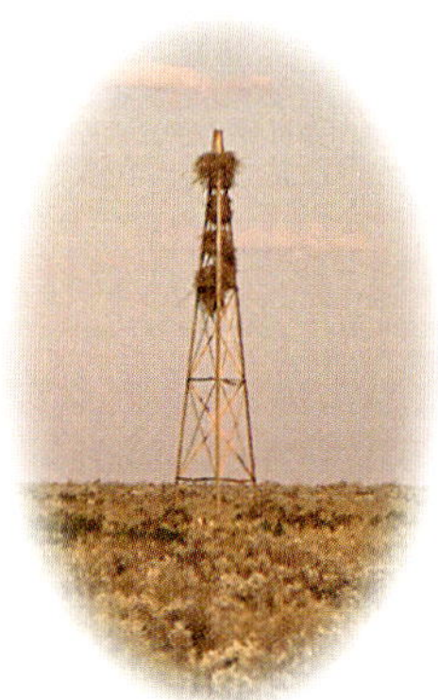

High rise birds nests, Nullarbor.

Many of the telegraph poles carried, as well as their working load of copper wires, the nests of Wedge Tail Eagles, the bird which is the logo of the Indian-Pacific and Australia's largest raptor. The eagles, displaced from their sturdy but untidy nests by removal of the poles, have colonised towers built for them by the railways close to their old nesting places, and their separate nests are built on many levels like a multistorey housing block.

The long straight of the Trans-Australia Railway, beginning with the Nullarbor itself around Ooldea, stretches west across the West Australian border. But still in South Australia, the Indian-Pacific makes the one stop on the Nullarbor crossing where passengers are able to leave the train and visit one of the few remaining railway villages. It's a refuelling point for locomotives, and the train's water

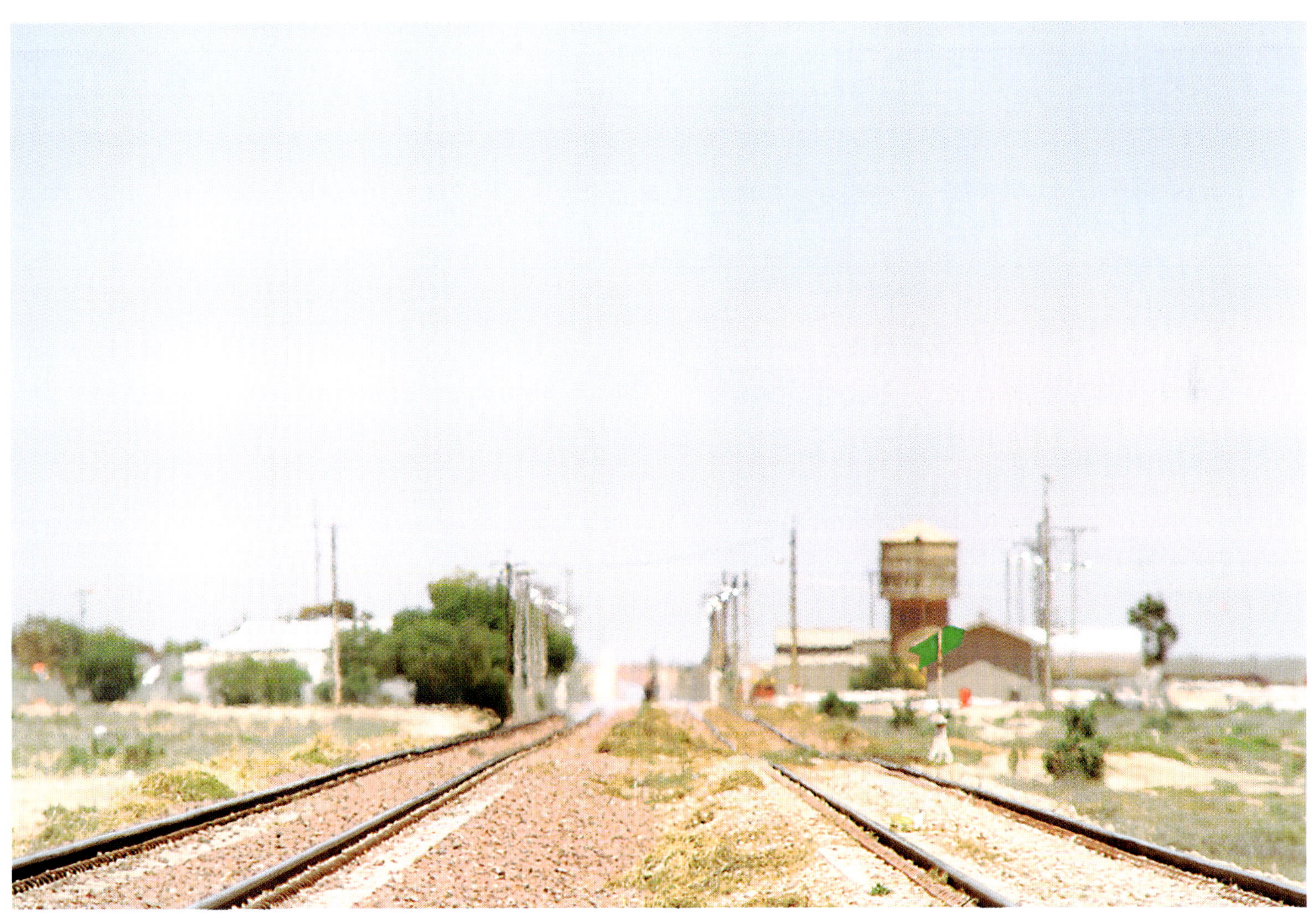

In the heat of the day: Cook.

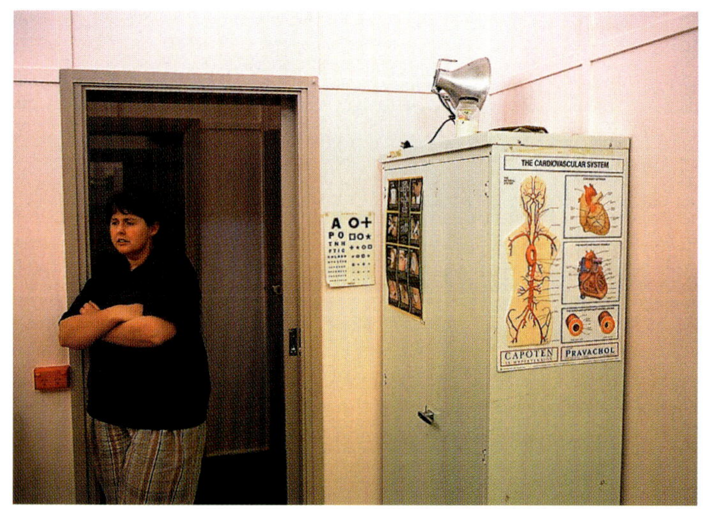

Nurse Joyce Kennedy is one of the two nurses of the Cook hospital, servicing about 80 ambulant cases and 10 inpatients per year. Serious cases are treated by the Flying Doctors who visit regularly. The hospital was opened in 1937 by the Bush Church Aid Society of Australia, a section of the Anglican Church.

supply is topped up with water railed from Port Augusta. There's no township anywhere else in Australia like the Nullarbor village of Cook.

There's an air of permanence about Cook: It has a school, and the only hospital between Port Augusta and Kalgoorlie. To the south, the sea, the Southern Ocean, is only 100 km away. To the north, there's nothing much at all for almost 2,000 km, then there's Darwin at the Top End of Australia. Cook is near enough to the half way point of the original Trans-Australia Railway.

Cook was the site, in 1982, of a cheeky challenge to the treeless Nullarbor. Railway volunteers from Port Augusta and Kalgoorlie met at this half way point for a weekend, and planted 600 young trees. They called their project The Greening of Cook and they hoped that in time an oasis would mark their effort. But the Nullarbor defeated them. Only some stunted survivors of the Greening remain. The plain remains *nulla arbor* (Latin: no trees) even at Cook.

About halfway along the long straight, at Deakin on the map, the train crosses the South Australia - West Australia border. Nothing changes except the time: The one-and-a-half hour time change is evidence of the distance the train has come. At the border, the Indian-Pacific is more than 2,500 km from Sydney, and with almost 1,400 km yet to go to Perth. The border country, for hundreds of kilometres east and west of the state boundary, is in normal seasons some of the most barren of the whole journey. Yet it needs only a rainstorm to bring the land to spectacular life, transformed by grasses and wildflowers. The rabbits go into fertility overdrive and very quickly there is a plague. They strip the country as bare of its growth as it was before the rain, then they starve again and suspend their breeding until next time the desert flowers.

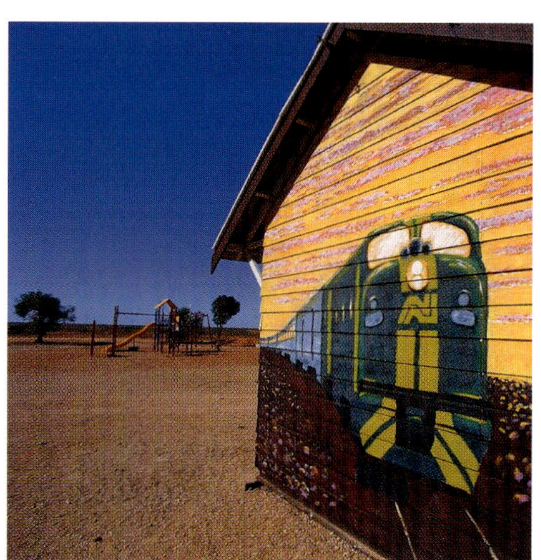

Mural at Cook school.

The first settlement inside West Australia is Forrest, named in small recognition of a notable explorer, later a politician who more than any other individual brought about the railway across Australia. Sir John Forrest, later again Lord Forrest, lived to see rails span the country he had first explored on foot.

The little railway township boasts the longest sealed and lit airstrip in Australia, apart from the capital cities'. Forrest was a necessary refuelling stop in the years when nonstop flight from Adelaide to Perth was beyond the range of the commercial aeroplanes of the time. It's about half way on the intercity flight, and light planes still refuel there. Forrest is also an emergency diversion should a commercial flight be forced into an unscheduled stop, but no-one at Forrest can remember when that last happened.

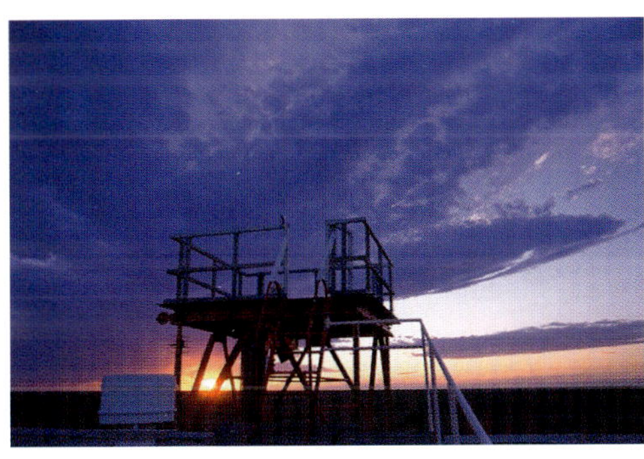

Forrest weather station.

On the edge of Forrest's airfield, a weather station takes half-hourly readings of conditions in an area which has some say in the future weather of the eastern half of Australia. And four times a day, Forrest sends aloft balloon-borne instrument packages to sample and radio back the temperatures, winds and humidity between 6 and 20 km above the earth. Their readings give early warning of what's coming on the Southern Ocean's weather streams and the possible effect two or three days later on the eastern population centres of Australia.

Forrest itself, like all the Nullarbor, has extremes of weather: Almost 50 degrees Celsius at its hottest, and down to zero on some winter nights. The almost constant winds, and their chill factor, can produce conditions well below zero.

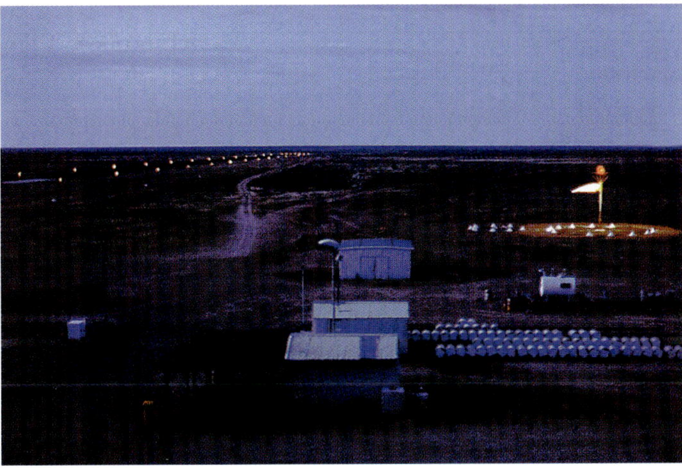

Forrest's air field. Runway lights can be switched on from the air by remote control.

After almost 480 km, the long straight ends about an hour and a half west of Forrest, with a barely perceptible curve at Nurina. An hour later, only a sign alongside the track marks the site of a World War II wartime prison so remote that it needed no walls. The place was called Wilban. The prisoners were Italians, driven to war on the side of Hitler by their own dictator Mussolini, captured in North Africa, shipped half way round the world, and deposited by train alongside a railway line in another desert at the end of the earth.

P.O.W.s

Australia was not experienced at taking and keeping prisoners of war. In earlier wars, someone else, usually the British, had dealt with any prisoners Australian soldiers captured. But in North Africa, 18,000 Italians surrendered to Australians, 'Barbarians in shabby shorts and cowboy hats,' one of the prisoners would write years later, ' men who dressed untidily, took orders grudgingly, and addressed their Italian captives as 'Tony', officer and common soldier alike.'

Taken initially to the major p.o.w. camp at Hay, NSW, 350 of the captured Italians were selected for work on the Trans-Australia railway, re-sleepering and other heavy maintenance on sections between Watson and Rawlinna. 'Strong labouring types should be selected,' Army Order 53/101/54 of March 13, 1942, Secret and Immediate, said, 'and care taken to exclude potential trouble makers and unwilling workers.'

In case of trouble, the Australian Army guards would carry rifles and side arms and 100 rounds of .303 ammunition. Each man, prisoner and guard alike, would be issued four blankets and one palliasse (without straw). Only the military mind would expect to find straw at the western end of the Nullarbor Plain. The prisoners were to be paid for their work, at one shilling threepence per day – about 12 cents – and by order of the Military Board itself, 'the hours and conditions of work for p.o.w.'s will be those stipulated in the appropriate award for railway workers, but will not exceed 8 hours in any one day and will include 24 consecutive hours rest in each 7 days.' And – a wise concession – p.o.w.'s were to provide their own cooks, and were thus spared the efforts of the infamous cooks of Australia's Army. It's almost certain that behind the barbed wire of Wilban, captives ate far better than captors.

In the hours beyond their working eight, Wilban's Italians has little to do and nowhere to go. To relieve the boredom, they gathered stones and used them to make borders along the paths of the camp. Elsewhere in Australia, Italian prisoners were so successful at farm work and public projects that Australia actually asked for more of them . Some never went home. Others, repatriated to Italy after the war, came back as fast as they could. But no-one ever returned to Wilban, on the Nullarbor, where if they had come back, even today, they'd find only rusting scraps of barbed wire, some traces of pathways edge in stone, and fragments of old razor blades and tobacco tins.

It was one of the ironies of war that while Italian prisoners worked on a railway in Australia, paid and under union conditions, far to the north in South-East Asia captured Australians worked on another railway for another, less considerate, captor. Their experiences, their starvation, their diseases, their ill-treatment and their deaths on the Burma-Siam Railway as slaves of the Japanese Emperor, are written indelibly on the list of atrocities of the 20th century.

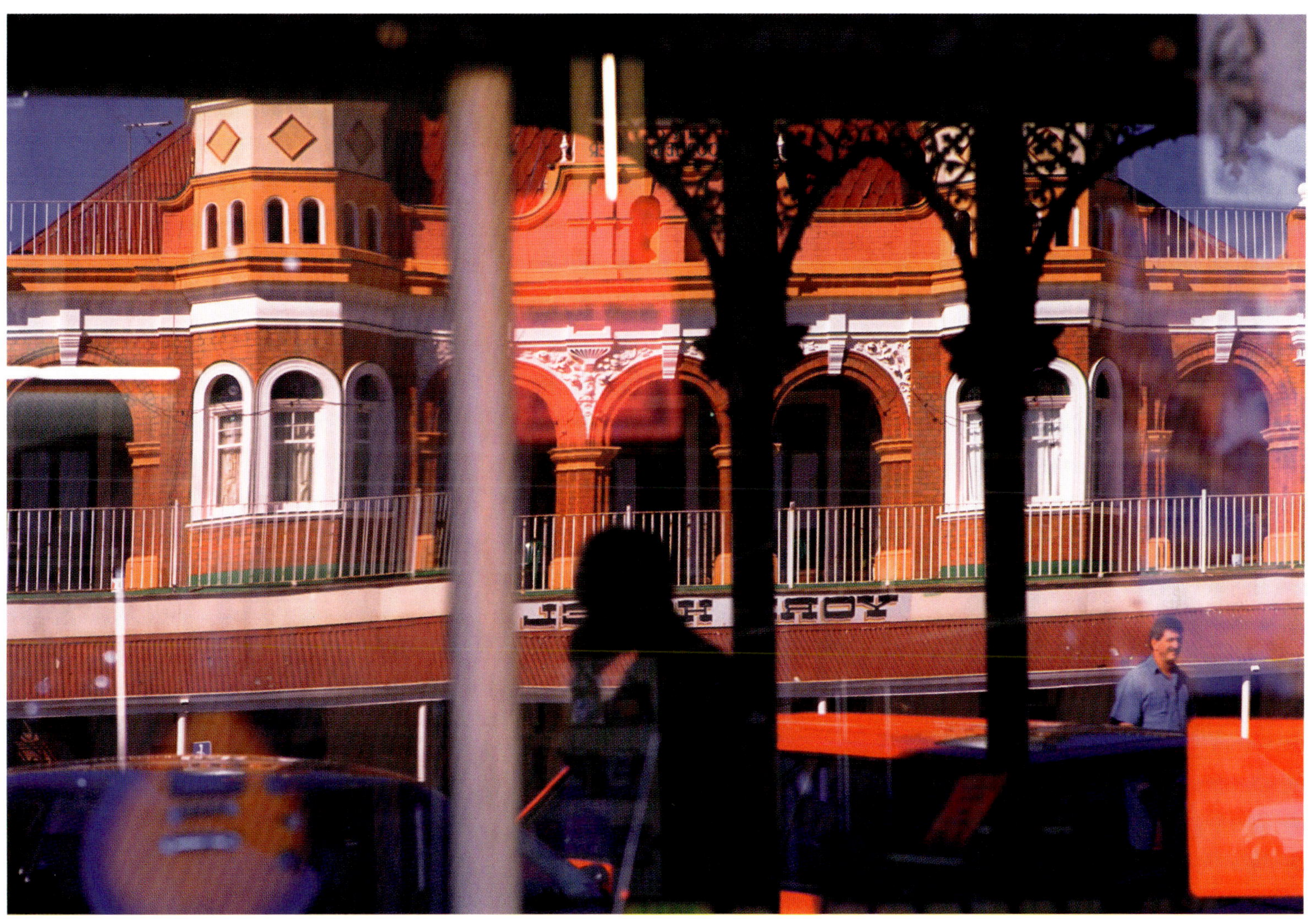

Reflections of Kalgoorlie: Italian influence in the facades...

Railwaying at its Wildest

Across the Nullarbor with the Tea 'n Sugar

by Berthold Daum

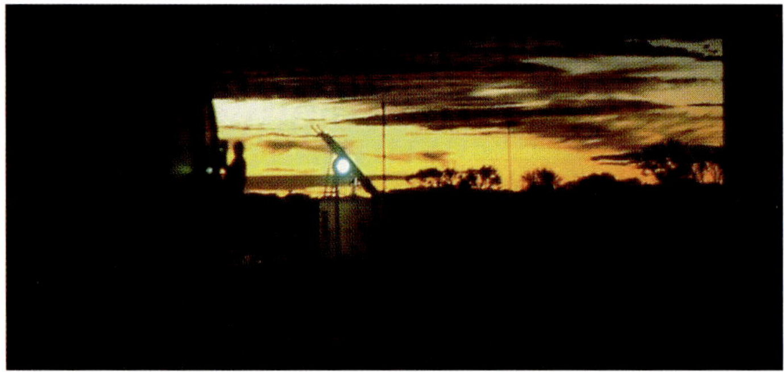

Night stop at a loop.

The week before Easter '96, I had the opportunity to travel on board the *Tea and Sugar* train from Port Augusta to Cook.

The *Tea and Sugar* was then a low priority supply train (officially 'Community Services Train') that followed the Transcontinental line from Pt. Augusta to Forrest. Running weekly it supplied the small communities along the line with food and other goods. The train once served 47 communities between Pt. Augusta and Kalgoorlie. Before the days of refrigeration it carried live sheep that were slaughtered along the way. Fortnightly, a dentist, a doctor, and a social worker would travel on the train. And once a year, it was Father Christmas. Wet towels helped to keep him cool in the searing heat.

Over the years the number of communities served by the *Tea 'n Sugar* dropped continuously. Running fortnightly the train served at last only Kingoonya, Barton, Watson, and Forrest. Tarcoola and Cook have their own stores and are supplied by regular freight trains.

1996 was the last year for the *Tea*. It officially stopped service with the 31st August '96, but a very last service was performed on Christmas Day for the children in Cook. I happened to be in Cook at this time and was able catch some glimpses of this historic event on film. But first my diary from that memorable trip earlier in the last year of the *Tea*.

Wed 8:00 am

I had been advised to report to the Spencer Junction Service Centre in Pt. Augusta at Wednesday 8:00 am, if possible earlier.

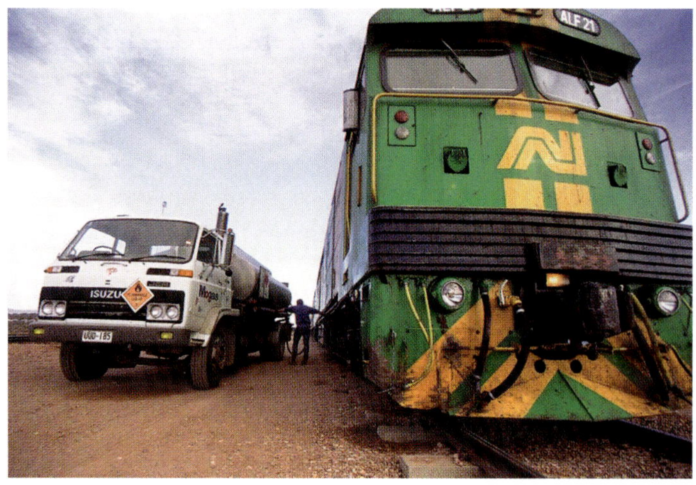

Fuelling up in Pt. Augusta.

The day before I had made the trip from Adelaide to Pt. Augusta on board the Indian-Pacific. The Indian-Pacific has all the amenities of modern life – showers, video on-board entertainment, a buffet car in the holiday class and a restaurant car and a lounge in the first class. Only poker machines are missing...

I had spent the night in a hotel in Pt. Augusta. Now I report to Graham Lancaster in the Service Centre. I am told to reappear at 11:00 am as the planned departure has been set to 12:00 noon. I use the time for a walk through Pt. Augusta.

Wed 11:00 am

I reappear at the Service Centre and we go out to the train in search of the storeman, who will be my host for the next day on board. The train has still to be shunted. Ron Davey, the store man, appears at 11:30 am. In his earlier life he has been a truck driver, and he has worked as a waiter and conductor on the Ghan train.

The crew consists of a total of 6 locomotive drivers working in 3 shifts. Ron is not exactly a crew member, but runs his business (the store) on the premises of the *Tea 'n Sugar*. The crew have their own car for accommodation (similar to a first class car from the Indian-Pacific, but with an integrated lounge and kitchen). The storeman sleeps in the store van. He also has a fully equipped kitchen and a shower.

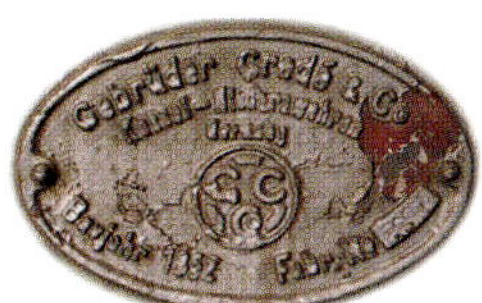

I am accommodated in an old coach built in 1952 in Germany. It is nicknamed the Volkswagen, probably because it still runs. These coaches were part of the reparations paid by Germany to Australia after World War II. There is a shower, but no air conditioning, and I have the whole coach to myself. During the trip the doors would stay open for ventilation, a fact that offers good opportunities for taking pictures.

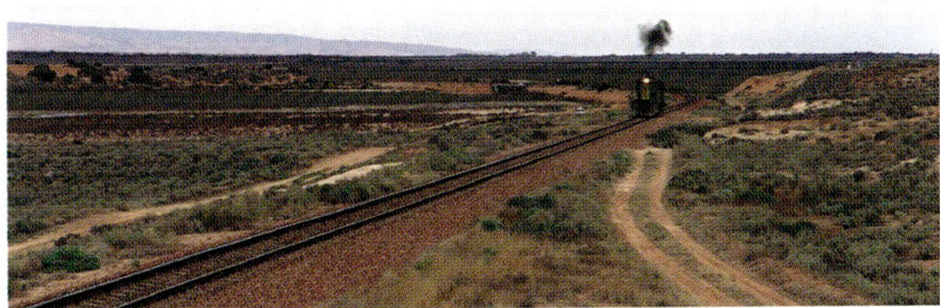

Relief in sight: The shunting loco arrives...

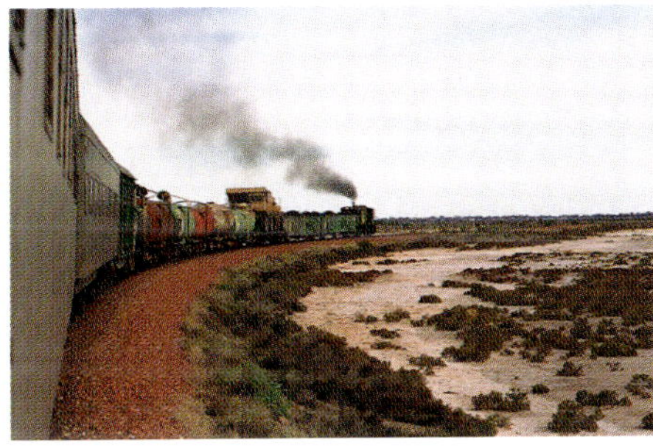

... and pulls us back to Pt. Augusta.

Wed 12:00 noon

We leave Pt. Augusta. Eight kilometres out of town the engine breaks down. We wait for a shunting loco to pull us back into Pt. Augusta.

Wed 4:00 pm

A replacement engine has been found and is now fuelled up. It takes 7000 litres until the tanks are full.

Wed 5:00 pm

A bolster plate on the store van was discovered to have dropped out of place (probably the bolster had hit a rock).

A crew arrives to jack up the van and put the plate into place. The process is similar to changing a flat tire on a car. The bolster is jacked up using an hydraulic jack, and the plate is pushed back into place.

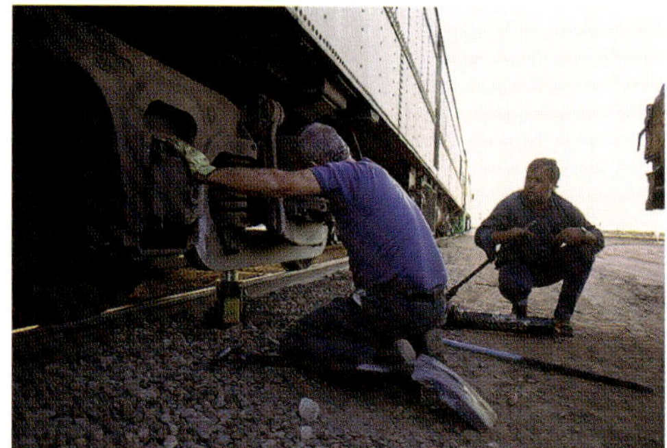

Roadside service, Pt. Augusta.

Wed 5:30 pm

After the bolster plate had been fixed, an air leak is discovered. We have to wait for the train examiners who are currently on another job at the other end of the town.

Wed 11:50 pm

An air leak is discovered in the brake system of the store van. The van is uncoupled and brought over a pit for repair. On the way back, the store van derails. Ron Davey, the storeman, who sleeps in the van, doesn't notice a thing. I decide to go to bed, too.

Thu 2:00 am

The train moves. The trip begins.

Thu 7:00 am

We are at Pimba, 80 km north of Pt. Augusta, which makes an average speed of 16 km per hour. We have stopped to let two freight trains cross. Freight trains have top priority, even before passenger trains. The *Tea 'n Sugar*, however, has the lowest priority which makes it prone to delays.

Thu 10:00 am

We arrive at Kingoonya, customers already waiting. Ron hands the goods out through a side door, and slowly the pick-up truck begins to fill. Later the men come in to sign for the goods in the store journal.

Thu 12:50 pm

We come into Tarcoola but we have to drop off two tractors at a quarry 100 km north of Tarcoola. It is not exactly on our route, but who cares. The quarry produces the ballast used for rail beds. The store van and rest of the train stay in Tarcoola. The locomotive is shunted to the cars carrying the tractors. I decide to join to take a few photos at the quarry. In the quarry we learn that we have to take some empty trucks back. This involves some more shunting, and the prospect that we may pay a visit to the Tarcoola pub diminishes.

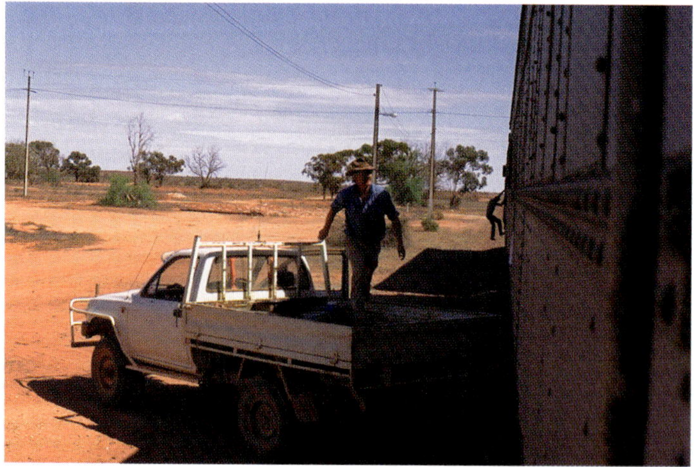

Shopping, Kingoonya style.

The Tea 'n Sugar

There's a mighty train a'puffin up and down the track,
It's the Tea 'n' Sugar with bread and butter on it's back,
Can't recall it being early, most times it's very late!
But to not arrive at all would surely seal our fate.

Trains will come and go out on this lonely track,
Not like the Tea 'n' Sugar, it keeps on coming back,
I can still recall the billowing smoke pouncing from its stack,
And all around are shouting; 'the "Sugar's" down the track!'

The children gather quickly, Dad too is in from work,
Mum to do the shopping and he's to visit the payory clerk,
I can see the butcher bent over his chopping block.
Hacking through meat orders, in a race against the clock.

The store-van takes the longest, for it has all the wares,
so long as he has lollies, forget the rest, who cares!
'Please Mum don't take your time, there'r others in the queue',
Just grab this and that, so long as I can have a chew.

If things go well I'll still have time to look,
The taking of coal and water before it heads for Cook,
Tom Sayers is the driver, I'm running, can't be late,
Please stop and let me ride; up on the cabin plate.

I love to see the fire-man building up the steam,
This old NM's a beauty, like Mother, she's a queen!
The shovel moves like lightning, forward and back it goes,
Every muscle is in motion from his head down to his toes.

With all this done, it's over, it's time to close the doors,
People have quit the butchers van, retired from the stores,
Guard Savill has blown his whistle, signals the "All-clear",
This happens every week, but the waiting is a year!

Rolly St.Clair, Tarcoola, 1986

Thu 6:00 pm

We are back in Tarcoola. As a railway town, Tarcoola will cease to exist in the near future. Its small gold mine will continue to operate. Tarcoola's bright red pub is up for sale, but it is more than doubtful if it will find a buyer.

Thu 7:30 pm

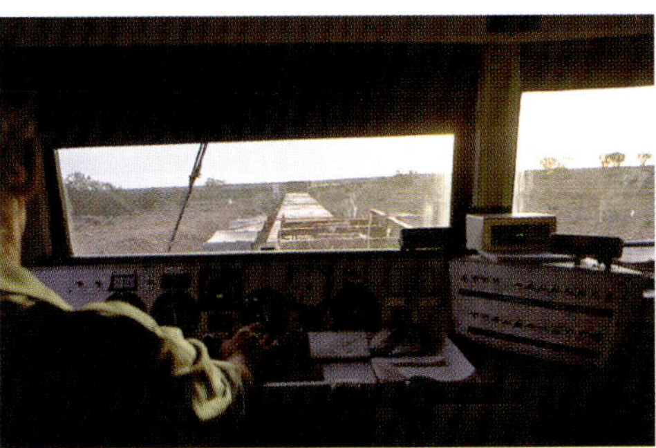

Pushing freight.

Shortly after we have left Tarcoola the train slows down and pulls over on a loop. Since the whole track has only a single pair of rails, 'loops' are provided in more or less regular distances to let trains with a higher priority overtake or to let trains going in the opposite direction pass. This is called a "crossing".

The switches at the beginning and end of these loops are operated manually. One of the two drivers jumps out (the one who doesn't drive) and throws the switch, the train moves across, then he switches back. After the crossing the train pushes back onto the main track and picks up the man outside.

Newer switches are semiautomatic. All that's left to do is press a button. The switch will return to its original position 15 seconds after the last car has passed. These switches are solar powered with a backup battery for operation at night.

As we stop, Ron, the storeman, says: "Probably another crossing". But the loco pushes us back again on the main track, decouples and starts some shunting. Probably they have to drop off some goods. In the meantime, Ron and I have dinner. Ron, who lives in Pt. Augusta, has brought some crabs, fresh caught out of Spencer Gulf.

We hear the loco coming in again and recoupling to the train. Then silence. Nothing happens. The train stands quietly on the main track. After half an hour Ron tries to find out what is going on and calls the loco crew on the two-way-radio. Nothing. No answer.

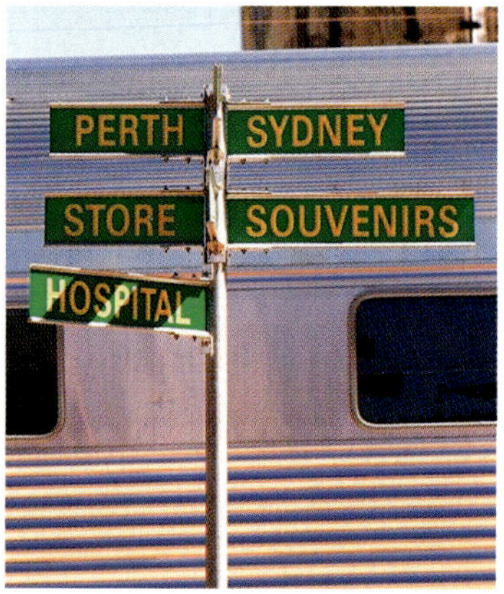

"Come with me" he says. We go to the back to the crew quarters. We find the crew having dinner. "Is there another crossing now" asks Ron. "Yes, something will cross our teeth" is the answer. They both smile.

Thu 11:50 pm

We arrive at Barton. Old Ziggy lives here with six dogs and some pigeons. He lives without water supply or electricity, but imports boxes of dog food via the *Tea 'n Sugar.*

First he lived in Mungala. When this siding was closed he moved all his belongings with his wheelbarrow ("Doesn't need petrol") to Barton, 27 km west.

As we stop at Barton a dog begins to bark. Ron uses a spotlight to signal Ziggy who already had been waiting for the *Tea 'n Sugar* to arrive. In the beam of the spotlight I see Ziggy appear with his wheelbarrow. Ron hands the boxes out, the wheelbarrow begins to fill.

Then Ziggy comes in to get his pay cheque and to sign for the goods. He is strongly built, with bushy eyebrows. He doesn't look like 72. He sees me and begins to talk. Talks to me, talks to Ron, talks of Belgium, and of God and the world. He doesn't even ask who I am and what I am doing on the train. He buys me a beer. He talks and talks, a lonely man living in the desert with his dogs and his pigeons.

Fri 3:00 am

The next customers are waiting in Watson. The men from the Australian Protective Services (Department of Defence) from Maralinga pick up their delivery (including a batch of the latest editions of R-rated magazines) . They are out here to clean up the area of the nuclear tests. The site will be reinforced by 80 new staff in October - after the British government agreed to pay for the job.

Fri 4:30 am

We arrive at Cook. For me it is the end of the journey on the *Tea 'n Sugar.* For the last hour I had been sitting in the open door of my coach watching the landscape pass by. We had entered the straight section of the line which is known to be the longest straight piece of rail in the world: 480 km without a curve or a bend. The horizon is just as even and the Nullarbor proves to be what the name says: without a tree. We have full moon and as the train moves the clouds change quicker than the landscape does.

On arrival in Cook I get the keys to a room in the Boongil guest house. This turns out to be a nice little apartment with air-conditioning, fully equipped kitchen, and TV. I go to bed and wake up 10:30 in the morning.

Fri 11:00 am

I had been told that I could buy food in the store. But I am a day late and it is Good Friday by now - the store keeper has gone fishing (a 5 hour drive to Pt. Fowler) - and I am stranded without food. So I go to the office ("all visitors report here"), and surprise, surprise, find Ron, my store man from the *Tea 'n Sugar*. The train still hasn't left town, now delayed for a full day. So I buy my supplies at the *Tea 'n Sugar* - the most natural thing in the world.

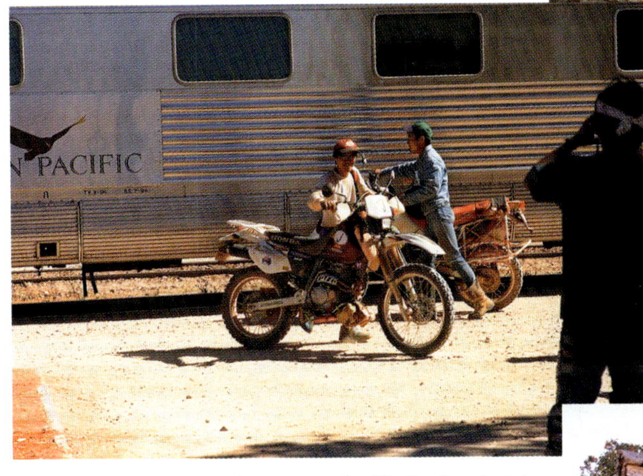

Japanese motorcyclists cross the Nullarbor beside the railway track. In Cook they re-provision and get a stamp in the travel diary. There may be easier ways to cross the desert.

About 80-90 people are living in Cook. There is a school, a hospital ("Our hospital needs help, get sick"), a store, a post office, and the souvenir shop run by community charities. In the middle of the township is a big sign "Evacuation point". The town people would gather there in case of an emergency, a fire or a derailment, to organise rescue actions. In former times, about 200 people lived in Cook. There was a coal train and a water train every week.

Sat 9:00 am

The westbound Indian Pacific passenger train to Perth arrives at Cook. While the coaches' tanks are refilled with water the tourists flood the little station of Cook, queuing in front of the souvenir shop and asking staff to pose for a photo. The children of Cook use the opportunity selling candies to raise funds for their school holiday camp.

Sat 11:30 am

The eastbound Indian-Pacific arrives and everything is repeated. It's a big day for Cook – happening only twice a week! I board the train and we leave at 12:30 pm. It is a very different world from the *Tea 'n Sugar*, a world of luxury, of fine cuisine, dessert forks and napkins, fresh towels and linen. It would eventually take me back to civilisation, meaning Adelaide.

After a night in Cook's historic gaol.

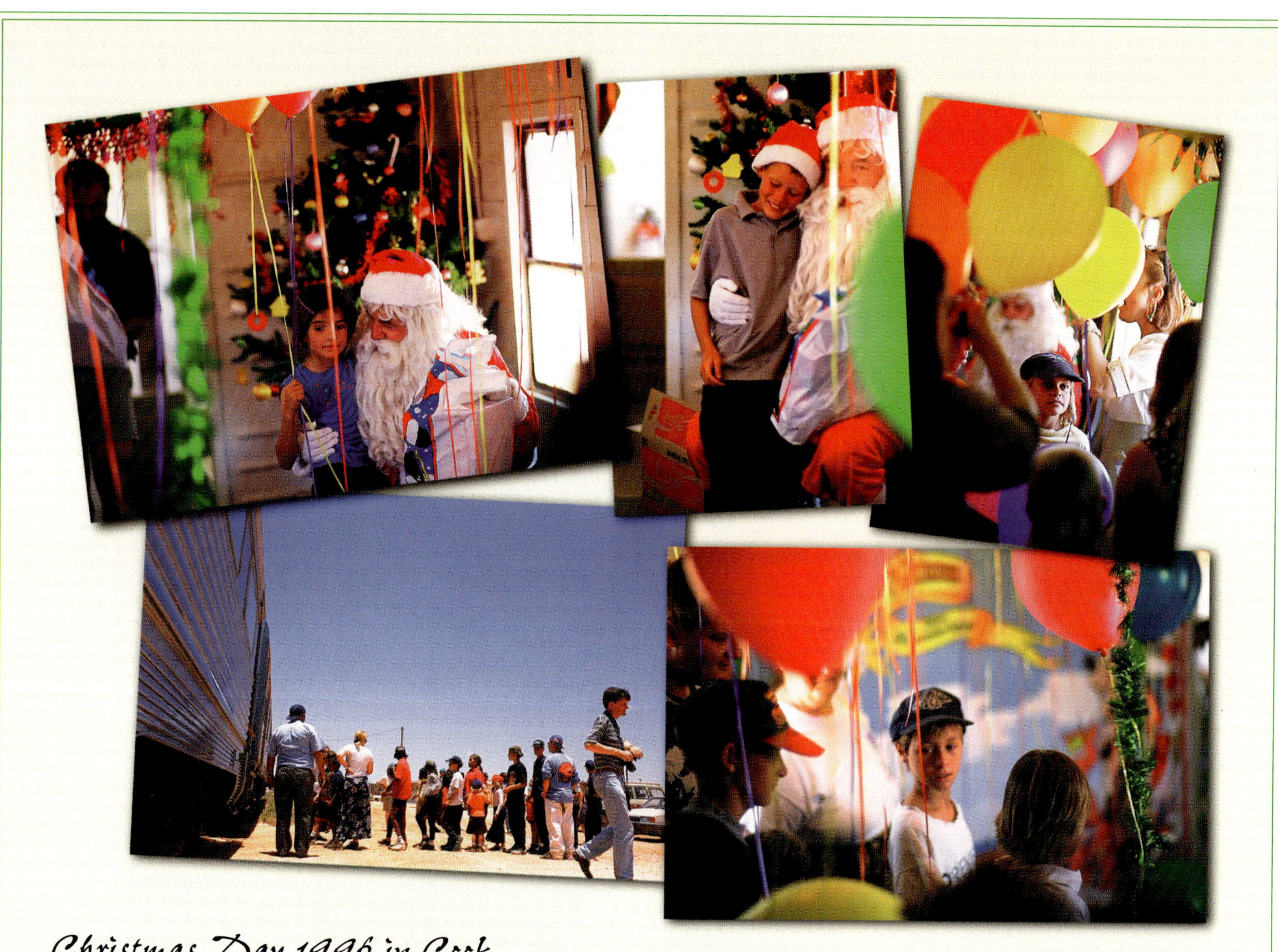

Christmas Day 1996 in Cook

The children queue up to visit Father Christmas in his 'cave'. This year should be the last one when Father Christmas will come all the way from Adelaide. The event also marked the end of the Tea and Sugar. Another Australian icon had become history.

The West

The western colony of the island of Australia was big, more than one third the total area of the whole island. And it was confident, brash even, from the wealth of its new-found goldfields. But the goldfields themselves were a problem to the colonial administrators in Perth, 600 km away, because their wealth from mines that seemed inexhaustible gave them their own sense of independence. Pressures existed for the goldfields to go their own political way. The administration in Perth was reluctant to join the Federating eastern colonies. The goldfields made it clear that given the choice between a breakaway Perth and the eastern Federation, they would join the proposed Commonwealth of Australia, taking their gold with them.

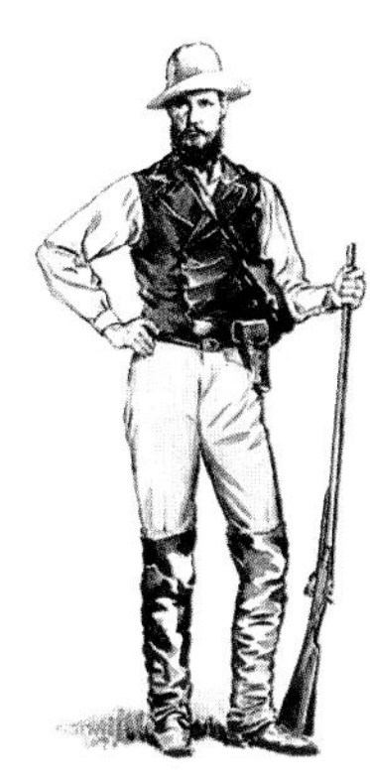

John Forrest

This was the threat to the Perth administration. The bribe came from the Federation, and essentially it said to the potential rebels in Perth: Join us, and we will build you a railway to the east as a sign of our union. Threat and bribe combined, as so often they do in such affairs, in an unrefusable offer. Western Australia joined the Federation.

But much talking remained to be done: From Federation in 1901, they talked about the transcontinental railway for the next eleven years before a sleeper was laid or a track spike driven. When it could decently delay no longer, the new Commonwealth Government looked around for a man who knew how to build a railway where nature would offer no help at all.

In Sydney they found the engineer Henry Deane, who'd built the impossible railway to the coal and shale mines of the Wolgan Valley in N S W. Deane was hired as Engineer In Chief, his assignment: To build 1,800 km of standard gauge railway across a little known desert with no trees for sleepers or buildings; no towns or villages for supplies and accommodation; no coal for fuel; no population for the human muscle he would need; no animals for work or food; and worst of all, no rivers, no creeks, no water: a climate of devastating heat, the certainty of drought, and rare but dangerous storms and local floods that could damage tracks in minutes and be gone within hours leaving behind little useful water.

The Perth explorer John Forrest had walked the approximate route of the railway in 1874, as leader of the first European crossing of the continent. Later, as Premier of Western Australia, he became a politician of national significance. Forrest was a strong and effective advocate of the Australian Federation, and he wanted his West to be part of it, despite the opposition of the Perth establishment. He gave his support to the railway project. Such support was not always given to the Engineer In Chief, Henry Deane, when he proposed to his federal master – and had rejected – ideas so far ahead of the time that the political mind could not admit them.

Had government listened to Deane, the trans-Australia could have been the first railway in the world powered by the

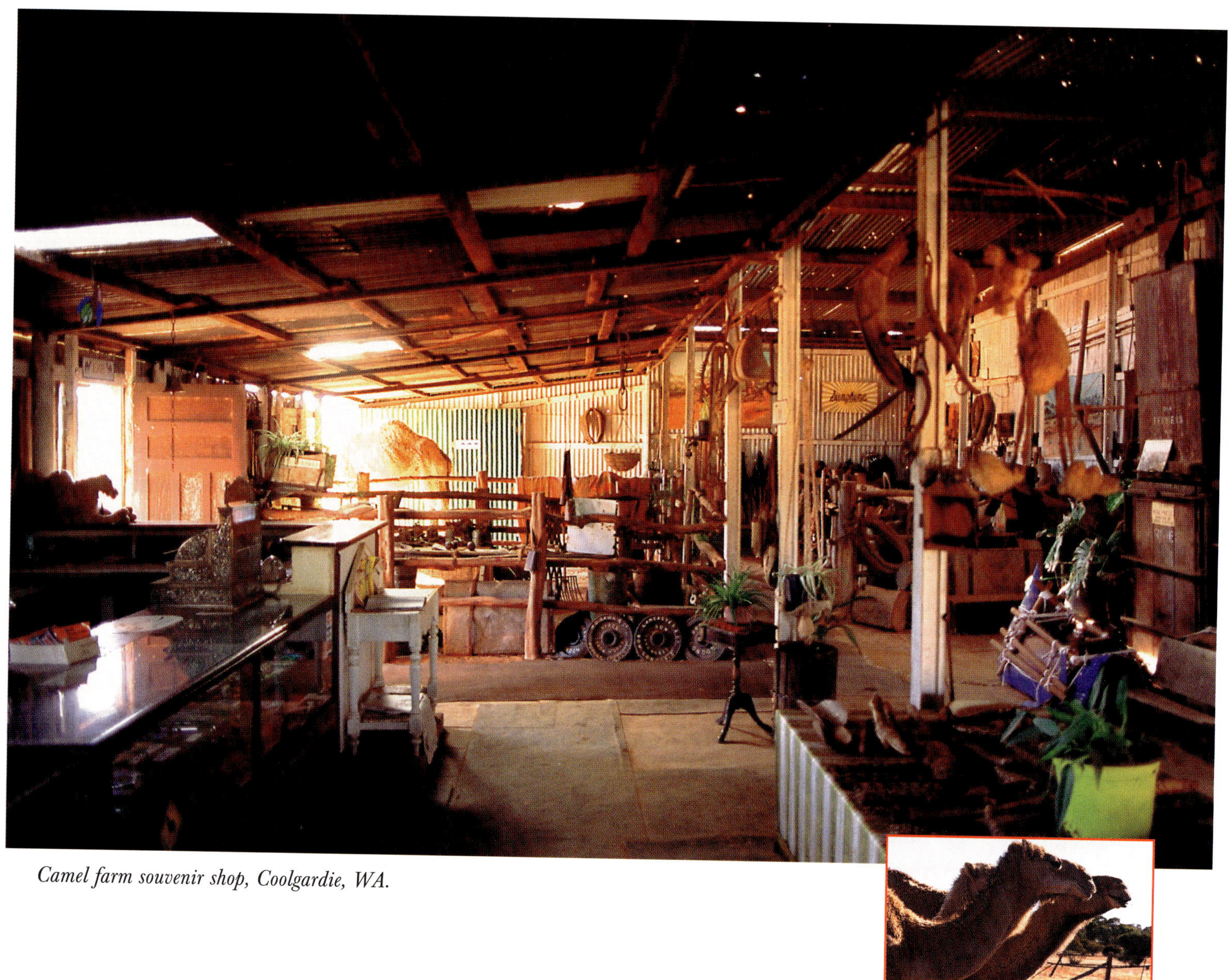

Camel farm souvenir shop, Coolgardie, WA.

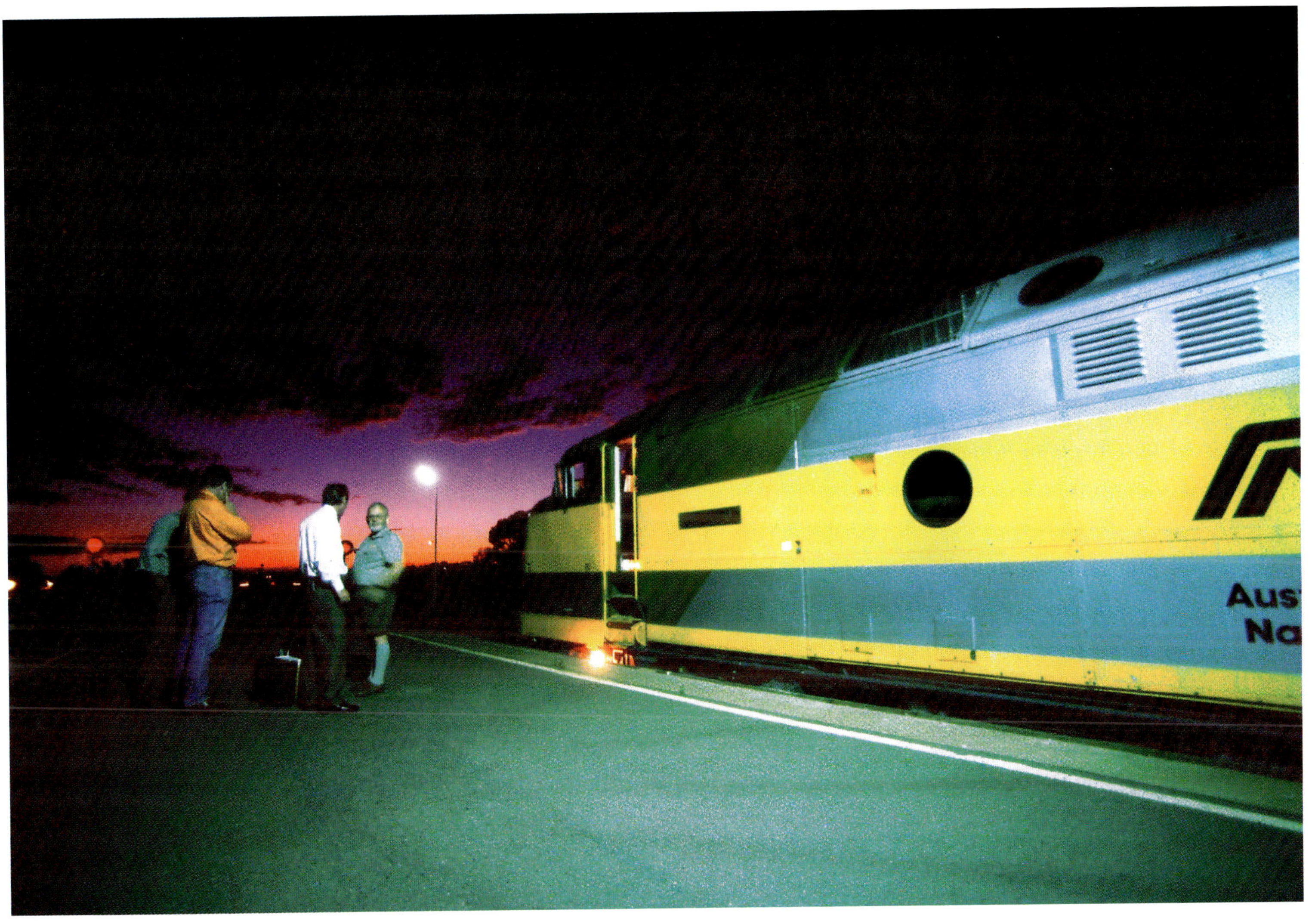

Break at Kalgoorlie.

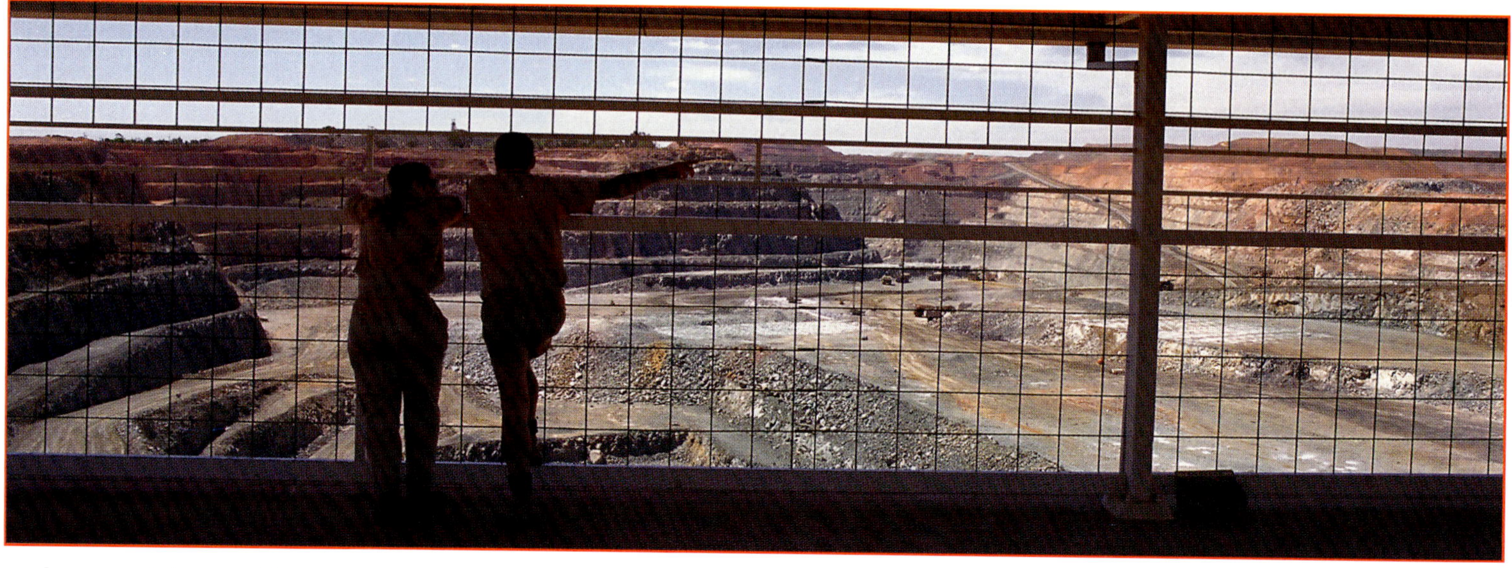

Superpit, Kalgoorlie, WA.

The Golden Mile

The vast Nullarbor Plain, an area larger than the state of Victoria, ends after 676 km at Naretha. The great plain ends as it began, imperceptibly, and there's no precise point to be described as the western end of it. But far to the right of the train, about half an hour west of Rawlinna, a distant tree line appears and a little further on a lineside cattle loading yard marks the beginning of the grazing leases of West Australia. Then, quite suddenly, the bush approaches the track and the treeless plain has ended.

Through Boonderoo, Kitchener, Zanthus and Coorana the train speeds westward. At Caronia, so unimportant now that it's been deleted even from railways maps, a pattern of drains on a hillside marks a brave attempt to gather water from the air, as the saltbush does, and channel it into storages to slake the thirst of steam engines. By all accounts, it was less successful than the saltbush.

The original Trans Australia line, as if a road to El Dorado, ended at Kalgoorlie. The westbound Indian-Pacific sees the Golden City of the Golden Mile by night, when the headframes of the working, and seemingly inexhaustible, mines are dramatically floodlit.

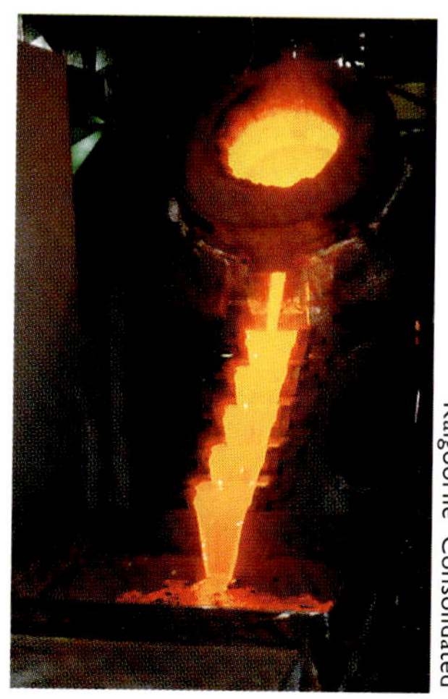

Kalgoorlie Consolidated

Gold pour.

This has been a gold field for more than a century. Paddy Hannan the prospector is honoured for its discovery, and although two other Irishmen were involved, Tom Flannagan and

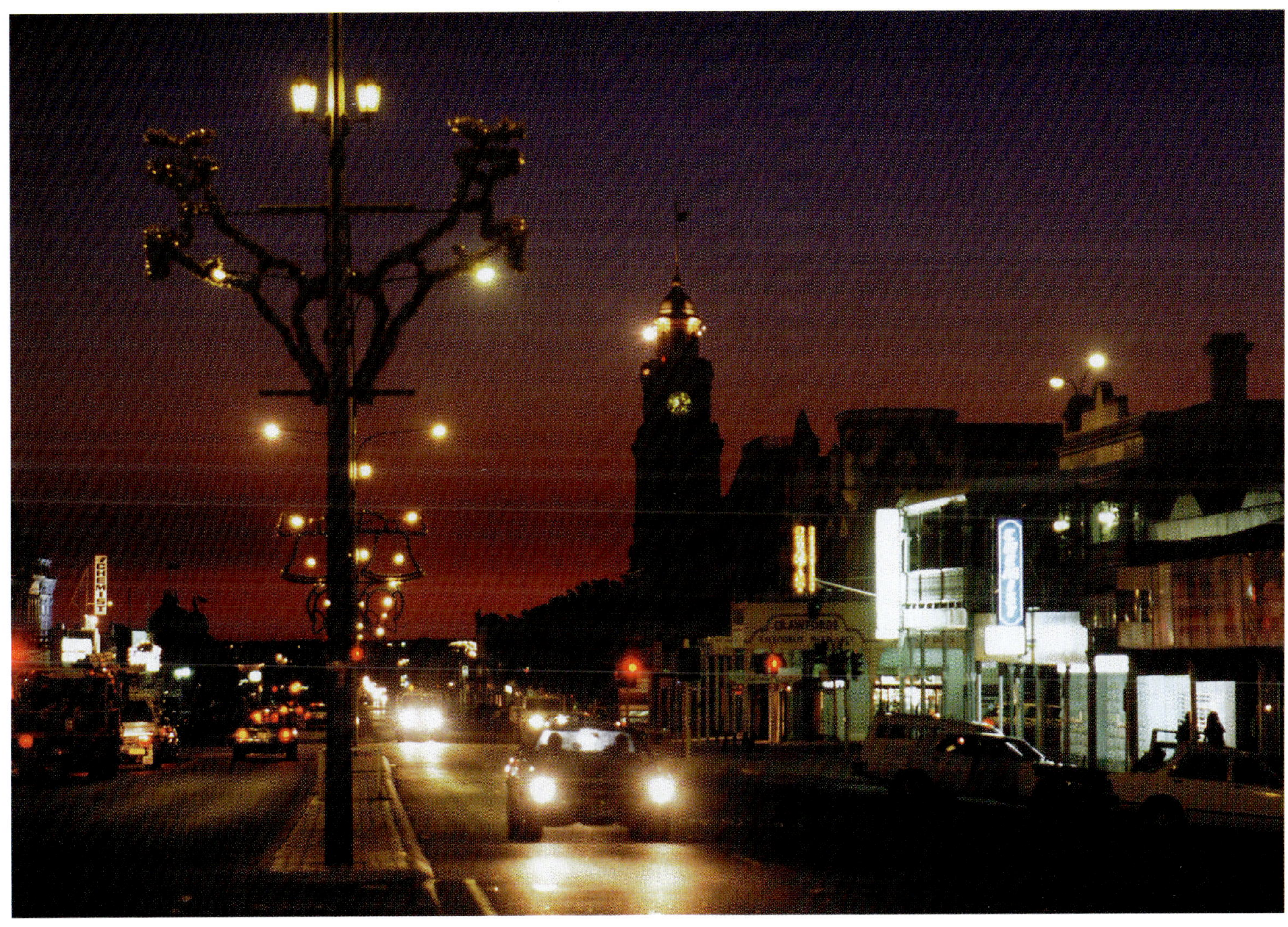

Kalgoorlie main street

Dan Shea, it's Hannan whose bronze statue decorates Kalgoorlie's main street.

The first gold of the Golden Mile was found in 1893, and there's been continuous and ever-expanding mining ever since. Every name on the map of these Eastern Goldfields (as the area is known in West Australia) has a mining story attached: Kalgoorlie to Boulder, the Golden Mile; Coolgardie, a ghost town now but once a thriving city with buildings bigger than any outside Perth; Kambalda, to the south, one of the richest known nickel mines on earth; and further south again, on the far side of the salt Lake Lefroy, the old goldfield Norseman, named, legend has it, for the horse whose hooves kicked up the golden nugget that set off the Norseman rush.

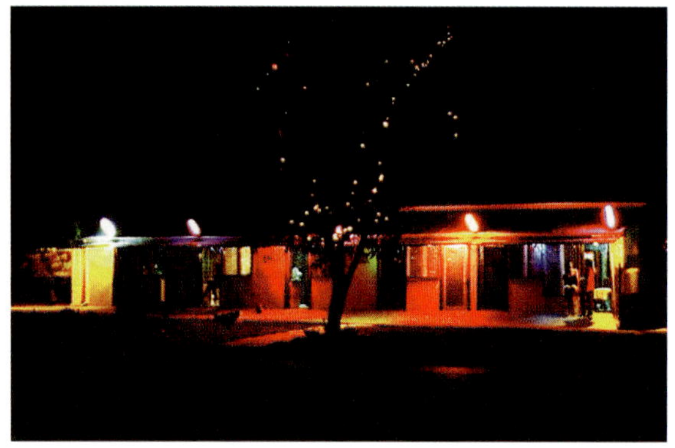

The tin shed brothels of Hay St., Kalgoorlie. Police station, Court house and Ministry of Justice are in the same street but in a section renamed Broockman St., and an illusion of respectability is preserved.

Coolgardie saw its first western gold rush in 1892, when a prospector rode into town from Fly Flat, in little known country 200 km to the east. He tied up his horse at the Mining Warden's office and produced 554 ounces of gold. Within days, a horde of hopefuls were pegging the district. Tent towns housing thousands of people marked the likely spots, and solely because of gold, the population of West Australia increased fourfold. Coolgardie alone had 16,000 people. The original strike, which came to be called Bayley's Reward, was productive for 70 years, but long before its gold was gone, the fabulous Golden Mile of Kalgoorlie-Boulder had stolen the old glamour of Coolgardie.

The Mile has yielded 45-million ounces of gold in just over a century of continuous mining, from deep underground mines for the first 90 years, then from vast open pit mining as well.

In 1989 all the mining leases of the Golden Mile were brought together by a joint venture company, Kalgoorlie Consolidated Gold Mines Pty Ltd, whose production of 700,000 ounces of gold per year makes it one of the world's top 20 gold producers.

Together with the treasure, the company took on the task of cleaning up the mess of a hundred years of mining. For most of those years, environmental concerns had little priority on the goldfield. The land was stripped bare of trees and all natural vegetation. Waste dumps, abandoned mine shafts and pits scarred the landscape. The fumes from chemical extraction polluted the air.

Drought is the rule, rather than the exception, on the Golden Mile. The city and its wealth are sustained only by a water pipeline that runs 600 km from catchments in the coastal ranges above Perth, and there's little water to spare for beautification. Nevertheless, a massive clean-up and plant regeneration program, now in its first decade, is showing results in scores of thousands of trees planted and the development of a green belt between mines and city. The long-term aim is that when mining ends, as in time it inevitably will, the Golden Mile will show none of the scars.

Through the Wheat Belt

The 650 km run from Kalgoorlie to Perth covers county of such variety that only the railway seems to tie it together. The aridity of Kalgoorlie continues far to the west. At Koolyanobbing, an iron ore mining town, the railway turns to the south and again is in gold country around Southern Cross. The gold strike at Southern Cross predated Kalgoorlie, but its glory was short lived. When all the easy gold was gone, there remained land fertile enough to grow wheat and rainfall enough, in most years, to water it.

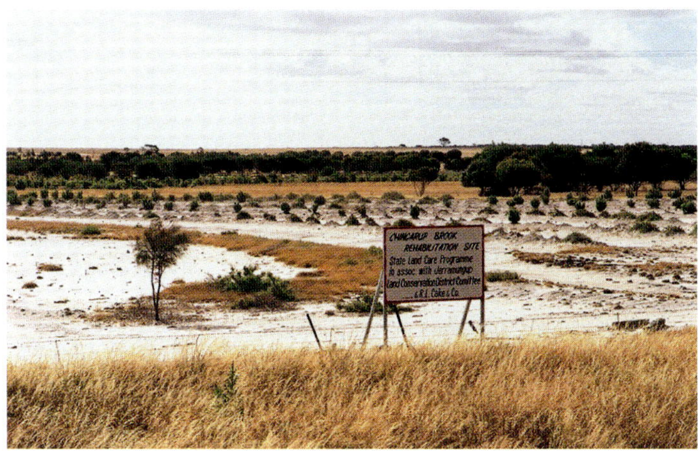

Revegetation near Jerramungup.

The wheat belt of West Australia has been enormously productive, but here, the width of Australia away from the Murray-Darling Basin, the land also is making a silent, threatening protest against misuse.

Dying gum trees are a warning sign: Eucalypts are hardy and rugged survivors, for they've evolved in a harsh land. Part of their role in the balance of nature is to act as pumps, drawing up water from underground and evaporating it into the atmosphere in the process called transpiration. When land is over-cleared and the pumps are gone, the underground water level rises and brings to the surface concentrated natural salts which destroy the fertility of the soil.

Belatedly, the salination problem has been recognised in West Australia's wheat lands. The national soil protection program, Landcare, aims to make all Australians, especially land holders, aware of the damage done to much of Australia's soils and to apply known measures of land protection.

One of the towns of the wheat belt, Meckering, was the victim in 1968 of the most severe earthquake ever recorded on mainland Australia. On the scale by which earthquakes are measured, Meckering is equal to the great earthquake of San Francisco. Though the centre was 9 km

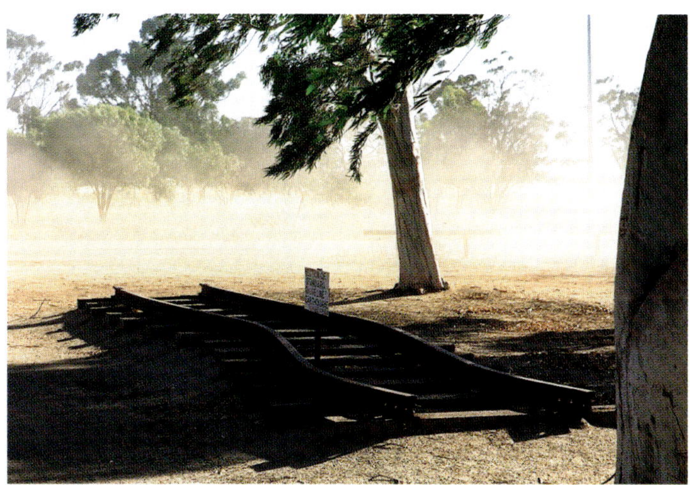

Monument to an earthquake, Meckering, WA.

out of town, practically every building in Meckering was damaged, and many destroyed. Mud brick and stone houses were worst affected. The railway line was lifted, twisted and wrecked, the water pipeline to Kalgoorlie ruptured. The 'quake left a 32 km long scar on the country southwest of Meckering to remind Australians that theirs is not necessarily the seismically safe, stable island they'd always thought.

Just west of Meckering, the railway enters the valley of the Avon River, the first river worthy of the name since the 2500 km distant Darling, east of Broken Hill. The Avon is a stream totally unlike its gentle English namesake. WA's Avon is usually not so much a stream as a series of water holes, but given good rain in its catchment, it can change in hours to a rushing torrent of white water which draws the adventurous for rafting and canoeing. The Avon joins the Swan, whose valley harbours some of the West's famous vineyards, and downstream at the coast, the Swan's estuary is the pride of Perth.

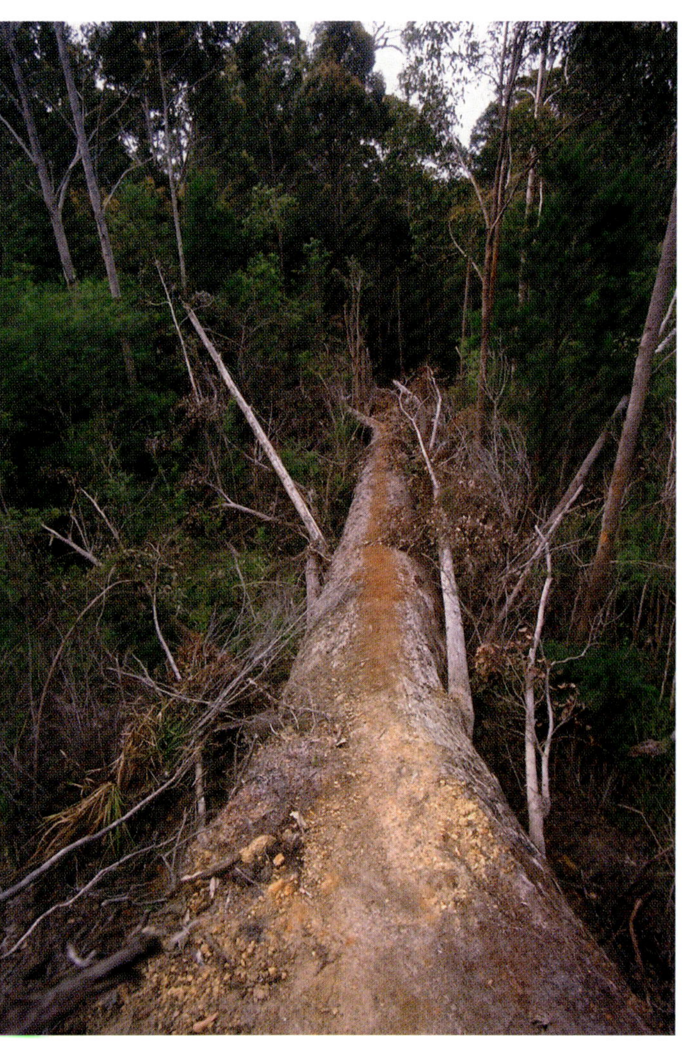

Even giants die: Fallen karri tree, Walpole, WA.

Many of the world's cities claim to be unique, often with good grounds. But the special nature of Perth is possibly best realised by people who've crossed Australia on the Indian-Pacific, who've taken a day and a half to travel from Adelaide, the better part of three days from Sydney, and who've seen the vastness of the country roll endlessly by.

The desert land bridge they've crossed creates a perception of distance, a sense of difference. And the West is different. This huge state is nearly half of mainland Australia. It grows pearls in its north, grapes in its south. Its forests are home to the biggest and best of Australia's hardwoods, the jarrah and karri. In its streams live the freshwater crayfish, the marron, a world delicacy if the world could get enough of them. Its beaches, in the southwest corner between Perth and Cape Leeuwin, are clean and almost empty of people and washed by a crashing Indian Ocean surf that's touched nothing since Africa. On the coastal plain are vineyards making wines so good the French import and sell them in Paris, and in villages and on small farms live and work potters and crafts people and settlers who, having visited the place, couldn't bear to leave.

Western Australia was first settled to keep it safe in British hands from possible colonisation by either the Americans, the French, or the Russians whose whaling and sealing ships were frequent visitors to the southwest corner of the Australian continent.

As the Southern Right whales have their breeding grounds at the eastern end of the Great Australian Bight, Humpback whales gathered off the southwestern coast and were hunted since last century by whalers from as far away as Norway. So many Norwegian ships came that a shore colony developed near Albany, and even today some of Albany's houses are painted in traditional Norwegian colours. Australia, too, had a whaling industry. It closed, as world opinion against whaling became overpowering, in 1978. The once active Cheyne's Beach Whaling Station has been preserved and restored as a museum of the industry.

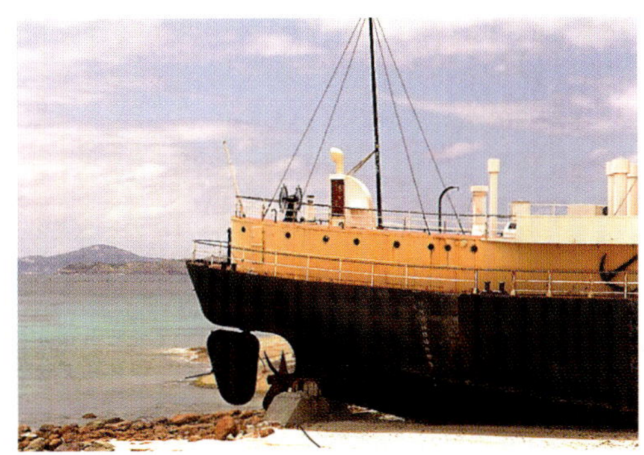

Albany: A whaler high and dry.

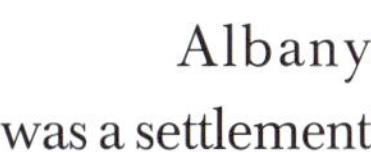

Albany was a settlement more than two years before Perth was established as the Swan River Colony. Albany's origins were as an outpost of the New South Wales Regiment, and soldiers and convicts from Sydney were its first residents.

Had the Dutch been as territorially acquisitive as the British and French, West Australia might well have been theirs. William Vlamingh was one of many Dutch navigators to visit its coast. He landed in 1696 on an island 20 km off the coast, inhabited only by animals he thought were the same as the rats that infested his ship, and in disgust he called the place Rats' Nest, Rottnest in Dutch. Three centuries later, Rottnest Island is a Perth playground, and the 'rats,' identified now as quokkas, a different animal altogether, are a protected species.

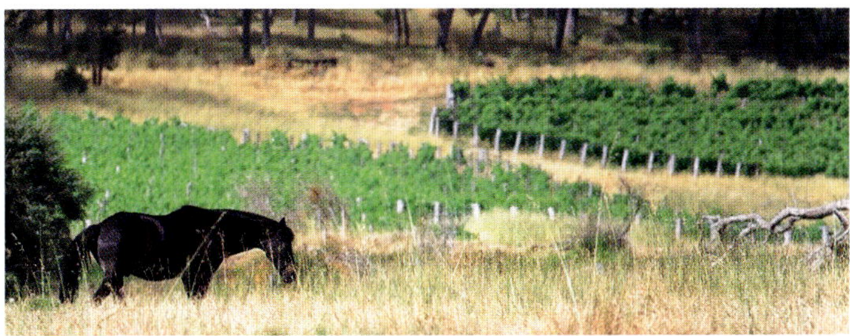

Vineyards, southwest WA.

Traces of the Dutch exploration of the West Australian coast are among the most prized exhibits at Fremantle's Maritime Museum, a feature of one of Australia's oldest port cities.

The site of Fremantle, as nature made it at the mouth of the Swan River, was less than ideal as a port. A rocky bar at its entrance

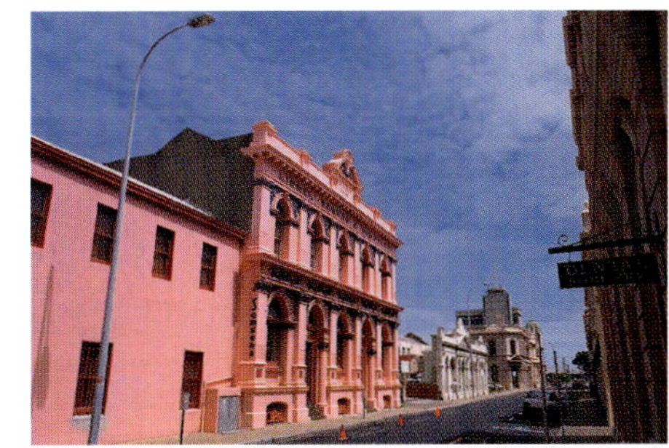

Fremantle street.

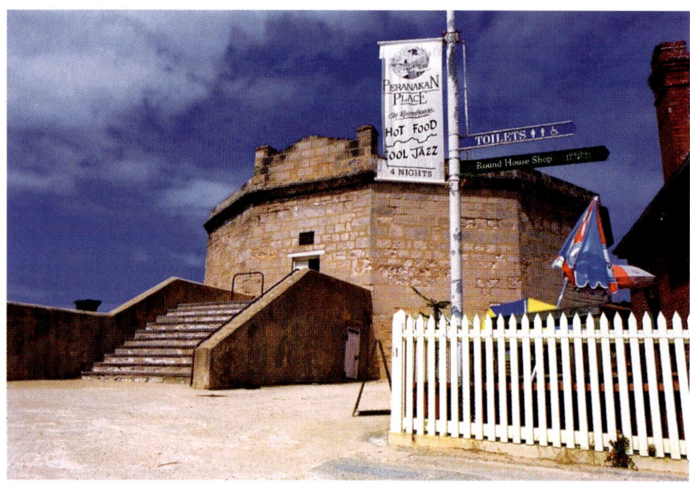

Fremantle Roundhouse.

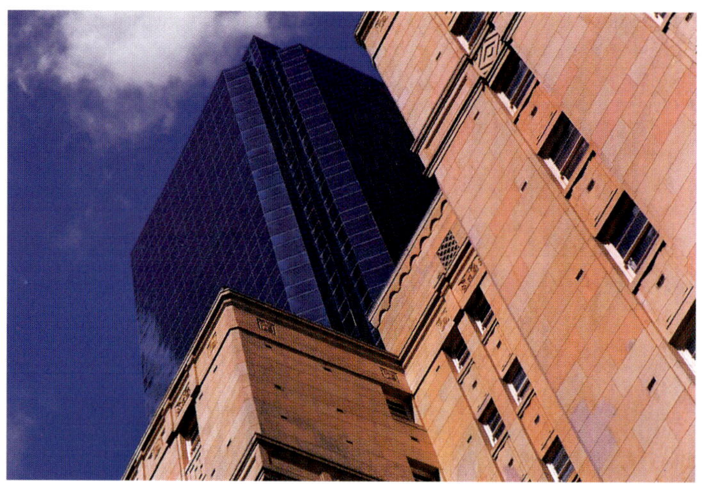

Perth facades.

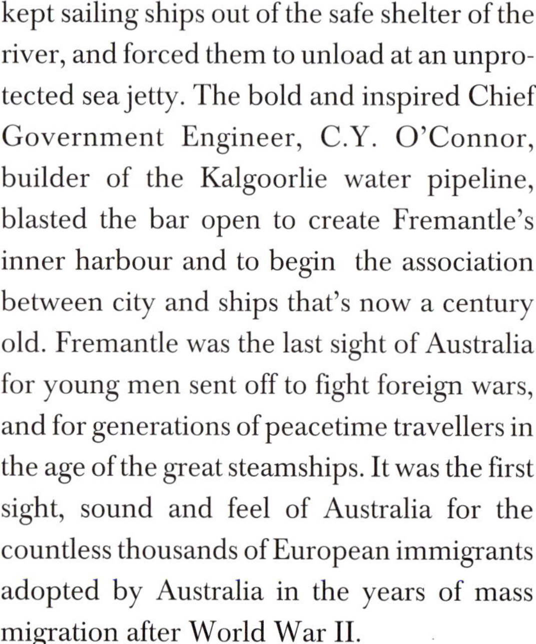

kept sailing ships out of the safe shelter of the river, and forced them to unload at an unprotected sea jetty. The bold and inspired Chief Government Engineer, C.Y. O'Connor, builder of the Kalgoorlie water pipeline, blasted the bar open to create Fremantle's inner harbour and to begin the association between city and ships that's now a century old. Fremantle was the last sight of Australia for young men sent off to fight foreign wars, and for generations of peacetime travellers in the age of the great steamships. It was the first sight, sound and feel of Australia for the countless thousands of European immigrants adopted by Australia in the years of mass migration after World War II.

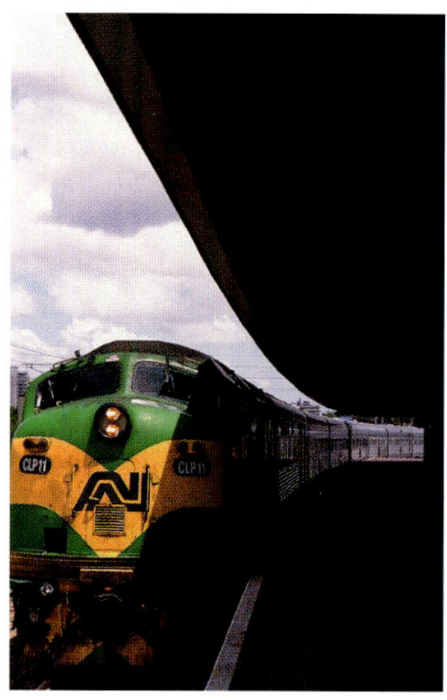

Perth Terminal: Journey's end.

The places they now live in are among the most melodious in all Australia: Fewer English politicians and minor royalty are found in the place names of West Australia, instead the gently musical words of all the Aboriginal languages once spoken here, in Wooroloo, Jumperkine, Moondyle and Tookyay; Dunderdin and Doodlakine; Kellerberrin, Meriden, Burracoppin, Carrabin, Moorine and Darrine and Looky-anobbing; Dambellup and Dwellingup.

Here is the end of the journey. And the beginning too, because the same day it arrives, the Indian-Pacific leaves again from Perth terminal, ahead of it the 4,000 km to the Pacific coast and the grand old sandstone station near the spot where Australia began.

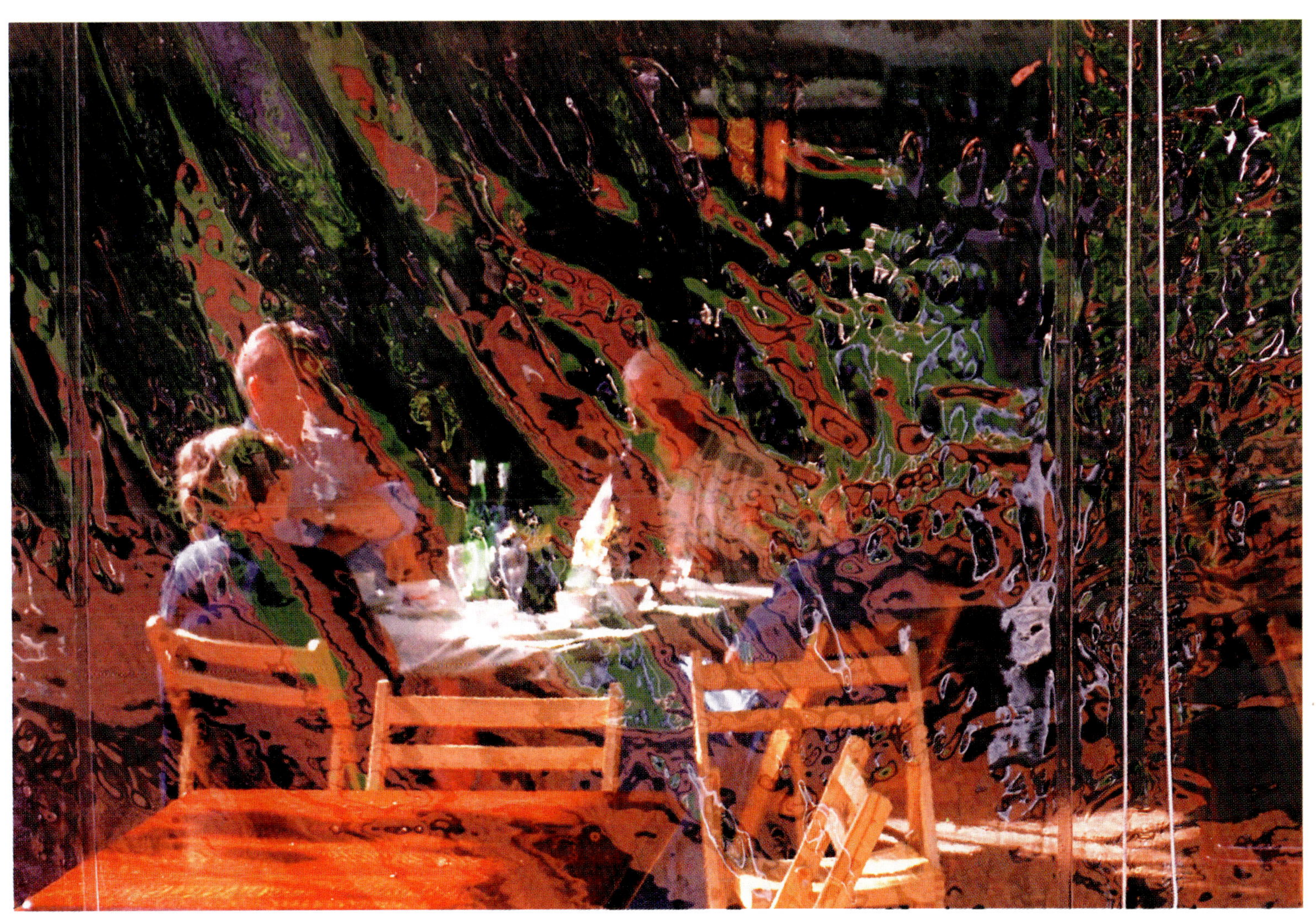

Lazy Sunday afternoon in the Swan Valley, WA: Patrons at a Winery.

Thank you

A great many people helped during the making of *The Indian-Pacific*. We wish to thank the following persons or organisations:

Bathurst: Bathurst Historical Society.

Adelaide: Christina Holmdahl and Graeme Dorling, Australian National; Steve Yorke, Port Dock Museum.

Pt.Augusta: Marion Ellis, Ron Davey, and Bryan Stewart, Australian National; Chris Flinn, E.T.S.A.

Quorn: Brian Powell.

Cowell: Bill Robins, Cowell Jade & Gemstones.

Pt.Lincoln: Linda Collins, Eyre Peninsula Tourism Association.

Kalgoorlie: Cecilia Camarri, Kalgoorlie Consolidated.

Coolgardie: Noel McKay, Coolgardie Camel Farm.

*Merredin:*Dr. Bob French and Malcolm Harper, Merredin Dryland Research Institute.

Perth: The Houghton Wine Company; The Rail Transport Museum; Robert Woldendorp.

Alice Springs: Dick Kimber.

Melbourne: Helen Smith, BHP Archives; Joyce Evans.

and: The people of Cook and Forrest.

Also available

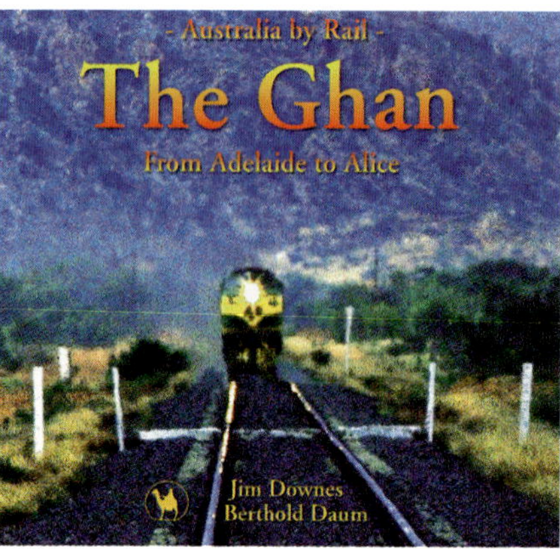

The Ghan
Hardcover
Dustjacket
250 by 230 mm
80 pages
full colour
ISBN 0646272888

On a Sunday morning in August, 1929, a mixed passenger and goods train steamed out of Adelaide railway station and through the sparse northern suburbs. Its destination was a thousand miles away, at the centre of Australia, and it carried, as well as more than a hundred through passengers, mail and fresh fruit.

This is how the story of a legend began. Built through one of the harshest regions in the world the Ghan served as a frontier railway opening up the Australian Outback.

It would quickly become infamous for its delays that were not measured in hours but in weeks – due to floodings, white ants, and rails buckling in the heat.

A new line was eventually completed in 1980 – the only major passenger line in the world built in this century. Passengers ride in the comfort of the 20th century – sometimes in stark contrast to the rugged and hostile world outside.

It still is a fascinating trip – a must in the agenda of every lover of railways.